A Treasury of Prayer

Also by Tony Castle

Christian Names for Boys and Girls

A TREASURY OF PRAYER

Prayers for Everyday and All Occasions

Compiled by
Tony Castle

Hodder & Stoughton
LONDON SYDNEY AUCKLAND

Copyright © 1983 by Tony Castle.
Based on material from *The Hodder Book of Christian Prayers*,
first published in Great Britain 1986.
This impression 1997

The right of Tony Castle to be identified as the Author of
the Work has been asserted by him in accordance with the
Copyright, Designs and Patents Act 1988.

3 5 7 9 10 8 6 4 2

British Cataloguing in Publication Data
A CIP catalogue record for this book is available from the British Library.

ISBN 0 340 57935 8

Printed and bound in Great Britain by
Clays Ltd, St Ives plc

Hodder and Stoughton Ltd
A Division of Hodder Headline PLC
338 Euston Road
London NW1 3BH

Dedicated

to

**Helena, Louise,
Angela and Thomas**

Contents

PRAYERS FOR THE CHRISTIAN'S LIFE

PRAYERS FOR THE SCHOOL ASSEMBLY

INTRODUCTION

As a child in primary school I learnt that prayer is the raising of the mind and heart to God. Nearly fifty years later, after reading numerous erudite and practical books on prayer, I cannot come up with any better definition of it. Being able to raise minds and hearts to God marks us out as distinctively human. Prayer is therefore more about the direction and orientation of human life than aiming wordy formulas heavenwards.

'Where your treasure is, there your heart will be also' Matthew 6:21. The Christian's heart belongs to Christ (Luke 14:26) and to treasure that love relationship is to treasure prayer, for without prayer the relationship cannot grow.

For nearly two millennia Christians have formulated and recorded prayers for use in public and private worship. Christianity is essentially a community faith, as the early Christians appreciated (Acts 2:42–47) and many of the prayers which have come down to us were originally composed for public worship. They are an essential and important part of our treasured heritage. It would be impossible to gather them all together into one volume. This compilation attempts to acknowledge our debt to the past while providing a practical and valuable treasury of Christian prayer for today.

While the ideal, in private prayer, is to express ourselves in our own words, or in the words of Scripture, there are occasions, for example in times of tiredness, sickness, grief or depression, when the desire and need to raise mind and heart to God is not matched by the ability. Then the prayers of others, praying from a like situation, are quite literally, a God-send.

There are prayers of saints and sinners, poets and playwrights, pastors and politicians, mums and mystics (the two are not mutually exclusive) – all of them sharing with us their struggle to give expression to and deepen their living relationship with God, in Christ.

The notes attempt to give a little information about the authors' names, dates and historical setting. As this treasury is a practical book of prayer and not an academic study the notes are not complete. By the very nature of prayer and the individuality of each Christian's spiritual journey, every compilation of prayers suffers from the limitation of being one person's selection, but the compiler hopes and prays that, like the teacher of the law who has been instructed (Matthew 13:52) in the kingdom of heaven, the reader will bring out of this treasury, 'new treasures as well as old' to deepen that all-important relationship with Father, Son and Holy Spirit.

Tony Castle
Harvest 1992

ACKNOWLEDGEMENTS

The editor and publishers wish to express their gratitude to the following for permission to reproduce material of which they are the publisher, author or copyright holder.

The British Broadcasting Corporation for prayers from *New Every Morning*.

Darton, Longman and Todd for two prayers by Metropolitan Anthony Bloom from *Living Prayer*, published and copyright © 1980, by Darton, Longman and Todd Ltd.

Oxford University Press for prayers by John Baillie from *A Diary of Private Prayer*; also for a verse of a hymn, 'Once from a European shore' by Brian Wren.

The Lutterworth Press for prayers by Beryl Bye from *Prayers for All Seasons*, published in 1971.

The International Bible Reading Association for prayers by Bernard Thorogood, Allen Birtwhistle and Michael Walker from the compilation *Everyday Prayers*, published in 1978.

William Heinemann Ltd for two prayers by Malcolm Boyd from his book *Are You Running with Me, Jesus?*

Augsburg Publishing House of Minneapolis for two prayers by J. Barrie Shepherd from *Diary of Daily Prayer*.

The Lutheran Publishing House of Adelaide, Australia, for the prayers of Bruce Prewer, first published in *Australian Prayers* and *Australian Psalms*; also the prayers of Terry Falla from *Be Our Freedom*.

The Presbyterian Publishing House of Atlanta, Georgia, for the prayers of William Kadel from *Prayers for Every Need*.

St Paul Publications for three prayers from *To Him Be Praise*, edited by Constante Berselli.

Holder & Stoughton Ltd for three prayers by Jamie Wallace from *A Month of Sundays*; also the prayers of Monsignor Michael Buckley, first published in *The Treasury of the Holy Spirit*; prayers by Canon Frank Colquhoun from *Parish Prayers* (1967), from *Contemporary Parish Prayers* and *New Parish Prayers*; three prayers of Leonard Barnett from *A New Prayer Diary*; also a prayer by Canon Michael Saward from *Contemporary Parish Prayers*; a prayer by Delia Smith, and one by Kenneth Lamplugh from *A Book of Graces*.

Fount Paperbacks (an imprint of HarperCollins Religious) for the prayers of William Barclay from *A Plain Man's Book of Prayers*, *Prayers for Young People* and *More Prayers for Young People*, also two prayers of Mother Teresa of Calcutta from *A Gift of God* and material from *Le Milieu Divin* by Teilhard de Chardin.

Fontana Paperbacks for the use of an extract from *Treat Me Cool, Lord* by Carl Burke.

Curtis Brown Ltd of New York for three prayers by Thomas Merton from *Thoughts in Solitude*.

SCM Press for the prayers of Rex Chapman taken from *A Kind of Praying*, *Out of the Whirlwind* and *Book of Prayers for Students*; the prayers of Caryl Micklem from *Contemporary Prayers for Modern Worship*; the prayers of Dietrich Bonhoeffer from *Letters and Papers from Prison*.

McCrimmon Publishing for the prayers of Rosa George, and Michael Hollings and Etta Gullick from *The Family Book of Prayer* compiled by T. Castle; also prayers by Michael Hollings and Etta Gullick (separately and together) from *The One Who Listens*, *The Shade of His Hand* and *You Must Be Joking*.

Sheed and Ward Ltd for the prayers of Caryll Houselander.

Gill and Macmillan Ltd of Dublin for the prayers of Michel Quoist from *Prayers of Life*.

The Rev. Dick Williams for contacting and obtaining approval from contributors to his *More Prayers for Today's Church*, published by Kingsway Publications Ltd.

The Rev. Llewellyn Cummings for prayers in *Family Prayers* published by Triangle/SPCK.

The Rev. Basil Naylor for the use of several of his prayers.

The Episcopal Church of the USA for prayers from their prayer book.

The Iona Community for the use of one of their prayers.

Prayers by Huub Oosterhuis are reprinted from *Your Word is Near*, copyright © the Missionary Society of St Paul the Apostle in the State of New York; used by permission of Paulist Press; first published in the Dutch language by Uitgeverij Ambo, copyright 1966.

Seabury Press for two prayers by Alan Paton taken from *Instrument of Thy Peace*.

Doubleday and Co. Inc. for a prayer by Henri Nouwen from *The Difficulties of Praying*.

Forward Movement Publications for two prayers by Monica Furlong.

Griffin House Press for a prayer by Jean Vanier from *Tears of Silence*.

While every effort has been made to trace copyright holders, and ascribe the prayers correctly, if there should be any error or omission, the publishers will be happy to rectify this at the first opportunity.

Prayers for the Christian's Day

Morning Prayers

1   We thank you, O Lord our God,
for making us rise from our beds
and setting upon our lips
these words of praise
so we may worship you and call upon your holy Name.
As you have continually blessed our lives
with goodness and mercy
so we pray to you now: send your help
to those who stand in your holy and glorious presence
awaiting your abundant mercy;
and may those who have served you unceasingly
in love and awe
praise, worship and adore
your unutterable goodness.

For to you belong
all glory, honour and praise,
Father, Son and Holy Spirit,
now and for ever,
to the ages of ages. Amen.

Orthodox prayer

2   O God, our Father, we thank you for waking us to see the light
of this new day. Grant that we may waste none of its hours; soil

none of its moments; neglect none of its opportunities; fail in none of its dûties. And bring us to the evening time undefeated by any temptation, at peace with ourselves, and with you. This we ask for your love's sake.

William Barclay

3 We give you heartfelt thanks, heavenly Father, for the rest of the past night, and for the gift of a new day with its opportunities of living to your glory. May we so pass its hours in the perfect freedom of your service that, when evening comes, we may again give you thanks; through Jesus Christ our Lord.

Orthodox Liturgy

4 The day returns and brings us the petty sound of irritating concerns and duties. Help us to perform them with laughter and kind faces. Let cheerfulness abound with industry. Give us to go happily on our business all this day, bring us to our beds weary and content and undishonoured, and grant us in the end the gift of sleep; for Jesus Christ's sake.

Robert Louis Stevenson

5 O Lord my God,
teach my heart this day where and how to see you,
where and how to find you.

You have made me and remade me,
and you have bestowed on me
all the good things I possess,
and still I do not know you.
I have not yet done that
for which I was made.

Teach me to seek you,
for I cannot seek you
unless you teach me,
or find you
unless you show yourself to me.

Let me seek you in my desire,
Let me desire you in my seeking.
Let me find you by loving you,
Let me love you when I find you.

Anselm of Canterbury

6 Lord God, this is your day;
    you created the sun, our light and energy;
    you give sleep as the renewal our minds and bodies need;
    each day you are the same God,
    always seeking the lost and wounded sheep,
    always speaking the creative word for each one.
    Help me to enter this day with you.
    May I begin to understand your presence
    in the events and people who come close to me today.

Bernard Thorogood

7 O Lord, we thank you for this new day with its new strength
    and vigour, its new hopes and its new opportunities. Help us
    to meet its joys with praise, its difficulties with fortitude, its
    duties with fidelity. Grant us wisdom and clear vision. Direct
    our steps and guard us from error. And of your great mercy
    deliver us from evil; through Jesus Christ our Lord.

H. Bisseker

8 For morning light and the gift of a new day,
    we praise you, our heavenly Father;
    and with thankful hearts we now entrust ourselves
    and those we love into your hands,
    praying that you will help us,
    guide us, and keep us
    in all that lies before us this day;
    for the sake of Jesus Christ our Lord.

Frank Colquhoun

9 Lord Jesus Christ, who alone are Wisdom, you know what is
    best for us; mercifully grant that it may happen to us only as
    it is pleasing to you and as seems good in your sight this day;
    for your Name's sake. Amen.

King Henry VI

10 Father, I offer you this new day,
    which is your gift to me.
    May your Son be within me today
    as I go about my normal routine.
    I want to unite myself to the

offering He makes of Himself to you;
may all I do at home or at work
be lifted from the level of routine habit
to a share in His offering.
May your Spirit purify my gift,
filling my mind with good thoughts
and my heart with love.

Anthony Castle

11 Almighty God, we bless and praise you that we have awakened
to the light of another day; and now we will think of what a day
should be.

Our days are yours, let them be spent for you.

Our days are few, let them be spent with care.

There are dark days behind us, forgive their sinfulness; there
may be dark days before us, strengthen us for their trials. We
pray you to shine on this day, the day which we may call
our own.

Lord, as we go about our daily work, help us to take pleasure
in it. Show us clearly what our duty is; help us to be faithful in
doing it. Let all we do be well done, fit for your eye to see.

Give us strength to do, patience to bear, let our courage
never fail.

When we cannot love our work, let us think of it as your
task, and by our true love for you make unlovely things shine
in the light of your great love, through Jesus Christ our Lord.

George Dawson

12 O God, I know that I am going to be very busy today.
Help me not to be so busy that I miss the most important things.

Help me not to be too busy to look up and to see a glimpse of
beauty in your world.

Help me not to be too busy listening to other voices to hear
your voice when you speak to me.

Help me not to be too busy to listen to anyone who is in trouble,
and to help anyone who is in difficulty.

Help me not to be too busy to stand still for a moment to think
and to remember.

Help me not to be too busy to remember the claims of my home, my children and my family.

Help me all through today to remember that I must work my hardest, and also to remember that sometimes I must be still.

This I ask for Jesus' sake. Amen.

William Barclay

13 O Lord, I have a busy world around me; eye, ear, and thought will be needed for all my work to be done in that busy world. Now, before I enter upon it, I would commit eye, ear, and thought, to you! Bless them and keep their work yours, such as, through your natural laws, my heart beats and my blood flows without any thought of mine for them, so may my spiritual life hold on its course at those times when my mind cannot consciously turn to you to commit each particular thought to your service. Hear my prayer for my dear Redeemer's sake. Amen

Thomas Arnold

14 God, make each moment of our lives a miracle; God, make us laugh at the utterly impossible; God, give us hope when all things seem hopeless, peace where no peace could be, love for the unlovable. Make us to gamble all on your Almightiness, and to dare everything in your great service.

M. E. Procter

15 Blessed are you, Lord, God of our fathers. You turn the shadow of death into morning, bringing light to my eyes. O Lord may your sun dispel the night-mist of my sins. Grant that I may become a child of the light and of the day. Keep me this day from sin. Uphold me when I stumble and pick me up if I should fall. Let this day add some knowledge or good deed to yesterday. O, let me hear your loving-kindness in the morning, for in you is my trust.

Lancelot Andrewes

16 O God, help me all through today
    To do nothing to worry those who love me;
    To do nothing to let down those who trust me;
    To do nothing to fail those who employ me;

To do nothing to hurt those who are close to me.

Help me all through this day
> To do nothing which would be a cause of temptation to someone else or which would make it easier for someone else to go wrong;
> Not to discourage anyone who is doing their best;
> Not to dampen anyone's enthusiasms, or to increase anyone's doubts.

Help me all through this day
> To be a comfort to the sad;
> To be a friend to the lonely;
> To be an encouragement to the dispirited;
> To be a help to those who are up against it.

So grant that others may see in me something of the reflection of the Master whose I am and whom I seek to serve.

This I ask for your love's sake. Amen.

William Barclay

17 O God, our Father, help us all through this day so to live that we may bring help to others, credit to ourselves and to the name we bear, and joy to those who love us, and to you.
> Cheerful when things go wrong;
> Persevering when things are difficult;
> Serene when things are irritating.

Enable us to be;
> Helpful to those in difficulties;
> Kind to those in need;
> Sympathetic to those whose hearts are sore and sad.

Grant that;
> Nothing may make us lose our tempers;
> Nothing may take away our joy;
> Nothing may ruffle our peace;
> Nothing may make us bitter towards anyone.

So grant that through all this day all with whom we work, and all those whom we meet, may see in us the reflection of the master, whose we are, and whom we seek to serve. This we ask for your love's sake.

William Barclay

18 Lord God, make us watchful to benefit, and not to injure the
minds and souls of those with whom we have to do this day;
and give us grace, by word and influence and good example to
promote their happiness and their good; through Jesus Christ
our Lord.

Charles J. Vaughan

19 Warm our cold hearts, Lord, we implore you. Take away all
that hinders us from giving ourselves to you.

Mould us according to your own image. Give us grace to obey
you in all things, and ever to follow your gracious leading.

Make us this day to be kind to everyone, to be gentle and
unselfish, careful to hurt no one by word or deed, but anxious
to do good to all, and to make others happy.

Give us a gentle and a loving spirit, which in your sight
is of great price. We would not live just for ourselves, but
for you.

Ashton Oxenden

20 O eternal Son of God, who came from the Father, the fountain
of light, to enlighten the darkness of the world. Shine upon us
today that in whatever we do we shall reflect your light, for
your Name's sake.

Jeremy Taylor

21 We commend to you, Lord,
our souls and our bodies,
our minds and our thoughts,
our prayers and our hopes,
our health and our work,
our life and our death;
our parents and brothers and sisters,
our benefactors and friends,
our neighbours, our countrymen,
and all Christian folk
this day and always.

Lancelot Andrewes

22 I want to begin this day with thankfulness, and continue it with
eagerness.

I shall be busy; let me set about things in the spirit of service to you and to my fellows, that Jesus knew in the carpenter's shop in Nazareth.

I am glad that he drew no line between work sacred and secular.

Take the skill that resides in my hands, and use it today;
Take the experience that life has given me, and use it;
Keep my eyes open, and my imagination alert, that I may see how things look to others, especially the unwell, the worried, the overworked. For your love's sake. Amen.

Rita Snowden

23 Make us of quick understanding and tender conscience, O Lord; that understanding, we may obey every word of yours this day, and discerning, may follow every suggestion of your indwelling Spirit. Speak, Lord, for your servant is listening through Jesus Christ our Lord. Amen.

Christina Rossetti

24 O my God, make me happy this day in your service. Let me do nothing, say nothing, desire nothing, which is contrary to your will. Give me a thankful spirit, and a heart full of praise for all that you have given me, and for all you have withheld from me. Amen.

Ashton Oxenden

25 Grant us, O Lord, to pass this day in gladness and peace, without stumbling and without stain; that, reaching the eventide victorious over all temptations, we may praise you, the eternal God, who are blessed, and govern all things, world without end. Amen.

Mozarabic Sacramentary

26 Father, may nothing this day come between us. May I will, do, and say, just what you, my loving and tender Father, will me to will, do, and say. Work your holy will in me and through me this day. Protect me, guide me, bless me, within and without, that I may do something this day for love of you; something which shall please you; and that I may, this evening, be nearer to you, though I see it not, nor know it. Lead me, O Lord, in a straight way to yourself, and keep me in your grace to the end. Amen.

E. B. Pusey

27 As I begin this day
become flesh again
in me, Father.
Let your timeless and everlasting love
live out this sunrise to sunset
within the possibilities,
and the impossibilities
of my own, very human life.

Help me to become
Christ to my neighbour,
food to the hungry,
health to the sick,
friend to the lonely,
freedom to the enslaved,
in all my daily living.

J. Barrie Shepherd

28 Lord Jesus, I thank you; you have watched over and protected
me, your unworthy servant, with your loving presence all
through the night. You have brought me safe and unharmed
to this morning hour. I thank you for all the blessings you have
given, of your great goodness, to me.

Edmund of Abingdon

29 Living each day to the full,
Lord, let me live this day
as if it were my first day,
or my last.
Let me bring to it
all the wonder and amazement of a new-born child;
the trust
that welcomes all I meet,
expects of them only the best,
and grants them the benefit
of every possible doubt;
But let me also bring
the wisdom and experience of the aged to this day;
the tenderness
that grows from years of care and gentle giving;

the hope
that has been forged through all the fires of doubt.

J. Barrie Shepherd

30   Be with me, Lord, at my rising in the morning. Have kindly
regard to me, my Lord, and guide my actions, my words and
my thoughts. Keep me in the right path, that I spend the
day according to your will. Give me reverence of you and a
repentant heart. Guide my hearing that I pay no attention to
backbiting, nor to untrue and foolish talk, but let my ears be
alert for the voice of God. Watch my steps that I go not about
from place to place with idle mind, but united with the thought
of God in my mind. Restrain my hands, that they be not ever
seeking undeserved rewards, but let them be, as it were in
service, offered to the Lord of this world, that the prophet's
prayer may be mine. The lifting up of my hands shall be my
evening sacrifice.

Book of Cerne
(of the tenth century)

31   Into your hands, O Lord, we commend ourselves this day.
Let your presence be with us to its close. Strengthen us to
remember that in whatsoever good work we do we are serving
you. Give us a diligent and watchful spirit, that we may seek in
all things to know your will, and knowing it, gladly to perform
it, to the honour and glory of your name; through Jesus Christ
our Lord.

Gelasian Sacramentary

32   Lord Jesus Christ, to whom belongs all that is in heaven and
earth. I desire to consecrate myself wholly to you and to be
yours for evermore. This day I offer myself to you in singleness
of heart, to serve and obey you always, and I offer you without
ceasing, a sacrifice of praise and thanksgiving. Receive me, O
my Saviour, in union with the holy oblation of your precious
blood which I offer to you this day, in the presence of angels,
that this sacrifice may avail unto my salvation and that of the
whole world.

Thomas à Kempis

33 Be Lord Jesus, a bright flame before me,
Be a guiding star above me,
Be a smooth path below me,
Be a kindly shepherd behind me,
Today – tonight – and forever.

Columba of Iona

34 Who can tell what a day may bring forth? Cause me therefore, gracious God, to live every day as if it were to be my last, for I know not but that it may be such. Cause me to live now as I shall wish I had done when I come to die. O grant that I may not die with any guilt on my conscience, or any known sin unrepented of, but that I may be found in Christ, who is my only Saviour and Redeemer.

Thomas à Kempis

35 Eternal God, who knows neither morning nor evening, yet wraps us in love both night and day, lift the curtain of night from the world and the veil from our hearts. Rise with your morning sun upon our souls and enliven our work and prayer. May we walk this day in the steps of him who worked in harmony with your will. Amen.

James Martineau

36 Eternal God, who commits to us the swift and solemn trust of life; since we know not what a day may bring forth, but only that the hour for serving you is always present, may we wake to the instant claims of your holy will; not waiting for tomorrow, but yielding today.

Lay to rest, by the persuasion of your spirit, the resistance of our passion, indolence or fear. Consecrate with your presence the way our feet may go; and the humblest work will shine, and the roughest places be made plain.

Lift us above unrighteous anger and mistrust into faith and hope and charity by a simple and steadfast reliance on your sure will. In all things draw us to the mind of Christ, that your lost image may be traced again, and you may own us as at one with him and you.

James Martineau

37 Teach us, O gracious Lord, to begin our daily tasks with fear,
to go on with obedience, and to finish them in love, and then to
wait patiently in hope, and with cheerful confidence to look up to
you, whose promises are faithful and rewards infinite; through
Jesus Christ our Lord.

George Hickes

38 Father in heaven, you have given us a mind to know you, a will
to serve you, and a heart to love you. Be with us today in all
that we do, so that your light may shine out in our lives.

We pray that we may be today what you created us to be,
and may praise your name in all that we do.

We pray for your Church: may it be a true light to all nations;
May the Spirit of your Son Jesus guide the words and actions
of all Christians today.

We pray for all who are searching for truth: bring them your
light and your love.

Give us, Lord, a humble, quiet, peaceable, patient, tender
and charitable mind, and in all our thoughts, words and deeds a
taste of the Holy Spirit. Give us, Lord, a lively faith, a firm hope,
a fervent charity, a love of you. Take from us all lukewarmness
in meditation, dullness in prayer. Give us fervour and delight in
thinking of you and your grace, your tender compassion towards
us. The things that we pray for, good Lord, give us grace to
labour for: through Jesus Christ our Lord.

Thomas More

Graces for Meal Times

39 Come Lord Jesus be our guest,
And may our meal by you be blest. Amen.

Attributed to Martin Luther

40 To God who gives our daily bread
A thankful song we raise,
And pray that he who sends us food
May fill our hearts with praise.

Thomas Tallis

41   Praise God from whom all blessings flow,
Praise him, all creatures here below,
Praise him above, angelic host,
Praise Father, Son and Holy Ghost.

Thomas Ken

42   Gracious God, may the food which we are about to receive
strengthen our bodies, and may your Holy Spirit strengthen
and refresh our souls; through Jesus Christ.

The Tent and the Altar

43   Be present at our table, Lord,
Be here and everywhere adored;
These creatures bless, and grant that we
May feast in paradise with thee.

John Cennick

44   We thank you, Father, for the holy resurrection, which you
made known to us through Jesus, your Child. As the ingredients
of the bread on this table, though once separate, were gathered
together and made one, so may your Church be built up from
the ends of the earth and gathered into your kingdom; for
power and glory are yours through all the endless succession
of ages. Amen.

Pseudo-Athanasius

45   O Lord our God, you are the Bread that is eaten in heaven, the
Bread that gives life, the Food that really nourishes the whole
world. You came down from heaven and gave the world life; you
guide us through this present existence, and you have promised
that there will be another for us to enjoy after this. Bless, then,
our food and drink and enable us to take them without sinning.
May we receive them thankfully and give you glory for them,
for you it is who confers all good gifts upon us.
    Blessed and glorious is your name, ever worthy of honour.

Third-century prayer

46   Bless, O Lord, this food to our use and us to your service
and provide for the wants of others less fortunate than ourselves,
for Jesus Christ's sake. Amen.

Traditional prayer

47 Bless us, O Lord, and these your gifts which we are about
to receive of your kindness, And keep us mindful of those in
want. Amen.

Traditional prayer

48 For food we eat, and those who prepare it,
For health to enjoy it and friends to share it.
We thank you, O Lord. Amen.

Kenneth Lamplugh

49 Thank you for the world so sweet,
Thank you for the food we eat.
Thank you for the birds that sing,
Thank you, God, for everything.

E. Rutter

50 We thank and praise you, Lord, for the gifts of your creation,
and ask your blessing on mankind that one day we can learn to
share with poorer nations so that no one will go hungry. We
ask this through Jesus Christ our Lord. Amen.

Delia Smith

51 For food in a world where –
many walk in hunger;
For faith in a world where –
many walk in fear;
For friends in a world where –
many walk alone,
we give you humble thanks, O Lord.

Girl Guide World Hunger Grace

52 Lord Jesus, who when you were on earth celebrated a meal
with joy, be with us now and fill us with your spirit as we share
food and fellowship together.

Michael Buckley

Evening Prayers

53 O Lord our God,
we come to you now with open hearts
to call upon your holy Name
and to give you thanks
for keeping us safe during this day
and for bringing us to the light of evening.
We pray that this evening and the approaching night
and all the days of our earthly life
may be free from sin:
clothe us with the armour of your Holy Spirit
to fight against the forces of evil
and the passions of the flesh;
put far from us all sin
and make us worthy of your eternal kingdom.

For to you belong
all glory, honour and praise,
Father, Son and Holy Spirit,
now and for ever
to the ages of ages. Amen.

Orthodox prayer

54 Holy Spirit, I thank you for the quiet moments of this busy day
when you spoke to me of your abiding love. Teach me now as
I lie down to rest how to listen to you when you speak in the
silence of the night, in the silence of my heart. Teach me waking
or sleeping how to watch and how to listen for your still, small
voice which gives meaning and direction to every moment of
my life.

Michael Buckley

55 My thanks, O holy Lord, Father Almighty, Eternal God, for
your divine mercy has kept me safe throughout this day; grant
that I pass this night tranquilly and in cleanness of mind and
body, that rising chaste in the morning hours, I may again do
you grateful service.

Alcuin

56 Holy Spirit, I thank you for being with me this day, for all the happiness your will has brought, and for all the toil and hardships I have had to accept. Forgive me for the times when I have forgotten you amid the cares of life. Forgive me also if I have not accepted any suffering in the same spirit as Christ my Lord. Help me to rest in peace this night, that I may wake truly refreshed and willing to spend a new day in your service. Guard me this night, as the good shepherd guards his flock. Grant that, in your mercy and love, when I close my eyes on this world for the last time, I may wake in the joy of your presence to a new everlasting day.

Harold Winstone

57 Dear God, you are always surprising me.
My day was just a few hours of life,
yet in it you were teaching me new things.
You showed me a fresh aspect of familiar people I met,
and new truth about myself.
Forgive my slowness to understand your word;
don't add up the wasted minutes;
judge all my work with a father's mercy.
Thank you, Lord, for the light and the night;
enable me to find renewal in sleep,
and let me know, deep in my heart,
that tomorrow I will be with you, through Jesus Christ.

Bernard Thorogood

58 O God, bless all my friends and my loved ones tonight:

Bless those whose lives are interwoven with mine, and without whom life could never be the same. Bless those to whom I owe my comfort, and without whom life would be very lonely.

Bless the one to whom I have given my heart to keep, and who has given me his/her heart to keep, and keep us for ever loyal, for ever loving, and for ever true to one another.

Bless my absent friends and loved ones, from whom for a time I am separated. Guard them, guide them, protect them, and grant that we may soon meet again.

I know that all for whom I am praying are also praying for me. Help me just now to feel very near to them, and not only to them, but even to those whom I have loved and lost awhile, and who have gone to be with you.

Hear this my prayer for your love's sake. Amen.

William Barclay

59 Forgive me, O God,
    For the time I have wasted today;
    For the people I have hurt today;
    For the tasks I have shirked today.

Help me
    Not to be discouraged when things are difficult;
    Not to be content with second bests;
    To do better tomorrow than I have done today.

And help me always to remember that Jesus is with me and that I am not trying all alone.

This I ask for Jesus' sake. Amen.

William Barclay

60 Before we go to rest, we would commit ourselves to God's care through Christ, beseeching him to forgive us for all our sins of this day past, and to keep alive his grace in our hearts, and to cleanse us from all sin, pride, harshness, and selfishness, and to give us the spirit of meekness, humility, firmness, and love. O Lord, keep yourself present to us ever, and perfect your strength in our weakness. Take us and ours under your blessed care, this night and evermore; through Jesus Christ our Lord.

Thomas Arnold

61 Into your hands, O Lord, we commend our souls and bodies, beseeching you to keep us this night under your protection, and to strengthen us for your service on the morrow, for Christ's sake.

William Laud

62 Abide with us, Lord, for it is towards evening and the day is far spent; abide with us and with your whole Church. Abide with us in the evening of the day, in the evening of life, in the evening of the world. Abide with us and with all your faithful ones, O Lord, in time and eternity.

Lutheran Manual of Prayer

63   O Lord our God, what sins I have this day committed in word, deed, or thought, forgive me, for you are gracious, and you love all men. Grant me peaceful and undisturbed sleep, send me your guardian angel to protect and guard me from every evil, for you are the guardian of our souls and bodies, and to you we ascribe glory, to the Father and the Son and the Holy Ghost, now and for ever and unto the ages of ages.

Orthodox prayer

64   Show your loving kindness tonight, O Lord, to all who stand in need of your help. Be with the weak to make them strong, and with the strong to make them gentle. Cheer the lonely with your company and the worried with your peace. Prosper your Church in the fulfilment of her mighty task, and grant your blessing to all who have toiled today in Christ's name.

John Baillie

65   O Lord my God, I thank you that you have brought this day to a close; I thank you for giving me rest in body and soul. Your hand has been over me and has guarded and preserved me. Forgive my lack of faith and any wrong that I have done today, and help me to forgive all who have wronged me. Let me sleep in peace under your protection, and keep me from all the temptations of darkness. Into your hands I commend my loved ones and all who dwell in this house; I commend to you my body and soul. O God, your holy name be praised.

Dietrich Bonhoeffer

66   Eternal and ever-blessed God, we give you thanks, as the day comes to an end, for those who mean so much to us, and without whom life could never be the same.

We thank you for those to whom we can go at any time and never feel a nuisance.

We thank you for those to whom we can go when we are tired, knowing that they have, for the weary feet, the gift of rest.

We thank you for those with whom we can talk, and keep nothing back, knowing that they will not laugh at our dreams or mock our failures.

We thank you for those in whose presence it is easier to be good.

We thank you for those in whose company joys are doubly dear, and sorrow's bitterness is soothed.

We thank you for those who by their warning counsel and their rebuke have kept us from mistakes we might have made, and sins we might have committed.

And above all we thank you for Jesus, the pattern of our lives, the Lord of our hearts, and the Saviour of our souls.

Accept this our thanksgiving, and grant us tonight a good night's rest; through Jesus Christ our Lord.

William Barclay

67 Into your hands, most blessed Jesus, I commend my soul and body, for you have redeemed both by your most precious blood. So bless and sanctify my sleep to me, that it may be temperate, holy, and safe, a refreshment to my weary body, to enable it so to serve my soul, that both may serve you with never-failing duty. Visit, I beseech you, O Lord, this habitation with your mercy, and me with your grace and favour. Teach me to number my days, that I may apply my heart unto wisdom, and ever be mindful of my last end. Amen

Jeremy Taylor

68 The busy day now takes its rest,
as mother evening enfolds us in embrace.
The distant stars and galaxies signal
messages about a Creator so vast
that our minds stagger
and our hearts are filled
with loving awe.

O Lord, our Lord,
glorious in your name in all the universe.
What are earth's children
that you notice us?
And what is the mystery of divine grace
that you love us?
You give us faith to trust you,
even though we cannot see you.
You touch our minds with fingers of light,
and our hearts with forgiveness and peace.

As the evening moves on,

we go to rest
able to sleep the sleep of children
who know that, in life or death,
we are surrounded by love eternal.

O Lord, our Lord, glorious is your name
on earth and in the heavens!

Bruce Prewer

69 Great and wonderful God,
in your unfathomable goodness and great providence
you have given us the good things of this world,
and furthermore
you have made us a pledge of your eternal kingdom;
during this past day
you have kept us safe from evil:
so grant us to end the day
without sin
in the presence of your divine glory
and to sing hymns to you
who are our God
and who alone are good and loving to everyone.

For you, O God,
are full of mercy
and deep love for mankind:
we give you glory,
Father, Son and Holy Spirit,
now and for ever,
to the ages of ages. Amen

Orthodox prayer

70 Today, Lord, has been awful!
It started badly.
Imps of depression sat on the bedposts
waiting for me to wake,
ready to pounce on me,
to harry me
and fill me with their gloom.

My head ached, my nerves were edgy
and I felt irritable.

And then it rained . . .
not a decent sort of rain, soon over and done with,
but a penetrating, miserable, drooling kind of rain,
that wet-blanketed soul as well as body.

There are days like that, Master.
Days when life is heavy, boring, meaningless;
days when no ray pierces the inward gloom,
just plain bad days.

What is your recipe for such hours, Lord?
I am reminded of some words which were often on your lips:
Take heart!'
They must have comforted your followers many times.

You used them when they were startled,
when they had lost their nerve,
when they needed encouragement.

I need encouragement, Master,
so I quieten my mind and wait to hear you say:
'Take heart!'
Thank you, Lord.

Flora Larsson

Children's Night Prayers

71 Thank you, God, for our home, with its welcome at the end of
the day. A lot of things have happened, and a lot of people have
helped us today.
Parents and teachers, bus-drivers and playmates;
People who kept the traffic flowing;
People who protected us from law-breakers.
Thank you for the fun we've had, for the chatter with friends,
for the new things learned.
Forgive us if we've been cheeky.
Forgive us if we've been selfish.
Forgive us if we've been untruthful.
We didn't mean to be like this – if we were –
now we're sorry.

Send us to sleep forgiven, secure in your love and keeping; and
waken us to a better day tomorrow.

Rita Snowden

72 My Prayer is such a little thing, it might get lost and go
astray.
Are you, dear God, now listening to what I say?
I wish to thank You for the sun that kissed, this morn, my
sleeping eyes;
for all the happy things I've done since I did rise.

For gift of sound and gift of sight; for feet that skip so
merrily;
for food and warmth, and each delight You gave to me.
I thank You for my mother dear; I thank You for my father
kind;
and for the star that watches near – behind the blind.

So many Grown-ups show me love, though I'm a child and still
quite small.
Look down upon them from above – and please God, bless
them all.
And, now, dear God, I'll say, 'Goodnight', and may Your angels
guard my bed
until You send Your morning light to wake this Sleepy Head.

Wilhelmina Stitch

73 Jesus, tender Shepherd, hear me,
Bless thy little lamb tonight;
Through the darkness be thou near me,
Watch my sleep till morning light.

All this day thy hand has led me,
And I thank thee for thy care;
Thou hast clothed me, warmed and fed me,
Listen to my evening prayer.

Let my sins be all forgiven;
Bless the friends I love so well;
Take me, when I die, to heaven,
Happy there with thee to dwell.

Mary L. Duncan

74   We thank you, O God, for our happy playtimes. Help us to play happily together, for Jesus Christ's sake. Amen.

We thank you, loving Father, for our home where we are loved, cared for, and are so happy. Bless our mother and father and all who love us. Help us to be kind and thoughtful and to love them dearly. Amen.

Madge E. Swann

PRAYERS FOR THE CHRISTIAN'S YEAR

Advent

75 Father, may this season of Advent renew our hope and the trust which we place in the future that you have prepared for us.

May our hope be strong in the face of all that makes for despair, fear and unbelief:

the cruelties that people inflict on one another,

the questions that cannot be answered,

the uncertainty of our tomorrows.

May our trust grow stronger, Father, as we celebrate the coming of Christ in glory,

when pain, suffering, parting and death will come to an end,

wars shall cease, hunger be no more,

and everyone live secure in your eternal love.

Forgive, Father, all within us that is unprepared for Christ's coming:

our neglect of other people's need,

our involvement in what is trivial and our indifference to what is of lasting importance in our lives,

our idleness in prayer and our lack of attention to your word.

Make us ready for his coming that we may run to meet him with love, adoration and gratitude.

Michael Walker

76 O Lord our God, make us watchful and keep us faithful, as we await the coming of your Son our Lord; that when he shall appear, he may not find us sleeping in sin, but active in his service and joyful in his praise, for the glory of your holy name.

Gelasian Sacramentary

77 Our God, God of the patriarchs, prophets, and apostles, of Abraham and Sarah, of Moses, of Hannah, of Joseph and Mary, of Simeon and Anna, put within us in this season of Advent the longing for your coming that was possessed by those who journeyed before us.

Awaken within us the richness of our origins and the depths of our past that we may be a people old in experience and young in hope.

Come to us as the breaking of the dawn, and dispel the darkness of our desolation and abandonment with a sense of expectancy and joy.

Help us to turn to you with eyes newly open, with hope reawakened, shrugging off the layers of care and doubt that have closed about us.

Lord, prepare us for your coming as pilgrims of the future, looking for the promise of your word: the Saviour of the world. Amen.

Terry Falla

78 O God, our loving Father, we thank you for giving us your Son to be the light of the world.
As we light our Advent candles and open the doors of our Advent calendars help us to gradually open our minds and hearts to his coming.
> Your love came as a baby, may we cherish our children and our families.
> Your love came as a preacher proclaiming the Good News of salvation, may we cherish our Christian faith and share it.
> Your love will come again as judge at the end of time, may we live by the law of love and walk in the light of the same Christ our Lord. Amen.

Anthony Castle

79 Merciful God, who sent your messengers the prophets to preach repentance and prepare the way of our salvation: give us grace to heed their warnings and forsake our sins, that we may greet with joy the coming of Jesus Christ our Redeemer; who lives and reigns with you and the Holy Spirit, now and for ever.

Episcopal Church, USA

80 Almighty God, we give you thanks for the mighty yearning of the human heart for the coming of the Saviour, and the constant promise of your word that he was to come. In our own souls we repeat the humble sighs and panting aspirations of ancient men and ages, and own that our souls are in darkness and infirmity without faith in him who comes to bring God to man and man to God. We bless you for the tribute we can pay to him from our very sense of need and dependence, and that our own hearts can so answer from their wilderness, the cry, 'Prepare the way of the Lord'. In us the rough places are to be made smooth, the crooked straight, the mountains of pride brought low and the valleys of despondency lifted up. O God, prepare the way in us now, and may we welcome anew your Holy Child. Hosanna! Blessed be he who comes in the name of the Lord. Amen.

Samuel Osgood

Christmas

81 Glory be to God in the highest, and on earth peace, good will towards men; for unto us is born this day a Saviour who is Christ the Lord. We praise, we bless, we glorify, we give thanks to you, for this greatest of mercies, O Lord God, heavenly King, God the Father Almighty.

Thomas Ken

82 God, who makes us glad with the yearly remembrance of the birth of your only Son Jesus Christ; Grant that as we joyfully receive him as our Redeemer, so we may with sure confidence behold him, when he shall come to be our Judge, who lives and reigns with you and the Holy Ghost, now and forever.

Book of Common Prayer, 1928

83   Loving Father, as we think of the little Child of Bethlehem,
make us glad that you the Almighty, the Creator, the Infinite,
whose Being is utterly beyond even the power of our loftiest
thought and most daring imagination, can speak to us in a little
human Child. Save us from being impressed too much by the
impressive. Help us to see you in simple things: a child's love,
birdsong, the quiet loveliness of dawn, human friendship and the
peace of our homes. We bow in worship before the majesty of
heaven revealed in a human life. Accept our worship and make
our lives more like his. We ask it for his sake. Amen.

Leslie D. Weatherhead

84   Sweet Child of Bethlehem, grant that we may share with all
our hearts in this profound mystery of Christmas. Pour into
the hearts of men the peace which they sometimes seek so
desperately, and which you alone can give them. Help them
to know one another better and to live as brothers, children
of the same Father. Awaken in their hearts love and gratitude
for your infinite goodness; join them together in your love; and
give us all your heavenly peace.

Pope John XXIII

85   O God, our loving Father, help us rightly to remember the birth
of Jesus, that we may share in the songs of the angels, the
gladness of the shepherds, and the worship of the wise men.
May the Christmas morning make us happy to be your children,
and the Christmas evening bring us to our beds with grateful
thoughts, forgiving and forgiven, for Jesus' sake. Amen.

Robert Louis Stevenson

86   O Christ, whose wondrous birth means nothing unless we be
born again, whose death and sacrifice nothing if you be risen
alone: raise up and exalt us, O Saviour, both now to the estate of
grace and hereafter to the seat of glory; where with the Father
and the Holy Spirit you live and reign, God for ever and ever.

Eric Milner-White

87 Thank you, Father, for this loved and familiar season:
     for tuneful carols,
     for reunions with families and friends,
     for giving and receiving,
     for a sense of celebration everywhere,
     for all the ways of saying, 'Christ is born'.
We ask that the familiarity of Christmas may not smother the truth that we celebrate together.

May Christ be amongst us, as real, as close, as warm as at that first Christmas:
    with Mary, may we open our hearts to the word of God, that Christ may be born in us;
    with the shepherds, may we hear in the world of our daily work what heaven is saying to us;
    may our experience of Christ be as real and enduring as theirs.
Save us from a faith so shallow that we put away our Christian commitment with the decorations or discard it like an unwanted present.

Father, in Christ you embrace our happiness and our need: give to us a love that shall exclude none.

Michael Walker

88 Jesus – Lord
for whom an inn could find no room,
whom your own world would not receive
never let me close my door against you
nor against the least of my brethren
   in their least need.

Stand not then at my door and knock,
though that be a miracle of mercy,
but lift the latch and enter,
Jesus – Lord.

Eric Milner-White

Epiphany

89 Almighty and everlasting God, the brightness of faithful people, who brought the Gentiles to your light, and made known to them Christ who is the true light, and the bright and morning star: fill, we implore you, the world with your glory, and show yourself by the radiance of your light to all the nations; through Jesus Christ our Lord.

Gregorian Sacramentary

90 May Jesus Christ, the king of glory, help us to make the right use of all the myrrh that God sends, and to offer to him the true incense of our hearts; for his name's sake. Amen.

Johann Tauler

91 O God, who made manifest your only begotten Son to the Gentiles, and commanded your Church to preach the gospel to every creature: bless all your servants who are working for you in distant lands. Have compassion upon those who do not know you. Lead them by the Holy Spirit to him who is the light of the world, that, walking in the light, they may at length attain to the light of everlasting life; through Jesus Christ our Lord.

Robert Nelson

92 Lord Jesus Christ, who in the offerings of the wise men received an earnest expression of the worship of the nations: Grant that your Church may never cease to proclaim the good news of your love, that all men may come to worship you as their Saviour and King, who lives and reigns world without end.

George Appleton

Week of Prayer for Christian Unity

93   O Lord God, the one God, make your people one. Whatever our differences, even in matters essential, may we ever realise that we are one in Christ Jesus. Let not Satan break the blessed bond of union between believers, but may it be increasingly strengthened in our own experience, and in all your people everywhere, for the sake of Jesus Christ our Redeemer.

Benjamin Jenks

94   Almighty and everliving God, lover of peace and unity, you have called us, in Christ, to the same love and unity. We pray that your Holy Spirit will so guide and direct our hearts that being released from human pride and fears we may serve you in mercy, humility and gentleness, united with our brothers and sisters, through your dear Son, Jesus Christ.

Christian K. J. Bunsen

95   Lord Jesus Christ, who prayed for your disciples that they might be one, even as you are one with the Father; draw us to yourself, that in common love and obedience to you we may be united to one another, in the fellowship of the one Spirit, that the world may believe that you are Lord, to the glory of God the Father.

William Temple

96   O God, the physician of men and nations, the restorer of the years that have been destroyed: look upon the distractions of the world, and be pleased to complete the work of your healing hand; draw all men to you and one to another by the bands of your love; make your Church one, and fill it with your Spirit, that by your power it may unite the world in a sacred brotherhood of nations, wherein justice, mercy and faith, truth and freedom may flourish, and you may be ever glorified; through Jesus Christ our Lord.

Acts of Devotion

97 O God, whose will it is that all your children should be one in Christ; we pray for the unity of your Church. Pardon all our pride and our lack of faith, of understanding and of charity, which are the causes of our divisions. Deliver us from narrow-mindedness, from our bitterness, from our prejudices. Save us from considering as normal that which is a scandal to the world and an offence to your love. Teach us to recognise the gifts of grace among all those who call upon you and confess the faith of Jesus Christ our Lord.

Liturgy of the French Reformed Church

98 Eternal God, look mercifully upon the broken body of your Church. Draw its members to you and one to another by the bands of your love; that its restored unity may bring healing to the nations, and the life of mankind may glorify you; through Jesus Christ our Lord.

New Every Morning

99 Jesus, Saviour of human activity to which you have given meaning, Saviour of human suffering to which you have given living value, be also the Saviour of human unity; compel us to discard our pettinesses, and to venture forth, resting upon you, into the undaunted ocean of charity.

Teilhard de Chardin

100 O Christ, may all that is part of today's encounter be born of the Spirit of truth and be made fruitful through love.
Behold before us: the past and the future.
Behold before us: the desires of so many hearts.
You, who are the Lord of history and the Lord of human hearts, be with us. Christ Jesus, eternal Son of God, be with us. Amen.

Prayed by Pope John Paul II in Canterbury Cathedral, 29th June 1982

(See also For Christian Unity, 586–587)

Mothering Sunday

101 On this day of sacred memories, our Father, we would thank
you for our mother who gave us life, who surrounded us early
and late with love and care, whose prayers on our behalf still
cling around the Throne of Grace, a haunting perfume of love's
petitions.

Help us, her children, to be more worthy of her love. We know
that no sentimentality on this one day, no material gifts – no
flowers or boxes of candy – can atone for neglect during the
rest of the year. So in the days ahead, may our love speak to
the heart who knows love best – by kindness, by compassion,
by simple courtesy and daily thoughtfulness.

Bless her whose name we whisper before you, and keep her
in your perfect peace, through Jesus Christ, our Lord. Amen.

Peter Marshall

102 Lord Jesus, nine months before the day we celebrate as
Christmas, your Father's message to Mary of Nazareth and
the presence of the Holy Spirit, began your human life within
her. She formed you, educated you, cared for you.

At the foot of the cross Mary witnessed your loving sacrifice
for us. You cared so much for her that your dying act was
to commend her to the care of the Apostle John. May we
continually thank the Father for our mothers who have formed
us, educated us and cared for us.

Anthony Castle

103 Please God, bless all mothers everywhere; the mothers of:
 the little white children,
 the little brown children,
 the little black children,
 the little yellow children,
 the children who live in the hot lands,
 the children who live in the lands of ice and snow.
Wherever there are mothers, please give them your blessing,
 dear God.

Vera Pewtress

Lent

104 Father, give to us the aid of your Holy Spirit
   that we may wisely use this season of Lent.
  It would be tempting, Lord, to make empty gestures, going
  without sugar, or cigarettes, or elevenses, dramatising what
  we do, giving it the appearance of sacrifice.
Father, if you would have us fast,
  then help us to be modest in our fasting,
  keeping what we do to ourselves,
  and not parading abstinence
  as a virtue for others to see
  and congratulate.
Help us to seek a deeper fellowship with Christ:
  may we read the scriptures with greater care,
  recognising those words that particularly speak to us,
  calling us to a greater obedience
  and more willing sacrifice;
  create within us a thirst for prayer,
  so that we may make more time to be with you,
  to listen for your voice in the silence,
  to renew our faith and love.
Help us to be more compassionate to others,
  to draw nearer to you by drawing nearer to them.
Father, may Lent teach us to be better Christians.
            Michael Walker

105 Heavenly Father,
we have decided for your kingdom
and dared to take your cup.

But we confess that we do not understand
the fearsome consequences of obedience.

When we are brought to the test,
steady our nerve and hold us in our faith,

That we may sail through heavy seas,

and ride the frightening storm.

Through Jesus Christ, our Lord. Amen.

Caryl Micklem

106 Almighty God, Father of our Lord Jesus Christ, Maker of all things, Judge of all men: we acknowledge and bewail our manifold sins and wickedness, which we, from time to time, most grievously have committed, by thought, word, and deed, against thy Divine Majesty, provoking most justly thy wrath and indignation against us. We do earnestly repent, and are heartily sorry for these our misdoings; the remembrance of them is grievous unto us; the burden of them is intolerable. Have mercy upon us, have mercy upon us, most merciful Father; for thy Son our Lord Jesus Christ's sake, forgive us all that is past: and grant that we may ever hereafter serve and please thee in newness of life, to the honour and glory of thy Name; through Jesus Christ our Lord.

Book of Common Prayer, 1548

107 O Lord, grant that we may not be conformed to the world, but may love it and serve it. Grant that we may never shrink from being instruments of your peace because of the judgement of the world. Grant that we may love you without fear of the world, grant that we may never believe that the inexpressible majesty of yourself may be found in any power of this earth. May we firstly love you and our neighbours as ourselves. May we remember the poor and the prisoner, and the sick and the lonely, and the young searchers, and the tramps and vagabonds, and the lost and lonely, as we remember Christ, who is in them all.

Alan Paton

108 Lord and Master of my life, take from me the spirit of sloth, faintheartedness, lust of power and idle talk. Give me rather the spirit of chastity, humility, patience and love. Grant me, my Lord and King, to see my own errors and not to judge my brother, for you are blessed for ever and ever.

Ephrem Syrus

109   Give me that tranquil courage which is content to await your
       gift. I live by what comes to me from you, your word proceeding
       forth from your mouth, at your own time, in your way: not
       by my deliberate self-occupied use of the power you give.
       Sometimes my need and exhaustion seem very great, and you
       seem very silent: surrounding conditions seem very stony, and
       hard. Those are the moments when my faith is purified, when
       I am given my chance of patience and fortitude and tranquillity:
       abiding among the stones in the wilderness and learning the
       perfection of dependence on you.

                                                    Evelyn Underhill

110   Bestow on me, O Lord, a genial spirit and unwearied forbear-
       ance; a mild, loving, patient heart; kindly looks, pleasant, cordial
       speech and manners in the intercourse of daily life; that I may
       give offence to none, but as much as in me lies live in charity
       with all men.

                                                       Johann Arndt

111   I pray you, Lord, the Father, and the Guide of our reason, that
       we may remember the nobleness with which you have adorned
       us; and that you would be always on our right hand and on our
       left, in the motion of our own wills; that so we may be purged
       from the contagion of the body and the affections of the brute,
       and overcome them and rule, and use, as it becomes men to use
       them, for instruments. And then that you would be in fellowship
       with us for the careful correction of our reason, and for the
       conjunction by the light of truth with the things that truly are.

                                                    George Chapman

112   Have mercy upon our efforts, that we
       Before you, in love and in faith,
       Righteousness and humility,
       May follow you, with self-denial,
       Steadfastness and courage,
       And meet you in the silence.
       Give us a pure heart that we may see you,
       A humble heart that we may hear you,
       A heart of love that we may serve you,
       A heart of faith that we may love you.

                                                  Dag Hammarskjöld

113   Christ,
      In this dark hour,
      Be near,
      Be swift to save:
      We thank you for the price which must be paid,
      We thank you for each stab which marks the cost,
      We thank you for all weariness, all pain
      Which lays upon us, all too late, our share,
      Our share so little of your cross;
      Oh, make us zealous, Lord, to bear, to pay
      In secret ways,
      That burden and that price:
      Oh, give us grace,
      That valiantly and uncomplainingly
      We may bear on, pay on,
      Unto the end,
      With you.

John S. Hoyland

114   O Lord Christ, Lamb of God, Lord of Lords,
      call us, who are called to be saints,
      along the way of your cross:
      draw us, who would draw nearer our king,
      to the foot of your cross:
      cleanse us, who are not worthy to approach,
      with the pardon of your cross:
      instruct us, the ignorant and blind,
      in the school of your cross:
      arm us, for the battles of holiness,
      by the might of your cross:
      bring us in the fellowship of your sufferings
      to the victory of your cross:
      and seal us in the kingdom of your glory
      among the servants of your cross,
      O crucified Lord;
      who with the Father and the Holy Ghost
      lives and reigns one God
      almighty, eternal,
      world without end.

Eric Milner-White

115   Thank you, Lord Jesus Christ,
for all the benefits which you have given me,
for all the pains and insults you have borne for me.
O most merciful redeemer, friend and brother,
may I know you more clearly,
love you more dearly,
and follow you more nearly,
day by day.

Richard of Chichester

116   O Christ, my Master, let me keep very close to you. When I am tempted to be undisciplined or self-indulgent, let me remember your forty days of prayer and fasting. When the fires of my spirit burn low, let me remember you continuing all night in prayer. When I flinch from hardship, let me go with you to your Gethsemane. When I am lonely, let me turn to you, my risen Lord. Whatever the outer facts may be, grant me your gift of inner joy; in your name and through your grace. Amen

Walter Russell Bowie

117   Son of Man, our Saviour, we remember that your sternest judgements were reserved for the religious people of your day, because they failed to live up to their profession.

Forbid it, Lord, that we, who so often and so readily take your name upon our lips, should come under the same condemnation.

Help us in this season of Lent to search our hearts and examine our lives and to have done with all hypocrisy and pretence; that we may be what we seem to be, put our creed into practice, and bear a witness that will honour you before men.

Frank Colquhoun

Holy Week

118   Lord Jesus Christ, who when you were about to institute your holy Sacrament at the Last Supper washed the feet of the

apostles, and taught us by your example the grace of humility:
Cleanse us, we beseech you, from all stain of sin, that we may
be worthy partakers of the holy mysteries; who lives and
reigns with the Father and the Holy Ghost, one God, world
without end.

The Royal Maundy

119 My God, I love thee: not because
I hope for heaven thereby,
nor yet because who love thee not
are lost eternally.

Thou, O my Jesus, thou didst me
upon the cross embrace;
for me didst bear the nails and spear
and manifold disgrace.

And griefs and torments numberless
and sweat of agony;
even death itself – and all for one
who was thine enemy.

Then why, O blessed Jesu Christ,
should I not love thee well;
not for the sake of winning heaven
or of escaping hell;
not with the hope of gaining aught,
nor seeking a reward:
but as thyself has loved me,
O ever-loving Lord!

Even so I love thee, and will love
and in thy praise will sing,
solely because thou art my God
and my eternal king.

Francis Xavier

120 Almighty and most merciful Father, we are about to commemorate
the death of your Son, Jesus Christ our Saviour and Redeemer.
Grant, O Lord, that our whole hope and confidence may
be in his merits and your mercy. Enforce and accept our
imperfect repentance, make this commemoration available to
the confirmation of our faith, the establishment of our hope,

and the enlargement of our love, and make the death of your dear Son Jesus Christ effectual to our redemption. Have mercy upon us, and pardon the multitude of our offences. Bless our friends. Have mercy upon all men. Support us by the Holy Spirit throughout life, and receive us at last into everlasting happiness.

Dr Samuel Johnson

121   O Jesus, poor and abject, unknown and despised, have mercy upon me, and let me not be ashamed to follow you.

O Jesus, hated, calumniated, and persecuted, have mercy upon me, and make me content to be as my master.

O Jesus, blasphemed, accused, and wrongfully condemned, have mercy upon me, and teach me to endure the contradiction of sinners.

O Jesus, clothed with a habit of reproach and shame, have mercy upon me, and let me not seek my own glory.

O Jesus, insulted, mocked, and spit upon, have mercy upon me, and let me not faint in the fiery trial.

O Jesus, crowned with thorns and hailed in derision;

O Jesus, burdened with our sins and the curses of the people;

O Jesus, affronted, outraged, buffeted, overwhelmed with injuries, griefs and humiliations;

O Jesus, hanging on the accursed tree, bowing the head, giving up the ghost, have mercy upon me, and conform my whole soul to your holy, humble, suffering Spirit.

John Wesley

122   O loving Saviour, we would linger by your cross, that the light of your perfect love may shine into the secret places of our souls, showing what is vile there, so that it may shrink away; and nurturing whatever there is pure or lovely or good, so that beholding you, we may become more like you, Revealer of God to men, Guide of men to God.

William Temple

123   Lord Jesus Christ, who for us endured the horror of deep darkness; teach us by the depth of your agony the vileness of our sin, and so bind us to yourself in bonds of gratitude and love, that we may be united with you in your perfect sacrifice, our Saviour, our Lord and our God.

William Temple.

124   Good, kind and gentle Jesus
      I kneel before you.
      I see and consider your five wounds.
      My eyes behold what David prophesied:
      'They have pierced my hands and my feet;
      they have counted all my bones'.
      Engrave upon me this image of yourself.
      Fulfil the yearnings of my heart;
      give me faith, hope, and love,
      repentance for all my sins
      and a true turning to you for life.

                                        Traditional prayer

125   I kiss the wounds in your sacred head,
      with sorrow deep and true,
      may every thought of mine this day
      be an act of love for you.

      I kiss the wounds in your sacred hands,
      with sorrow deep and true,
      may every touch of my hands this day
      be an act of love for you.

      I kiss the wounds in your sacred feet,
      with sorrow deep and true,
      may every step I take this day
      be an act of love for you.

      I kiss the wound in your sacred side,
      with sorrow deep and true,
      may every beat of my heart this day
      be an act of love for you.

                                        George Spencer

126   Soul of Christ, sanctify me.
      Body of Christ, save me.
      Blood of Christ, fill me.
      Water from the side of Christ, wash me.
      Passion of Christ, strengthen me.
      O good Jesus, hear me.
      Within your wounds hide me.

Suffer me not to be separated from you.
From the malicious enemy defend me.
In the hour of my death call me.
And bid me come unto you.
That with your saints I may praise you.
For ever and ever.

Fourteenth-century prayer

Easter

127 It is the Pasch; the Pasch of the Lord . . .
O you, who are truly all in all! . . .
The joy, the honour, the food and the delight of every
    creature;
through you the shadows of death have fled away,
and life is given to all,
the gates of heaven are flung open.
God becomes man
and man is raised up to the likeness of God.

O divine Pasch! . . .
O Pasch, light of new splendour . . .
The lamps of our souls will no more burn out.
The flame of grace,
divine and spiritual,
burns in the body and soul,
nourished by the resurrection of Christ.

We beg you, O Christ, Lord God,
eternal king of the spiritual world,
stretch out your protecting hands
over your holy Church
and over your holy people;
defend them, keep them, preserve them . . .

Raise up your standard over us
and grant that we may sing with Moses
the song of victory,
for yours is the glory and the power for all eternity! Amen.

Hippolytus of Rome

128 O Lord, who by triumphing over the power of darkness prepared our place in the New Jerusalem; grant us, who have this day given thanks for your resurrection, to praise you in that city of which you are the light; where with the Father and the Holy Spirit you live and reign, now and for ever.

William Bright

129 God, through the mighty resurrection of your Son Jesus Christ you have liberated us from the power of darkness and brought us into the kingdom of your love; grant that as he was raised from the dead by the glory of the Father, so we may walk in newness of life, and look for those things which are in heaven, where with you, Father, and the Holy Spirit, he is alive and reigns for ever and ever.

Gelasian Sacramentary

130 O heavenly Father, whose blessed Son has 'risen from the dead, and become the first fruits of them that slept', grant that we may so live and die in him that when he shall appear again in his glory we may rise to everlasting life. We pray also for all our brethren in Christ, especially our relations and friends, and neighbours, that we may all share in a joyful resurrection, and be partakers of thy heavenly kingdom, through Christ our Lord.

W. Walsham How

131 Merciful and gracious God, who deigned to make Mary Magdalene the first witness and herald of the glorious resurrection of your Son. Grant to those who have fallen into the torment and captivity of sin to hear that wondrous voice of Jesus, which is able to subdue and cast out all evil passions, that there may be none without hope of mercy, or beyond help of grace, through the same Jesus Christ our Saviour.

William E. Orchard

132 O God of unchangeable power and eternal light, look favourably on your whole Church, that wonderful and sacred mystery, and carry out the work of man's salvation; and let the whole world feel and see that things which were cast down are being raised up, and things which had grown old are being made new, and all things are returning to perfection, through Jesus Christ our Lord. Amen.

Gelasian Sacramentary

133 O God, who by the glorious death and resurrection of your Son Jesus Christ has brought life and immortality to light; grant us so to die daily to sin that we may evermore live with you in the joy of his resurrection; through the same Jesus Christ our Lord, to whom be glory and dominion for ever and ever.

Gregorian Sacramentary

134 Lord Jesus, risen from the dead and alive for evermore: Stand in our midst today as in the upper room; show us your hands and your side; speak your peace to our hearts and minds; and send us forth into the world as your witnesses; for the glory of your name.

John R. W. Stott

135 God of the inner light,
come to us
on the golden rays of the morning,
warming moods that are frosty,
enlightening minds that are gloomy;
and, as the sun swings higher,
so may our lives rise to you
in the active praise of this day's duties:
through Jesus, our risen Light.

Bruce Prewer

136 Lord of creation and God of grace, we thank you for the yearly miracle of the spring, as the earth awakes from its winter sleep and is arrayed again in the glory of resurrection life.

May a similar miracle of grace take place in our lives this Easter. Send into our hearts the Spirit of the living Christ, to raise us to newness of life and to clothe us with the beauty of his holiness, for your honour and glory.

Frank Colquhoun

137 Pour upon us, O Lord, your heavenly blessing, that we may be armed with the faith of the resurrection so as not to fear any army of men sent against us.

Matthew Parker

138 Lord Jesus, our risen Saviour, we rejoice in your mighty victory
over sin and death. You are the Prince of life: you are alive for
evermore. Help us to know your presence, not only as we
worship you here, but at home, and at work, and wherever
we go; for your great name's sake. Amen.

Michael Botting

139 O risen and victorious Christ, whose power and love destroyed
the darkness and death of sin; ascend, we pray, the throne of
our hearts, and so rule our wills by the might of that immortality
wherewith you have set us free, that we may evermore be alive
to God, through the power of your glorious resurrection, world
without end.

John W. Suter

140 Lord, come alive within my experience,
within my sorrows and disappointments and doubts,
within the ordinary movements of my life.
Come alive as the peace and joy and assurance that is
stronger than the locked doors within, with which we
try to shut out life.
Come alive as the peace and joy and assurance that
nothing in life or death can kill.

Rex Chapman

141 O Risen Saviour, bid me rise with Thee
and seek those things which are above;
not only seek, but set my whole heart upon them.

Thou art in heaven, ever raising lives to Thyself;
O, by Thy grace, may mine be making that ascent
not in dreams, but in truth,
now, tomorrow, always.

Daily in spirit, in Thy Holy Spirit,
Let me behold Thee on the throne of God,
Thou King reigning in holiness,
Thou Conqueror of all evil,
Thou Majesty of love,
very God and very Man,

of glory unimaginable and eternal,
in whom all hope is sure.

Eric Milner-White

Ascension

142 Glory to our ascended Lord that he is with us always.
Glory to the Word of God, going forth with his armies conquering and to conquer.
Glory to him who has led captivity captive and given gifts for the perfecting of his saints.
Glory to him who has gone before to prepare a place in his Father's home for us.
Glory to the Author and Finisher of our Faith; that God in all things may be glorified through Jesus Christ,
To whom be all worship and praise, dominion and glory; now and for ever and ever. Amen

Sursum Corda

143 O Glorious Christ, who in your ascension entered into your kingdom: Remember the countless millions who have not heard of the redemption which you have won for them.

Grant that they may learn, through your Church, of the new and living way which you have opened for them. Let them draw near in fullness of faith, to enter with you into the holy place of the Father's presence, and receive forgiveness and peace. So may they worship, with the innumerable company of angels and with the spirits of just men made perfect, Father, Son and Holy Spirit, one God, blessed for evermore.

George Appleton

144 O God, who has exalted the Crucified, the Son, by a triumphant resurrection and ascension into heaven: May his triumphs and glories so shine in the eyes of our hearts and minds, that we may more clearly comprehend his sufferings, and more courageously pass through our own; for his sake who with Thee and the Holy Ghost lives and reigns, one God, for ever and ever.

Eric Milner-White

145 Almighty and merciful God, into whose
ascend, not by the frailty of the flesh, but
soul: make us ever seek after the courts ᴏ
where our Saviour Christ has ascended, aᴎ
confidently enter them both now and hereaᵭ
same Jesus Christ our Lord.

ʙ   . Brooks

146 You are not only risen and alive, you are Lord.
This your ascension, your ascendency over the whole
universe.
You stand over and above all that is best in life as its source.
You stand above all that is worst as ultimate victor.
You stand above all powers and authorities as judge.
You stand above all failure and weakness and sin as forgiveness
and love.
You alone are worthy of total allegiance, total commitment.
You are Lord,
'My Lord and my God'.

Rex Chapman

Pentecost

147 Come, Holy Spirit, fill the hearts of your faithful, and kindle in
them the fire of your love.
Send forth your Spirit and they shall be created.
And you shall renew the face of the earth.
O God, who has taught the hearts of the faithful by the light
of the Holy Spirit, grant that by the gift of the same Spirit we
may be always truly wise and ever rejoice in his consolation.

Traditional prayer

148 Breathe the Spirit into our hearts, Father.
Set us free from habits or traditions that no longer allow the
Spirit to move freely among us. Touch our tongues with holy
fire that we may more effectively proclaim the gospel. Fill all

our activities with the love of Christ that what we do may serve
the increase of your kingdom.
Father, give us the Spirit and help us to receive him.

Michael Walker

149 O God, may the fire of the Holy Spirit burn up the dross in our
hearts, warm them with love and set them on fire with zeal for
your service.

Ancient collect

150 O Lord Jesus Christ, who on the first day of the week rose
again: Raise up our souls to serve the living God; and as
you also on this day sent down on your apostles your most
Holy Spirit, so take not the same Spirit from us, but grant
that we may be daily renewed and plentifully enriched by
his power; for your own mercy's sake, who lives and reigns
with the Father and the Holy Spirit, ever one God, world
without end.

Lancelot Andrewes

151 Lord Jesus, we thank you that you have fulfilled your promise
and given us your Spirit to abide with us for ever: grant us to
know his presence in all its divine fullness.
    May the fruit of the Spirit be growing continually in our
lives;
    may the gifts of the Spirit be distributed among us as he wills
to equip us for your service;
    and may the power of the Spirit be so working in us that the
world around may increasingly come to believe in you.
    We ask it, Lord, in your victorious name.

Michael Botting

152 Holy Spirit of God,
    great gift of our exalted Lord,
    on the day of Pentecost you came to the Church
    as he promised, to abide with us for ever.
    Come to us in your grace and power today,
    to make Jesus real to us,
    to teach us more about him,
    and to deepen our trust in him;
    that we may be changed into his likeness

and be his witnesses in the world,
to the glory of God the Father.

Unknown source

153 Praise to the Holy Spirit who alone enables us to call God
     our Father and Jesus our Lord.
     May we live and walk by the same Spirit,
     that we may grow in the likeness of Jesus Christ
     and pray with the freedom of the sons of God.

     Praise to the Holy Spirit for his fruit of love and joy and
       peace.
     May he put to death in us the works of the flesh,
     that his fruit may grow and prosper
     and our lives be lived to the glory of God.

     Praise to the Holy Spirit for his gifts of power and inspiration.
     May he lead the Church to desire the best gifts
     and to distinguish the true from the false,
     for the sake of the health of the Body.

     Praise to the Holy Spirit who is the promise of the Father and
       the gift of the Son, in whose name we pray, Jesus
       Christ our Lord.

Christopher Idle

154 O Lord our God,
     you poured out the grace of your Holy Spirit
     upon your holy and glorious apostles:
     so purify our minds,
     and let them be without stain or blemish,
     that approaching your fearful Name
     with cleansed hearts
     we may enjoy
     the good things promised to us.

     Through the mercy of your Christ
     with whom and the most holy and life-giving Spirit
     you are to be worshipped
     now and for ever
     to the ages of ages. Amen.

Orthodox Liturgy

155 O heavenly Father, the author and fountain of all truth, the bottomless sea of all understanding, send, we beseech you, your Holy Spirit into our hearts and lighten our understanding with the beams of your heavenly grace. We ask this, O merciful Father, for your dear Son, Our Saviour, Jesus Christ's sake. Amen.

Nicholas Ridley

156 Strengthen me, O God, by the grace of your Holy Spirit. Grant me to be strengthened with might in the inner man, and to empty my heart of all useless care and anguish. O Lord, grant me heavenly wisdom, that I may learn above all things to seek and to find you, above all things to relish and to love you, and to think of all other things as being, what indeed they are, at the disposal of your wisdom. Amen.

Thomas à Kempis

157 Give me, O Lord, purity of lips, a clean and innocent heart; humility, fortitude, patience.

Give me the Spirit of wisdom and understanding, the Spirit of counsel and strength, the Spirit of knowledge and godliness, and of your fear.

Make me ever to seek your face with all my heart, all my soul, all my mind; grant me to have a contrite and humble heart in your Presence.

Most high, eternal and ineffable Wisdom, drive away from me the darkness of blindness and ignorance; most high and eternal Strength, deliver me; most high and eternal Light, illuminate me; most high and infinite Mercy, have mercy on me.

Gallican Formularies

158 O Lord, my God, teach me to pray for the right blessings. Steer the vessel of my life towards yourself, the peaceful harbour for storm-tossed souls. Show me the course I should sail, renew a willing spirit within me. May your Spirit curb my wandering senses and help me to observe your laws. Gladden my heart with your glorious presence within. For yours is the glory and the praise of all the saints forever.

Basil the Great

159 O God, renew our spirits by your Holy Spirit, and draw our hearts to yourself, that our work may not be a burden, but a delight. Let us not serve as slaves, with the spirit of bondage, but with freedom and gladness as your sons, rejoicing in your will; for Jesus Christ's sake.

Benjamin Jenks

160 Your Spirit, O God, came to the disciples through Jesus Christ our Lord: bless your disciples today with the same gift from the same Master, that they may find fullness of life in him, and serve him with joy and power all the days of their life, for his truth and mercy's sake. Amen.

Dick Williams

161 O Lord, grant us the power of your Holy Spirit in our lives
even as you have promised.
Remove from our hearts and minds and lives those things
which hinder,
And increase and nourish all that is good.
Give us courage to speak for you,
Energy to work for you,
And strength to face the troubles of each day.
So that, through us, your Kingdom may increase and your Name
be glorified. Amen.

Beryl Bye

162 O Spirit of God
who speaks to spirits
created in your own likeness;
penetrate into the depths of our spirits,
into the storehouse of memories,
remembered and forgotten,
into the depths of being,
the very springs of personality,
and cleanse and forgive,
making us whole and holy,
that we may be thine
and live in the new being
of Christ our Lord.

George Appleton

163   These are the gifts I ask
      Of Thee, Spirit serene;
      Strength for the daily task,
      Courage to face the road,
      Good cheer to help me bear the traveller's load;
      And for the hours that come between,
      An inward joy in all things heard and seen.

                                    Henry van Dyke

164   Lead, Kindly Light, amid the encircling gloom,
      Lead Thou me on!
      The night is dark, and I am far from home;
      Lead Thou me on!
      Keep Thou my feet; I do not ask to see
      The distant scene; one step enough for me.

      I was not ever thus, nor pray'd that Thou
      Shouldst lead me on.
      I loved to choose and see my path; but now
      Lead Thou me on!
      I loved the garish day, and, spite of fears,
      Pride ruled my will: remember not past years.

      So long Thy power hath blest me, sure it still
      Will lead me on,
      O'er moor and fen, o'er crag and torrent, till
      The night is gone;
      And with the morn those angel faces smile
      Which I have loved long since, and lost awhile.

                                    John Henry Newman

165   O Come, O Holy Spirit, come!
      Come as holy fire and burn in us,
      Come as holy wind and cleanse us,
      Come as holy light and lead us,
      Come as holy truth and teach us,
      Come as holy forgiveness and free us,
      Come as holy love and enfold us,
      Come as holy power and enable us,
      Come as holy life and dwell in us.
      Convict us, convert us,

Consecrate us, until we are wholly Thine
for Thy using, through Jesus Christ our Lord.

Adapted by Charles Francis Whiston
from an ancient prayer

166   Spirit of the Living Christ, come upon us in the glory of your
risen power; Spirit of the Living Christ, come upon us in
all the humility of your wondrous love; Spirit of the Living
Christ, come upon us that new life may course within our
veins, new love bind us together in one family, a new vision
of the Kingdom of God spur us on to serve you with fearless
passion.

Iona Community

167   Come, thou Father of the poor,
Come with treasures which endure,
Come thou light of all that live!
Thou of all consolers best.
Thou the soul's delightful guest,
Dost refreshing peace bestow.
Thou in toil art comfort sweet,
Pleasant coolness in the heat,
Solace in the midst of woe.
Light immortal, light divine,
Visit thou these hearts of thine,
And our inmost being fill.
If thou take thy grace away
Nothing pure in man will stay;
All his good is turned to ill.
Heal our wounds, our strength renew.
On our dryness pour thy dew,
Wash the stains of guilt away.
Bend the stubborn heart and will;
Melt the frozen, warm the chill;
Guide the steps that go astray.
Thou on us, who ever more
Thee confess and thee adore,
With thy sevenfold gifts descend:
Give us comfort when we die,

Give us life with thee on high;
Give us joys that never end.

Attributed to Stephen Langton
Translated E. Caswall

Trinity

168 Blessing and honour, thanksgiving and praise
more than we can utter be unto you,
O most adorable Trinity, Father, Son and Holy Ghost,
by all angels, all men, all creatures
for ever and ever Amen and Amen.
To God the Father, who first loved us,
and made us accepted in the Beloved;
To God the Son who loved us,
and washed us from our sins in his own blood;
To God the Holy Ghost,
who sheds the love of God abroad in our hearts
be all love and all glory for time and for eternity. Amen.

Thomas Ken

169 I am bending my knee
In the eye of the Father who created me,
In the eye of the Son who purchased me,
In the eye of the Spirit who cleansed me,
In friendship and affection.
Through Thine own Anointed One, O God,
Bestow upon us fullness in our need,
Love towards God,
The affection of God,
The smile of God,
The wisdom of God,
The grace of God,
The fear of God,
And the will of God,
To do on the world of the Three,
As angels and saints
Do in heaven;

Each shade and light,
Each day and night,
Each time in kindness,
Give Thou us Thy Spirit.

Gaelic prayer

170 Batter my heart, three-person'd God, for you
As yet but knock, breathe, shine, and seek to mend.
That I may rise and stand, o'erthrow me, and bend
Your force to break, blow, burn, and make me new.
I, like an usurp'd town, to another due
Labour to admit you, but O, to no end!
Reason, your viceroy in me, me should defend,
But is captiv'd and proves weak or untrue.
Yet dearly I love you, and would be loved fain,
But am betrothed unto your enemy;
Divorce me, untie, or break that knot again,
Take me to you, imprison me, for I
Except you enthral me, never shall be free,
Nor ever chaste, except you ravish me.

John Donne

171 Almighty God, you have revealed to your Church your eternal
Being of glorious majesty and perfect love as one God in Trinity
of Persons: give us grace to continue steadfast in the confession
of this faith, and constant in our worship of you, Father, Son,
and Holy Spirit; for you live and reign, one God, now and
for ever.

Episcopal Church, USA

172 Glory be to the Father
and to the Son
and to the Holy Spirit
as it was in the beginning
is now and ever shall be
world without end.
Amen.

Traditional prayer

Harvest Thanksgiving

173 O God, from whose unfailing bounty we draw our life and all
that we possess, forgive our pride and self-sufficiency. Teach
us to reverence the earth, which you have made fruitful. Help
us to remember our unity with those by whose work we are
fed and clothed. Touch us with compassion for all who have not
enough to eat. As you have given us the knowledge which can
produce plenty, so give us also the wisdom to bring it within
the reach of all: through Jesus Christ our Lord.

John H. Oldham

174 Creator of heaven and earth, you have studded the sky with
stars and made it bright with lights, enriched the earth with
fruits to satisfy men's needs, given to the race that took shape
under your hands the clear light and the shining stars to enjoy,
the earth's produce to feed on. We pray you, send us rain,
abundant, plentiful, fertilising; and make the earth yield fruit
and to spare; for we know how you love men, we know what
your kindness is.

Hear our petitions and prayers and bless the whole earth,
through your only Son, Jesus Christ. Through him may glory
and power be yours, in the Holy Spirit, now and age after
age. Amen.

Serapion of Thmuis

175 Creator God, we thank you for your promise that while the
earth endures seed time and harvest, summer and winter, day
and night, shall not fail. We thank you for the reliability of this
good earth, for the variety of the seasons and for all the unity
and contrasts of creation. We thank you for this world's agenda
for the labours of men and for permitting us to be partners to the
earth's activity. We thank you that we can nourish the miracle
of life upon the miracle of harvest and we praise you for the
dignity of sharing in the work of your almighty hands, O God
our Father, blessed for ever. Amen.

Dick Williams

176 Almighty God, Lord of heaven and earth, in whom we live and move and have our being; who does good to all men, making your sun to rise on the evil and on the good, and sending rain on the just and on the unjust: favourably behold us your servants, who call upon your Name, and send us your blessing from heaven, in giving us fruitful seasons, and satisfying us with food and gladness; that both our hearts and mouths shall be continually filled with your praise, giving thanks to you in your holy Church; through Jesus Christ our Lord.

John Cosin

177 Lord, there is joy in this season. The earth again has performed her miracle and out of the seed buried in darkness has brought to birth our daily bread.
Thank you, Lord, for rain and sun that have summoned the seed out of the earth.
Thank you for those who have harvested the crops and those who have brought them to us.
Thank you, Lord, for our food and drink.

Michael Walker

178 We thank You, O God, for all the joys of harvest time.
For the satisfaction we gain from making jam and jelly and chutney and preserving and freezing tomatoes, fruit and vegetables.
For the beauty of the fields of ripe corn and the tints of autumn leaves.
For the smell of wood fires and ripe apples.
For the feel of a crisp morning and dry leaves crunching under our feet.
For these and many other blessings, accept our grateful thanks, O Lord. Amen.

Beryl Bye

179 Lord of the harvest,
we rejoice in the bounty of your world;
we thank you for the rich harvests it produces.
As we do so, we remember those who do not have enough,
the thousands who are daily dying of hunger.
We pray for those who have more than they require,
for ourselves and our churches.

Show us what needs to be done,
and how to share the world's harvest more fairly.
Teach us to value people more than things.
Above all, help us to set our hearts
on your kingdom of love and justice,
and to seek to do your will here on earth,
as servants of Jesus Christ our Lord.

Adapted from Christian Aid

Prayers for the Christian's Life

For the Family

180 O God, our heavenly Father, from whom every family in heaven and on earth is named: We entrust to your loving care the members of our families, both near and far. Supply their needs; guide their footsteps; keep them in safety of body and soul; and may your peace rest upon our homes and upon our dear ones everywhere; for Jesus Christ our Saviour's sake.

Frank Colquhoun

181 We thank you, Father, for the gift of Jesus your Son who came to our earth and lived in a simple home. We have a greater appreciation of the value and dignity of the human family because he loved and was loved within its shelter. Bless us this day; may we grow in love for each other in our family and so give thanks to you who are the maker of all human families and our abiding peace.

Michael Buckley

182 Father in heaven, pattern of all parenthood and lover of children, we pray for homes and families across the world (or in this community).

Sustain and comfort them in need and sorrow.

In times of bitterness, tension and division, draw near to heal.

May parents and children together be learners in the school of Christ, daily increasing in mutual respect and understanding, in tolerance and patience, and in all-prevailing love; through Jesus Christ our Lord.

Timothy Dudley-Smith

183   Lord God, from you every family in heaven and on earth takes its name.
Father, you are Love and Life.
Through your Son, Jesus Christ, born of woman,
and through the Holy Spirit, fountain of divine charity,
grant that every family on earth
may become for each successive generation
a true shrine of life and love.
Grant that your grace may guide
the thoughts and actions of husbands and wives
for the good of their families
and of all the families in the world.
Grant that the young may find in the family
solid support for their human dignity
and for their growth in truth and love.
Grant that love,
strengthened by the grace of the sacrament of marriage,
may prove mightier than all the weaknesses and trials
through which our families sometimes pass.
Through the intercession of the Holy Family of Nazareth,
grant that the Church may fruitfully carry out her worldwide
mission in the family and through the family.
We ask this of you, who are Life, Truth, and Love,
with the Son and the Holy Spirit. Amen.

Pope John Paul II

184   Lord God, to come to you is to come home, for you are eternally the Father of all men. From you every family takes its name, and your household of faith gives the pattern for every human household.
We thank you for showing us, in Jesus, that we belong to you and that you care for us. Help us to believe it, and to believe that we ought not to live so selfishly. Show us the deeper joy of

service, and give us pardon and peace through the Holy Spirit.
For Jesus Christ's sake.

Caryl Micklem and Roger Tomes

185 Almighty God, by whose goodness we were created, and whose
mercies never fail, we commend to you all who have a place
in our hearts and sympathies; all who are joined to us by the
sacred ties of kindred, friendship, and love; keep them both
outwardly in their bodies and inwardly in their souls; through
Jesus Christ our Lord.

John Hunter

186 O Lord, we pray for those who, full of confidence and love, once
chose a partner for life, and are now alone after final separation.
May they receive the gift of time, so that hurt and bitterness
may be redeemed by healing and love, personal weakness by
your strength, inner despair by the joy of knowing you and
serving others; through Jesus Christ our Lord.

Susan Williams

187 Lord, behold our family here assembled.
We thank you for this place in which we dwell,
for the love that unites us,
for the peace accorded us this day,
for the hope with which we expect the morrow;
for the health, the work, the food and the bright skies
that make our lives delightful;
for our friends in all parts of the earth.
Give us courage and gaiety and the quiet mind.
Spare us to our friends, soften us to our enemies.
Bless us, if it may be, in all our innocent endeavours;
if it may not, give us the strength
to endure that which is to come
that we may be brave in peril,
constant in tribulation, temperate in wrath
and in all changes of fortune
and down to the gates of death,
loyal and loving to one another.
We beseech of you this help and mercy
for Christ's sake.

Robert Louis Stevenson

188 Dear Lord, who has blessed us with the gift of family life, that we may learn to love and care for others: We praise you for the example of your Son Jesus Christ, who even when deserted and betrayed by closest friends took thought for his mother and his disciple. Open our eyes to recognise in all men the claims of kinship, and stir our hearts to serve them as brethren called with us into the sonship of your love.

Basil Naylor

189 Heavenly Father, from whom all parenthood comes, teach us so to understand our children that they may grow in your wisdom and love according to your holy will. Fill us with sensitive respect for the great gift of human life which you have committed to our care, help us to listen with patience to their worries and problems and give us the tolerance to allow them to develop, as individuals, as your Son did under the loving guidance of Mary and Joseph.

Michael Buckley

190 Lord God, to come to you is to come home, for you are eternally the Father of all men. From you every family takes its name, and your household of faith gives the pattern for every human household.
We thank you for showing us, in Jesus, that we belong to you and that you care for us. Help us to believe it, and to believe that we ought not to live so selfishly.
Show us the deeper joy of service, and give us pardon and peace through the Holy Spirit. For Jesus Christ's sake.

Frank Colquhoun

191 Lord, I want above all to bring up my children to know and love you. It is not easy to explain to them that you love them and care for them, especially when things go wrong and they are hurt physically or wounded mentally. I know I must show my trust in you and go on serenely and lovingly when I too am hurt. Take me over, Lord, completely, rule my life and shine through me with your light so that they may know that you are a living and loving God. Please let me forget myself through loving you, for this is the way that they will grow to see the depth of your love. Help me dear Lord.

Michael Hollings and Etta Gullick

192 Almighty God and heavenly Father, we thank you for the
children whom you have given to us; give us also grace to
train them in your faith, fear and love; that as they advance
in years they may grow in grace, and be found hereafter in the
number of your elect children; through Jesus Christ our Lord.
John Cosin

193 O Lord Jesus, be near to all young children, that in the peril
and confusion of this age their growing spirits may take no
hurt at our hands, and grant to parents such sure knowledge
of your love that they may guide their children with courage
and faith.
New Every Morning

194 Bless my children with healthful bodies, with good under-
standings, with the grace and gifts of your Spirit, with sweet
dispositions and holy habits, and sanctify them throughout in
their bodies, souls and spirits, and keep them unblameable to
the coming of the Lord Jesus.
Jeremy Taylor

195 God our Father, we pray for our young people growing up in
an unstable and confusing world.
     Show them that your ways give more meaning to life than
the ways of the world, and that following you is better than
chasing after selfish goals.
     Help them to take failure not as a measure of their worth but
as a chance for a new start.
     Give them strength to hold their faith in you, and to keep alive
their joy in your creation; through Jesus Christ our Lord.
Episcopal Church, USA

196 O Lord God, whose will it is that, next to yourself, we should
hold our parents in highest honour; it is not the least of our
duties to beseech your goodness toward them. Preserve, we
pray, our parents and home, in the love of your religion and in
health of body and mind. Grant that through us no sorrow may
befall them; and finally as they are kind to us, so may you be
to them, O supreme Father of all.
Erasmus

197 Heavenly Father, creator and giver of life, there is such joy in our hearts at the news of a baby's birth, a most special and complete gift of your love, a new being and a wonder of creation.

Be with the mother and father of this little baby in their happiness, and accept their praise and ours as we give thanks to you, through Jesus Christ our Lord.

Mothers' Union

198 Lord Jesus, who loved the little ones, bless the children of this family, guide and protect them through their growing years and throughout their lives. Be to them a true shepherd and suffer them not to fall away from your love and service. May they always listen to your voice, because they know you as their Lord and Saviour.

Michael Buckley

199 Lord Christ,
We bring before you the world of children.
We bring their openness and friendliness,
their sense of inquiry and curiosity,
their creativity and freshness.
Forgive our voices of experience,
our demand for their conformity.
Help us to stimulate and encourage and cheer,
to inspire and understand.
That their spirits may be lifted, their imaginations quickened,
their vision broadened. For your world's sake. Amen.

J. Dickson Pope

200 Father, hear us, we are praying,
Hear the words our hearts are saying,
We are praying for our children.

Keep them from the powers of evil,
From the secret, hidden peril,
From the whirlpool that would suck them,
From the treacherous quicksand pluck them.

From the worldling's hollow gladness,

From the sting of faithless sadness,
Holy Father, save our children.

Through life's troubled waters steer them,
Through life's bitter battle cheer them,
Father, Father, be Thou near them.
Read the language of our longing,
Read the wordless pleadings thronging,
Holy Father, for our children
    And wherever they may bide,
        Lead them Home at eventide.

                                          Amy Carmichael

201 Lord, guard our children from the dangers that beset them on
        every side, and help us to give them the right values.
     Help us to impress upon them the necessity of telling
        the truth.
     Help us to demonstrate the satisfaction gained from doing a
        job well.
     Help us to show them that hard work brings its own
        reward.
     Help us to teach them the meaning of real love.
     Help us to be honest about our own shortcomings, and to
        have the wisdom to introduce our children to the only One
        who can uphold and uplift them at all times, Jesus Christ
        our Lord. Amen.

                                              Beryl Bye

202 Lord,
     teach me to love my grandchildren
     as a grandmother should:
     not interfering,
     only understanding;
     not pushing myself,
     just being there when wanted.
     Teach me to be the sort of grandmother
     my children
     and my children's children
     would want me to be.

                                          Rosa George

For Friends

203 May the God of love
who is the source of all our affection
for each other formed here on earth
take our friendships into his keeping,
that they may continue and increase
throughout life and beyond it,
in Jesus Christ our Lord.

William Temple

204 Lord, I thank you for my special friends:
those with whom I share secrets and private names;
those who know my moods and yet still offer their affection
and understanding;
those to whom I can unburden the weakness of my nature,
and who can strengthen me against myself;
those who delight in my successes, and encourage me to rise
again from my failures.
Lord, for these special friends I pray.
May I keep such friendships in good repair.
May I never forget them or dishonour them.
May they and I, together, be held within the circle of your
love.

Stanley Pritchard

205 I thank you for my friends,
For those who understand me better than I understand myself,
For those who know me at my worst and still like me,
For those who have forgiven me when I had no right to expect
to be forgiven.
Help me to be as true to my friends as I would wish them to
be to me.

William Barclay

206 Lord Jesus, thank you for being our friend,
and for enriching our lives

with so many gifts of your love.
Thank you for human friends
and for all they mean to us.
Thank you especially for those
who have helped us
and stood by us in difficult times.
Help us, who have received so much,
to give true friendship to others,
in your name
and for your sake.

Frank Colquhoun

For the Married

207 Lord, it's wonderful being married and we do thank you for
the joy of it. We haven't much furniture and the flat needs
decorating badly, but it is an adventure doing things together
so as to make it look nicer. We may never have much money,
but we have each other. This is wonderful. Help us always to
be loving and able to share things. Whatever happens help us
to remember that you are with us in our love, and will help us
with all our problems.

Michael Hollings and Etta Gullick

208 Heavenly Father,
Marriage is of your making.
It is you who have joined us together
   as man and wife.
We pray that throughout our married life
   you will give us grace at all times
      to be true to one another,
      to consider one another's needs,
      to support one another in trouble,
      to forgive one another's mistakes,
      to love one another to the end.
So may we as man and wife enjoy your constant
   blessing and live together for your glory.

Frank Colquhoun

209 Eternal God, author of harmony and happiness, we thank you
for the gift of marriage in which men and women seek and find
fulfilment, companionship, and the blessing of family life.
    Give patience to those who look forward to
      marriage.
    Give courage to those who face trials within their
      marriage.
    Give comfort to those whose marriage has
      broken.
    Give gratitude to those whose marriages are
      successful and fruitful, and let their lives reflect your love
      and glory.
Through Jesus Christ our Lord.

Michael Saward

210 Lord, we've quarrelled and I'm utterly miserable. I don't know
what to do! He treats me like a stranger; whatever I do or say
makes no difference. When I try to be amusing, he just looks
at me coldly. I've tried to apologise but he does not respond,
not even to tell me that it was my fault! I am frozen inside and
weary, and without any idea what to do now. I love him so much
and it hurts. Lord, I love you too; don't leave me, but give me
your peace so I can keep going and break this deadlock in our
lives. Amen.

Michael Hollings and Etta Gullick

For the Elderly

211 Lord, Jesus Christ, King of kings; you have power over life
and death, you know even what is uncertain and obscure, our
secret thoughts and feelings are not hidden from you. Cleanse
me from my faults, for I have done evil in your sight.

    Day by day my life draws nearer to its end and my sins seem
to increase as time passes. O Lord, God of soul and body, you
know how frail I am. Give me strength, Lord, in my weakness

and uphold me in my sufferings. Give me a prudent judgement, good Lord, and let me always remember your blessings. Do not think of my many sins; put my faults out of your mind.

Lord, do not disdain my prayer, a sinner though I am; but leave with me that grace of yours that has been my protection until now. Your grace it was that taught me wisdom. Blessed are they that keep to its paths, a glorious crown awaits them.

I am unworthy and sinful, Lord, but I still want to bless and praise you, for you have poured your mercies lavishly over me, you have been my Helper and Protector; your great name deserves eternal glory.

Glory to you, O Lord, our God.

Ephrem Syrus

212 When the signs of age begin to mark my body and still more when they touch my mind; when the illness that is to diminish me or carry me off strikes from without or is born within me; when the painful moment comes in which I suddenly awaken to the fact that I am ill or growing old; in all those dark moments, O God, grant that I may understand that it is you, provided only my faith is strong enough, who are painfully parting the fibres of my being in order to penetrate to the very marrow of my substance and bear me away within yourself.

Teilhard de Chardin

213 It's not very nice to be an old fogey, Lord.
I don't feel an old fogey,
even if I might look one.
Inside one doesn't feel old,
it's the outside that decays so quickly.
Lined face,
sagging muscles,
greying hair
And young folk class you as an old fogey,
thinking that you have forgotten what it is to be young.
You were never old, Master.
You died in young manhood,
so You never felt the slackening of the life-lines as the years mounted.
But Your mother stood near the Cross, with tired face and greying hair.

And You loved her,
cared for her,
provided for her.
So You will be compassionate with those of us termed 'old
    fogies', won't You?
Even if we are slow on the uptake . . .
for the will to do still exists when the power to do departs.
The tenant remains youthful while the house decays.

It is Your own law, Master,
and You know best.

Flora Larsson

214   Eternal God, who through the passing years remain ever the
        same, be near to all who are aged or infirm. Though their bodies
        fail let their spirits be strong in you, that with patience they may
        bear weariness and distress, and at the last may meet death
        unafraid, through Jesus Christ our Lord.

New Every Morning

215   O Lord Jesus Christ, who heard the prayer of your two disciples
        and stopped with them at eventide: Stay, we pray, with all your
        people in the evening of life. Make yourself known to them, and
        let your light shine upon their path; and whenever they shall
        pass through the valley of the shadow of death, be with them
        unto the end; through Jesus Christ our Lord.

George Appleton

216   Jesus, who never grew old, it is not easy for any of us to face
        old age. It is fine to be young, attractive, strong. Old age
        reminds us of weakness and dependence upon others. But to be
        your disciple means accepting weakness and interdependence.
        Because of you we can rejoice in weakness in ourselves, and
        be tender to it in others.

Monica Furlong

217   May Christ-Omega keep me always young 'to the greater glory
        of God'.
            For
                old age comes from him,
                old age leads on to him, and

old age will touch me only in so far as he wills.

To be 'young' means to be hopeful, energetic, smiling – and clear-sighted.

May I accept death in whatever guise it may come to me in Christ-Omega, that is within the process of the development of life.

A smile (inward and outward) means facing with sweetness and gentleness whatever befalls me.

Jesus-Omega, grant me to serve you, to proclaim you, to glorify you, to make you manifest, to the very end through all the time that remains to me of life, and above all through my death. Desperately, Lord Jesus, I commit to your care my last active years, and my death; do not let them impair or spoil my work I have so dreamed of achieving for you.

Teilhard de Chardin

218   Lord, as I grow old,
help me to keep
all that I have learnt
in wisdom and experience
through the years,
as a book
to be dipped into
when asked,
and not flaunt
what little I know
as knowing better.
Let me be firmly and gently
at the other end;
about, if wanted,
ready to listen,
to counsel,
and to have
a pocket full of comfort,
encouragement
and strength.

Rosa George

219   Lord, you know better than I know myself that I am growing older, and will some day be old. Keep me from getting talkative,

and particularly from the fatal habit of thinking that I must say
something on every subject and on every occasion.

Release me from craving to straighten out everybody's
affairs. Make me thoughtful but not moody; helpful but not
bossy. With my vast store of wisdom it seems a pity not to
use it all, but you know, Lord, that I want a few friends at the
end. Keep my mind from the recital of endless details – give
me wings to come to the point.

I ask for grace enough to listen to the tales of others'
pains. But seal my lips on my own aches and pains – they
are increasing, and my love of rehearsing them is becoming
sweeter as the years go by. Help me to endure them with
patience.

I dare not ask for improved memory, but for a growing
humility and a lessening cocksureness when my memory seems
to clash with the memories of others. Teach me the glorious
lesson that occasionally it is possible that I may be mistaken.

Keep me reasonably sweet. I do not want to be a saint –
some of them are so hard to live with – but a sour old woman
is one of the crowning works of the devil.

Give me the ability to see good things in unexpected places,
and talents in unexpected people. And give me, O Lord, the
grace to tell them so.

Unknown source
(Attributed to a seventeenth-century nun)

220 Almighty and Everlasting God,

We know that all who are granted a full span of life must one
day experience the limitations of old age.

If we are old, Lord, grant us a sweetness of nature that will
attract others to us when we are unable to go to them.

Give us the patience with human shortcomings that comes
as a result of experience.

Show us when to stop talking, so that we can listen instead.

Help us to bear pain silently.

And to share our joys and not our complaints,

So that as we grow in age, we may grow also in grace.
Amen.

Beryl Bye

Daily Work

221   O Lord, give me grace and strength to do your will, to begin the
day and to end it with prayer and searching of my own heart,
and with reading of your word. Make me to understand it, to
understand you; to bring home to my heart the reality of your
perfect Godhead and perfect humanity, and, above all, of my
entire need of a Saviour; of my utter inability to do anything
that is right by my own strength; make me humble, reasonable,
contented, thankful, just, and considerate. Restrain my tongue
and my thoughts; may I act as ever in your sight, as if I may die
this day. May I not fear man nor man's opinions, but remember
that you know my motives and my thoughts, and that you will
be my Judge. Let me do today's work as well as I can today;
so living in humility, thankfulness, and contentment.

Henry Lawrence

222   Lord, I desire that, at all times, those who profit by my labour
may be not only refreshed in body, but may be also drawn to
your love and strengthened in every good.

Mechthild of Magdeburg

223   Take from me, Lord, all slothfulness, and give me a diligent
and active spirit, and wisdom to choose my employment, that
I may do works suitable to my person, and to the dignity of a
Christian. Fill up the spaces of my time with actions of religion
and charity; that when the Devil assaults me, he may not find
me idle, and my dearest Lord at His sudden coming may find
me busy in lawful, necessary, and pious actions. May I improve
my talent entrusted to me by you, my Lord; that I may enter
into the joy of my Lord.

Jeremy Taylor

224   O Lord, renew our spirits and draw our hearts to yourself that
our work may not be to us a burden, but a delight; and give us
such a mighty love for you as may sweeten all our obedience.
Let us not serve you with the spirit of bondage as slaves, but
with cheerfulness and gladness, delighting ourselves in you and
rejoicing in your work, for the sake of Jesus Christ.

Benjamin Jenks

225   Lord, as we go to our work this day, help us to take pleasure therein. Show us clearly what our duty is, help us to be faithful in doing it. May all we do be well done, fit for your eye to see. Give us enthusiasm to attempt, patience to perform. When we cannot love our work, may we think of it as your task, and make what is unlovely beautiful through loving service; for your Name's sake.

George Dawson

226   Lord, teach us to work with love, knowing that work is love made visible.

Teach us to weave the cloth with threads drawn from our heart, even as if you our beloved were to wear that cloth.

To build a house with affection, even as if you were to dwell in that house.

To sow seeds with tenderness and reap the harvest with joy, even as if you were to eat the fruit.

To charge all things we fashion with a breath of our own spirit,

And to know that all the blessed dead are standing about us and watching.

Kahlil Gibran

227   Lord, our attitude to work changes with our moods;
we are as variable as the weather.
Some days we enjoy every moment of our work;
other days we feel tired and resentful of it.
There are mornings when we dread the thought of getting up;
but there are also times when we go to work gladly.

Lord, some of us get paid for doing the things we enjoy;
others must work at distasteful tasks for their living.
Some of us work with kind and interesting people;
others must work with sour and ugly characters.
Some who long for company must work alone;
others who yearn for privacy must work with a crowd.

Lord, whether we work for love or pleasure,
or whether it is only for duty or money,

we thank you for the privilege of daily work,
for the rewards of labour in whatever form.
In a world where millions are unemployed,
we count ourselves as richly blessed.

As products of the work of a loving Creator,
we thank you for skills of eye, brain, and hand.
As friends of the carpenter's Son of Nazareth,
we offer to you our work as an act of praise.
As children of the Spirit who has never ceased to work,
we seek to honour you in everything we do.

Bruce Prewer

228   Lord Christ, you said to your disciples, 'My Father has worked
till now, and I work': we pray for those who through no fault of
their own have been deprived of the work that leads towards
the fulfilment of their lives.

Inspire and guide those who bear the responsibility of finding
the answer to our industrial problems.

Open their minds to the truth, that they may discern in the
events of our time the direction of your will; and give them
the courage to declare what they believe to be right, and the
power to carry it through.

Basil Naylor

Adoration and Praise

229   O most high, almighty, good Lord God, to thee belong praise,
glory, honour and all blessing!

Praised be my Lord God with all his creatures, and especially
our brother the sun, who brings us the day and who brings us
the light; fair is he and shines with a very great splendour;

O Lord, he signifies to us thee.

Praised be my Lord for our sister the moon, and for the
stars, the which he has set clear and lovely in heaven.

Praised be my Lord for our brother the wind, and for air and
cloud, calms and all weather, by the which thou upholdest life
in all creatures.

Praised be my Lord for our sister water, who is very serviceable unto us and humble and precious and clean.

Praised be my Lord for our brother fire, through whom thou givest us light in the darkness; and he is bright and pleasant and very mighty and strong.

Praised be my Lord for our mother the earth, the which doth sustain us and keep us, and bringeth forth divers fruits, and flowers of many colours, and grass.

Praised be my Lord for all those who pardon one another for his love's sake, and who endure weakness and tribulation; blessed are they who peaceably shall endure, for thou, O Most Highest, shall give them a crown.

Praised be my Lord for our sister the death of the body, from which no man escapeth. Woe to him who dieth in mortal sin!

Blessed are they who are found walking by thy most holy will, for the second death shall have no power to harm them.

Praise ye and bless ye the Lord, and give thanks unto him, and serve him with great humility. Amen.

Francis of Assisi

230 Glory be to God for dappled things –
For skies of couple-colour as a brinded cow;
For rose-moles all in stipple upon the trout that swim;
Fresh-firecoal chestnut-falls; finches' wings;
Landscape plotted and pieced – fold, fallow and plough;
And all trades, their gear and tackle and trim.
All things counter, original, spare, strange;
Whatever is fickle, freckled (who knows how?)
With swift, slow; sweet, sour; adazzle, dim;
He fathers-forth whose beauty is past change:
Praise him.

Gerard Manley Hopkins

231 God of bright colours: rainbows, peacocks,
And the shot-silk gleam of springing
Wind-shaken wheat
On rolling red-ribbed Earth:
Thou Who dost bring to birth
From out the womb
Of darkness golden flowers,
Filling the hollows

With daffodils in March,
Cowslips in April,
Dog-roses in May;
Who in the smouldering forest
Makes the huge
Red flare of Autumn:
God of all the colours
On Earth, and hues (too bright for mortal eyes)
In Paradise –
Unblind me to Thy glory,
That I may see!

F. W. Harvey

232　May none of God's wonderful works
keep silence, night or morning.
Bright stars, high mountains, the depths of the seas,
sources of rushing rivers:
may all these break into song as we sing
to Father, Son and Holy Spirit.
May all the angels in the heavens reply:
Amen! Amen! Amen!
Power, praise, honour, eternal glory
to God, the only Giver of grace.
Amen! Amen! Amen!

Third-century prayer

233　Holy, holy, holy, Lord God almighty!
Early in the morning our song shall rise to thee;
Holy, holy, holy, merciful and mighty,
God in three persons, blessed Trinity!
Holy, holy, holy, though the darkness hide thee,
Though the eye of sinful man thy glory may not see,
Only thou art holy; there is none beside thee,
Perfect in power, in love and purity.

Reginald Heber

234　Blessing and honour, and thanksgiving and praise, more than
we can utter, more than we can conceive, be yours, holy and
glorious Trinity, Father, Son and Holy Spirit, by all angels, all
men, all creatures, for ever and ever.

Lancelot Andrewes

235 O God,
without ever growing weary
you accept the praise
of the incorporeal powers of heaven,
who have no need of physical light,
having been given
the eternal brightness
of your impenetrable glory:
with your consent
they celebrate your holiness
in unending worship.

On our knees we glorify you,
beseeching you to set us free
from the darkness of sin,
and to bless us eternally
with the light of your countenance.

For yours is the greatness,
the majesty, the power and the glory,
Father, Son and Holy Spirit,
now and for ever,
to the ages of ages. Amen.

Orthodox Liturgy

236 I offer thee
Every flower that ever grew,
Every bird that ever flew,
Every wind that ever blew.

Good God!

Every thunder rolling,
Every church bell tolling,
Every leaf and sod.

Laudamus Te!

I offer thee
Every wave that ever moved,
Every heart that ever loved,
Thee, thy Father's well-beloved.

Dear Lord!

Every river dashing,
Every lightning flashing,

Like an angel's sword.

Benedicimus Te!

I offer thee
Every cloud that ever swept
O'er the skies, and broke and wept
In rain, and with the flowerets slept.

My King!

Every communicant praying,
Every angel staying,
Before thy throne to sing.

Adoramus Te!

I offer thee
Every flake of virgin snow,
Every spring of earth below,
Every human joy and woe,

My love!

O Lord! And all thy glorious
Self o'er death victorious,
Throned in heaven above.

Glorificamus Te!

(*Ancient Irish prayer*)

237 You are holy, Lord, the only God,
And your deeds are wonderful.
You are strong,
You are great.
You are the Most High,
You are almighty.
You, holy Father, are
King of heaven and earth.
You are Three and One,
Lord God, all good.
You are good, all good, supreme good,
Lord God, living and true.
You are love,
You are wisdom.
You are humility,
You are endurance.
You are rest,
You are peace.

You are joy and gladness,
You are justice and moderation.
You are all our riches,
And you suffice for us.
You are beauty,
You are gentleness.
You are our protector,
You are our guardian and defender.
You are courage,
You are our haven and our hope.
You are our faith,
Our great consolation.
You are our eternal life,
Great and wonderful Lord,
God almighty,
Merciful Saviour.

Francis of Assisi

238 O Light Invisible, we praise Thee!
Too bright for mortal vision.
O Greater Light, we praise Thee for the less;
The eastern light our spires touch at morning,
The light that slants upon our western doors at evening,
The twilight over stagnant pools at batflight,
Moon light and star light, owl and moth light,
Glow-worm glowlight on a grassblade.
O Light Invisible, we worship Thee!

We thank Thee for the lights that we have kindled,
The light of altar and of sanctuary;
Small lights of those who meditate at midnight
And lights directed through the coloured panes of windows
And light reflected from the polished stone,
The gilded carven wood, the coloured fresco.
Our gaze is submarine, our eyes look upward
And see the light that fractures through unquiet water.
We see the light but see not whence it comes.
O Light Invisible, we glorify Thee!

T. S. Eliot

239   O Lord, how wonderful you are!
Your greatness and love overwhelms me.
You catch and hold me in your shining darkness.
You take me out of myself into the light of your being
which blinds me with its brightness.
You fill me with yourself, and my being is suffused
with the beauty of your glory.
I am speechless, silent, held by your overwhelming love.
Lord, never let me go, keep me hidden in yourself, always.
                                                            Etta Gullick

240   O God, whose name is holy of itself, we pray that it may be
hallowed also by us. To this end help us, O blessed Father in
heaven, that thy word may be taught in truth and purity, and
that we, as thy children, may lead holy lives in accordance with
it; through Jesus Christ, thy Son, our Lord. Amen.
                                                            Martin Luther

241   Justify my soul, O God, but also from your fountains fill my
will with fire . . . Let my eyes see nothing in the world but
your glory, and let my hands touch nothing that is not for your
service . . . let me use all things for one sole reason; to find
my joy in giving You great glory.
                                                            Thomas Merton

242   We praise you, God our Father, for the richness of your
                creation,
for the uniqueness of each person,
for the creativity which sustains and renews our cultures,
for your faithfulness towards your people.
We praise you, Jesus our Lord, for your constant meddling in
                our affairs,
for your identification with the poor,
for your sacrifice for all men on the cross,
for revealing the true man to all people.
We praise you, God the Spirit, for your inspiration of life,
for your insistence to draw us always to Christ,
for the infusion of unrest among men,
for your patient preparation of the fulfilment of history.
We praise you, blessed Trinity, for not doing for us according
                to our sins,

for continuing your love to all that lives,
for continuing your disturbing call to repentance,
for continuing life on earth.

WCC Bangkok Conference, 1973

In Praise of Creation

243 Lord, may we love and respect all your creation, all the earth
and every grain of sand in it. May we love every leaf, every
ray of your light.

May we love the animals: you have given them the rudiments
of thought and joy untroubled. Let us not trouble them; let us
not harass them, let us not deprive them of their happiness, let
us not work against your intentions.

For we acknowledge that to withhold any measure of love
from anything in your universe is to withhold that same measure
from you.

F. Dostoevsky
(*adapted from* The Brothers Karamazov)

244 God bless the field and bless the furrow,
Stream and branch and rabbit burrow,
Hill and stone and flower and tree,
From Bristol town to Wetherby –
Bless the sun and bless the sleet,
Bless the lane and bless the street,
Bless the night and bless the day,
From Somerset and all the way
To the meadows of Cathay;
Bless the minnow, bless the whale,
Bless the rainbow and the hail,
Bless the nest and bless the leaf,
Bless the righteous and the thief,
Bless the wing and the fin,
Bless the air I travel in,
Bless the mill and bless the mouse,
Bless the miller's bricken house,
Bless the earth and bless the sea,

God bless you and God bless me.

An old English rhyme

245 Now we must praise the Ruler of Heaven,
The might of the Lord and His purpose of mind,
The work of the Glorious Father; for He,
God Eternal, established each wonder,
He, Holy Creator, first fashioned the heavens
As a roof for the children of earth.
And then our Guardian, the Everlasting Lord,
Adorned this middle-earth for men.
Praise the Almighty King of Heaven.

Caedmon

246 O God of mountains, stars, and boundless spaces!
O God of Freedom and of joyous hearts!
When Thy Face looketh forth from all men's faces,
There will be room enough in crowded marts:
Brood Thou around me, and the noise is o'er;
Thy universe my closet with shut door.

George Macdonald

247 Lord, purge our eyes to see
Within the seed a tree,
Within the glowing egg a bird,
Within the shroud a butterfly.
Till, taught by such we see
Beyond all creatures, Thee
And hearken to Thy tender word
And hear its 'Fear not; it is I'.

Christina Rossetti

248 Teach me, Father, how to go
Softly as the grasses grow;
Hush my soul to meet the shock
Of the wild world as a rock;
But my spirit, propt with power,
Make as simple as a flower.
Let the dry heart fill its cup,
Like a poppy looking up;

Let life lightly wear her crown,
Like a poppy looking down,
When its heart is filled with dew,
And its life begins anew.

Teach me, Father, how to be
Kind and patient as a tree.
Joyfully the crickets croon
Under shady oak at noon;
Beetle, on his mission bent,
Tarries in that cooling tent.
Let me, also, cheer a spot,
Hidden field or garden grot –
Place where passing souls can rest
On the way and be their best.

Edwin Markham

249 O Thou, who fillest heaven and earth, ever acting, ever at
rest, who art present everywhere and everywhere art wholly
present, who art not absent even when far off, who with thy
whole being fillest yet transcendest all things, who teachest
the hearts of the faithful without the din of words; teach us,
we pray Thee, through Jesus Christ our Lord.

Augustine of Hippo

250 Lord
isn't your creation wasteful?
Fruits never equal
the seedlings' abundance.
Springs scatter water.
The sun gives out
enormous light.
May your bounty teach me
greatness of heart.
May your magnificence
stop me being mean.
Seeing you a prodigal
and open-handed giver
let me give unstintingly
like a king's son
like God's own.

Helder Camara

251   Thou takest the pen – and the lines dance.
      Thou takest the flute – and the notes shimmer.
      Thou takest the brush – and the colours sing.
      So all things have meaning and beauty in that space beyond
          time
      where Thou art. How, then, can I hold back anything from
          Thee?

                                                    Dag Hammarskjöld

252   For all the first sweet flushings of the spring;
      The greening earth, the tender heavenly blue;
      The rich brown furrows gaping for the seed;
      For all thy grace in bursting bud and leaf . . .
      For hedgerows sweet with hawthorn and wild rose;
      For meadows spread with gold and gemmed with stars,
      For every tint of every tiniest flower,
      For every daisy smiling to the sun;
      For every bird that builds in joyous hope,
      For every lamb that frisks beside its dam,
      For every leaf that rustles in the wind,
      For spiring poplar, and for spreading oak,
      For queenly birch, and lofty swaying elm;
      For the great cedar's benedictory grace,
      For earth's ten thousand fragrant incenses,
      Sweet altar-gifts from leaf and fruit and flower . . .
      For ripening summer and the harvesting;
      For all the rich autumnal glories spread –
      The flaming pageant of the ripening woods,
      The fiery gorse, the heather-purpled hills,
      The rustling leaves that fly before the wind
      and lie below the hedgerows whispering;
      For meadows silver-white with hoary dew;
      For sheer delight of tasting once again
      That first crisp breath, of winter in the air;
      The pictured pane; the new white world without;
      The sparkling hedgerows' witchery of lace,
      The soft white flakes that fold the sleeping earth;
      The cold without, the cheerier warmth within . . .
      For all the glowing heart of Christmas-tide,
      We thank thee, Lord!

                                                    John Oxenham

253   If I have faltered more or less
In my great task of happiness;
If I have moved among my race
And shown no glorious morning face;
If beams from happy human eyes
Have moved me not; if morning skies,
Books, and my food, and summer rain
Knocked on my sullen heart in vain:
Lord, thy most pointed pleasure take
And stab my spirit broad awake.

Robert Louis Stevenson

254   Almighty One, in the woods I am blessed. Happy everyone in
the woods. Every tree speaks through Thee. O God! What
glory in the woodland! On the heights is peace – peace to
serve Him.

Ludwig van Beethoven

255   Let my soul praise you that it may love you, let it praise you
for your mercy and kindness. Without ceasing, your whole
creation speaks your praise. Man speaks his praise, animals
and lifeless things praise you through those who see and speak
on their behalf. Your creation helps our souls rise up to you
and wonder at your love. In that wonder we find strength and
refreshment.

Augustine of Hippo

256   *Prayer of the Butterfly*

Lord!
Where was I?
Oh yes! This flower, this sun,
thank you! Your world is beautiful!
This scent of roses . . .
Where was I?
A drop of dew
rolls to sparkle in a lily's heart.
I have to go . . .
Where? I do not know!
The wind has painted fancies
on my wings.

Fancies . . .
Where was I?
Oh yes! Lord,
I had something to tell you:
Amen.

Carmen Bernos de Gasztold

257 *Prayer of the Tortoise*

I am coming.
One must take nature as she is!
It was not I who made her!
I do not mean to criticise
this house on my back –
It has its points –
but you must admit, Lord,
it is heavy to carry!
Still,
let us hope that this double enclosure,
my shell and my heart,
will never be quite shut to You.

Carmen Bernos de Gasztold

258 *Prayer of the Elephant*

Dear God,
it is I, the elephant,
your creature,
who is talking to you.
I am so embarrassed by my great self,
and truly it is not my fault
if I spoil your jungle with my big feet.
Let me be careful and behave wisely,
always keeping my dignity and poise.
Give me such philosophic thoughts
that I can rejoice everywhere I go
in the lovable oddity of things.

Carmen Bernos de Gasztold

259 *Prayer of the Ox*

Dear God, give me time,

Men are always so driven!
Make them understand that I can never hurry.
Give me time to eat.
Give me time to plod.
Give me time to sleep.
Give me time to think.

Carmen Bernos de Gasztold

260   O Little Brother Bird, that brimmest with full heart, and having
naught, possessest all, surely thou dost well to sing! For thou hast
life without labour, and beauty without burden, and riches without
care. When thou wakest, lo, it is dawn; and when thou comest
to sleep it is eve. And when thy two wings lie folded about thy
heart, lo, there is rest. Therefore sing, Brother, having this great
wealth, that when thou singest thou givest thy riches to all.

Francis of Assisi

Faith

261   I believe in God, the Father almighty, creator of heaven and
earth, and in Jesus Christ, his only Son, our Lord, who was
conceived by the Holy Spirit, born of the Virgin Mary, suffered
under Pontius Pilate, was crucified, died, and was buried. He
descended into hell. The third day he rose again from the dead.
He ascended into heaven, sitteth at the right hand of God the
almighty Father. From thence he shall come to judge the living
and the dead. I believe in the Holy Spirit, the holy Catholic
Church, the Communion of Saints, the forgiveness of sins, the
resurrection of the body, and life everlasting. Amen

Traditional Apostles' Creed

262   I believe in Jesus as a perfect revelation of God and the only
sure Master for my life.

Because of Jesus, I believe in forgiveness – in the forgiveness
of God to man, and from man to man, and from me to anyone
who needs my forgiveness.

I believe that love is stronger than all other forces – that to
love is better than to be angry, that it is better to give than to

receive; better to serve than to be served; better to forget myself than to assert myself.

I believe that God's kingdom can come on earth, and that everything that is wrong in the life of the nation, or of the Church, or in my life can be conquered by the power of God.

I believe that nothing that is wrong need be permanent.

A. Herbert Gray

263 I believe that I cannot by my own reason or strength believe in Jesus Christ my Lord, or come to him; but the Holy Ghost has called me through the gospel, enlightened me by his gifts, and sanctified and preserved me in the true faith; in like manner as he calls, gathers, enlightens, and sanctifies the whole Christian Church on earth, and preserves it in union with Jesus Christ in the true faith; in which Christian Church he daily forgives abundantly all my sins, and the sins of all believers, and will raise up me and all the dead at the last day, and will grant everlasting life to me and to all who believe in Christ. This is most certainly true. Amen.

Martin Luther

264 I believe in the love of God revealed in Jesus Christ.

I believe that behind the clouds of life shines the love of God.

I believe that God has a purpose for the world and a purpose for my life.

I believe that God wills the blessedness of all lives and of every single life.

I believe that Jesus Christ saves life from the power of sin and sorrow and death.

I believe in the life-giving power and grace of the Holy Spirit.

I believe that through faith and prayer and Sacrament I can live the life which is life indeed.

I believe that God calls my life to love and service.

I believe that through Christ life leads at last to the fullness of goodness, truth, and beauty.

I believe in the grace of our Lord Jesus Christ, and the love of God, and the fellowship of the Holy Spirit.

Frederick B. Macnutt

265   We believe that God is spirit; and they that worship him must worship him in spirit and truth.

We believe that God is light: and if we walk in the light as he is in the light, we have fellowship one with another.

We believe that God is love: and that everyone that loves is born of God and knows God.

We believe that Jesus is the son of God: and that God has given us eternal life, and this life is in his son.

We believe that if we confess our sins: he is faithful and just to forgive our sins.

We believe that he who does the will of God shall abide for ever.

H. Stobart

266   Father, I thank you for giving me faith,
for that is the foundation of my prayers.
I believe that I am your child,
living in your world in your day.
My faith is shaky and suffers many knocks.
There are times when I push you out of my mind
and days when I cannot hear your voice.
Yet deep in my heart I believe in you,
your abiding, your holy love.
Thank you for giving me that seed of faith.

As I pray, I know that the little seed
is also fruit of a great tree of faith,
which stretches across the years and the continents
and links me to the apostles.

Great God, faith is the powerful bond
which links all Christian people.
We praise you for faith and faithfulness
    in the ages of darkness,
    in disappointments and disasters,
    in hostile societies where faith is called madness,
    amid affluent agnostics,
    expressed in every human language,
    victorious in pain and in death,
this is the work of your Spirit.
May this great tree of faith continue to grow,

deeply rooted in your word,
and offering to all a living faith
for the healing of the nations.

Bernard Thorogood

267   Give me, Lord, eyes to behold the truth;
A seeing sense that knows the eternal right;
A heart with pity filled, and gentlest ruth;
A manly faith that makes all darkness light.

Theodore Parker

268   Behold, Lord, an empty vessel that needs to be filled. My Lord,
fill it. I am weak in the faith; strengthen me. I am cold in love;
warm me and make me fervent, that my love may go out to
my neighbour. I do not have a strong and firm faith; at times I
doubt and am unable to trust you altogether. O Lord, help me.
Strengthen my faith and trust in you.

Martin Luther

269   God in heaven, I thank you that you have not required of
man that he should comprehend Christianity; for if that were
required, I should be of all men most miserable. The more I
seek to comprehend it, the more incomprehensible it appears
to me, and the more I discover merely the possibility of offence.
Therefore I thank you that you only require faith, and I pray you
to increase it more and more. Amen.

Søren Kierkegaard

270   Father, as we remember the victorious faith of your servants
of old, we acknowledge that we are not people of faith.

Sometimes your promises seem so unlikely as to be laugh-
able. They are almost more than we can believe.

Father, forgive us. Increase our faith, and save us from
concentrating on our doubts.

Open our eyes to see what you can do with us when we put
ourselves at your disposal.

Help us to hold firm to your promises, to laugh at impossibilities, and to believe that all things are possible, through Jesus
Christ our Lord.

Frank Colquhoun

271   We read in one of the Psalms, O God, the assertion of your
       saint of old who said, 'I have trusted in the Lord without
       wavering.' We thank you for his certain faith and for his
       strength of conviction whereby nothing could move him from
       his implicit trust. And we pray for that kind of faith to be in
       us. Our lives are beset by many challenges. When sorrow
       comes, or disappointment, or failure, or discouragement, we
       tend to lose faith. It is as if a little voice within us says,
       'Where is your God now?' But we know that in all these
       experiences, you are faithful. Make us as unwavering in our
       trust as you are unwavering in your care over us. We pray in
       Jesus' name. Amen.

                                                    William H. Kadel

272   Most merciful and gracious Father, I bless and magnify your
       name that you had adopted me into the inheritance of sons,
       and have given me a portion of my elder Brother. You who are
       the God of patience and consolation, strengthen me that I may
       bear the yoke and burden of the Lord, without any uneasy and
       useless murmurs, and ineffective unwillingness. Let me pass
       through the valley of tears, and the valley of the shadow of
       death with safety and peace, with a meek spirit, and a sense
       of the divine mercies, through Jesus Christ. Amen.

                                                      Jeremy Taylor

Hope

273   My Lord God, give me once more the courage to hope;
       merciful God, let me hope once again, fructify my barren and
       infertile mind.

                                                  Søren Kierkegaard

274   My God, who has graciously promised every blessing, even
       heaven itself, through Jesus Christ, to those who keep your
       commandments. Relying on your infinite power, goodness, and

mercy, and confiding in your sacred promises, to which you
are always faithful, I confidently hope to obtain pardon of all
my sins, grace to serve you faithfully in this life, by doing the
good works you have commanded, which, with your assistance,
I will perform; and eternal happiness in the next, through my
Lord and Saviour Jesus Christ. Amen.

Michael Buckley

275 Lord God,
the scripture says you make all things new.
Make all things new this day.
Give us such hope in you
that we become optimistic about everyone and everything
  else,
Lord of all hopefulness, Lord of the future,
lead us forward with a light step and a courageous heart;
to your honour and glory,
and for the sake of Jesus Christ,
your Son, our Saviour.

Jamie Wallace

276 You are the Lord of fire
Present in the fiery furnace,
Present in the heat of life,
Present in situations of horror and despair,
Present in the prisons that incarcerate men for their beliefs.
Shadrach, Meshach and Abednego were lucky ones, Lord.
They came out unscathed.
Not all are so lucky,
Not all understand the tyrannies of life and remain unharmed.
You are with men in their suffering, in their aloneness and
  ignominy and death.
Be with them.
Be with them through us who are your limbs.
Give us a glimmering óf hope in hopeless situations;
For where there is no hope there is nothing.

Rex Chapman

277 Lord, it's just when we most need the light of your love in our
lives that we least feel like asking for it. When things go wrong

and life seems dismal and grey, be with us, Lord, to support and
strengthen us. Help us never to give up hope, but to place all
our trust in your love, confident that your Son will lift us up and
fill our lives again with joy. Please hear our prayer through the
same Christ our Lord. Amen.

Anthony Castle

Love for God

278 Lord Jesus Christ, that our prayer may be rightly directed,
we pray first for one all-important need. Help us to love you,
increase our love, inflame it. This prayer you will surely hear,
for you are not love of a crude, selfish sort, merely an uncaring
object of regard. If you were you would not be the love that
casts out all fear. No, you are compassionate love; more than
that, you are love of such a sort that draws out the love that
loves you, nurturing and encouraging us to increase daily in
your love. Love divine, increase our love.

Søren Kierkegaard

279 O God, reign over us in spite of our infidelities; may the fire
of your love quench every other fire. What can we see that
is lovable outside of you, and which we do not find perfectly
in you, who are the source of all good? Grant us the grace of
loving you; we shall then love you only, and we shall love you
eternally.

François Fénelon

280 O God, my God and my all,
without you I am nothing, less than nothing,
a rebel to your love,
a despiser of your grace.
O God, have pity on me a sinner;
grant me a new vision of your love
and of your will for me;

give me a stillness in my soul
that I may know you and love you,
and grant me strength to do your will, O my God,
my all.

Gilbert Shaw

281 Open Thou my heart for Thy love, keep Thy love in me,
prepare me by Thy love for greater fullness of Thy love,
until I have reached the fullest measure of love, which Thou,
in Thine eternal love, hast willed for me.

Make me, in thought, word, and deed, to love Thee, and
thank Thee, and praise Thee, and praising Thee to love Thee
more, and know Thee more, how worthy Thou art of all love
and praise, until I be fitted with all Thy saints and angels to love
Thee and praise Thee everlastingly, and breathe out my soul to
Thee in loving Thee and praising Thee for all Thy boundless,
undeserved love to me, Thy poor sinner, yet, though a sinner,
Thine, O God my God. Amen.

E. B. Pusey

282 Lord,
How do I love thee? Let me count the ways.
I love thee to the depth and breadth and height
my soul can reach, when feeling out of sight
for the ends of being and of ideal grace.
I love thee to the level of every day's
most quiet need, by sun and candlelight.
I love thee purely, as they turn from praise.
I love thee with a passion put to use
in my old griefs, and with my childhood faith.
I love thee with a love I seemed to lose
with my lost saints – I love thee with the breath,
smiles, tears, of all my life!
And, God, if thou dost choose
I shall love thee better after death.

Elizabeth Barrett Browning

283 Lord, it is my chief complaint,
That my love is weak and faint;

Yet I love you and adore,
Oh for grace to love you more.

William Cowper

284   You who are love itself give me the grace of love, give me
      yourself, so that all my days may finally empty into the one
      day of your eternal life.

Karl Rahner

285   Teach us, O Lord, to fear without being afraid; to fear you in
      love that we may love you without fear; through Jesus Christ
      our Lord.

Christina Rossetti

286   O Lord, who has taught us that all our doings without love are
      worth nothing, send your Holy Ghost, and pour into our hearts
      that most excellent gift of love, the very bond of peace and of
      all virtues, without which whoever lives is counted dead before
      you: Grant this for your Son Jesus Christ's sake.

Thomas Cranmer

287   O Father, help us to know that the hiding of your face is wise
      love. Your love is not fond, doting and reasonless. Your children
      must often have the frosty cold side of the hill, and set down
      both their bare feet amongst the thorns: your love has eyes,
      and in the meantime is looking on. Our pride must have winter
      weather.

George Macdonald

288   You know better than I how much I love you, Lord. You know
      it and I know it not, for nothing is more hidden from me than
      the depths of my own heart. I desire to love you; I fear that I
      do not love you enough. I beseech you to grant me the fullness
      of pure love. Behold my desire; you have given it to me. Behold
      in your creature what you have placed there. O God, who loves
      me enough to inspire me to love you for ever, behold not my
      sins. Behold your mercy and my love.

François Fénelon

289 Dear Lord,
Love is kind and suffers long,
Love is meek and thinks no wrong,
Love than Death itself more strong,
Therefore give us Love!

Christopher Wordsworth

290 O God, the God of all goodness and all grace, you are worthy
of a greater love than we can either give or understand; fill my
heart, I implore you, with such love towards you as may cast
out all sloth and fear, that nothing may seem too hard for me
to do or to suffer in obedience to you; and grant that, by thus
loving, I may become daily more like you, and finally obtain the
crown of life, which you have promised to those who love you;
through Jesus Christ our Lord. Amen

Pocket Manual of Prayers

291 O God, we have known and believed the love that you have for
us. May we, by dwelling in love, dwell in you and you in us.
Teach us, O heavenly Father, the love wherewith you have
loved us; fashion us, O blessed Lord, after your own example
of love; shed abroad, Holy Spirit of love, the love of God and
man in our hearts. For your name's sake.

Henry Alford

292 Lord, you are the living flame, burning ceaselessly with love
for man. Enter into me and inflame me with your fire so that
I might be like you.

John Henry Newman

293 Give us, O Lord God, a deep sense of your wonderful love
towards us; how you would not let us alone in our ruin, but
came after us, in the Person of your Son Jesus Christ to bring
us back to our true home with you.

Quicken in us, O Lord, the Spirit of gratitude, of loyalty and
of sacrifice, that we may seek in all things to please him who
humbled himself for us, even to the death of the Cross, by dying
unto sin and living unto righteousness; through the same Jesus
Christ our Lord.

Charles J. Vaughan

294   My God, I love you with my whole heart and soul, and above
all things, because you are infinitely good and perfect, and most
worthy of all my love; and for your sake I love my neighbour as
myself. Mercifully grant, O my God, that having loved you on
earth, I may love and enjoy you for ever in heaven. Amen.

Traditional prayer

295   Late have I loved you, O beauty so ancient and so new;
late have I loved you.
For behold you were within me, and I outside;
and I sought you outside and in my ugliness fell
upon those lovely things that you have made.
You were with me and I was not with you.
I was kept from you by those things,
yet had they not been in you, they would not have been at all.
You called and cried to me and broke upon my deafness;
and you sent forth your light and shone upon me,
and chased away my blindness;
You breathed fragrance upon me,
and I drew in my breath and do now pant for you:
I tasted you and I now hunger and thirst for you;
you touched me, and I have burned for your peace.

Augustine of Hippo

296   O God, who by love alone are great and glorious, who are
present and live with us by love alone: grant us likewise by
love to attain another self, by love to live in others, and by
love to come to our glory to see and accompany your love
throughout all eternity.

Thomas Traherne

297   O that my Lord Jesus would grant me but a tiny spark of that
charity which is his gift! So might all that is close to his heart
be my care also, yet always with the surety that I give myself,
before all else, to what I know he asks of me, or whatever my
clear duty lays upon me.

Bernard of Clairvaux

298   O Jesus, Master and Lord, pour into our hearts your own heroic
love; that being filled with love we may know the love which

passes knowledge, and live in the unknown power of love to
win men to trust in love, to the glory of God who is love.

William Temple

299   Lord Jesus, may the sweet burning ardour of your love absorb
my soul entirely and make it a stranger to all that is not you or
for you.

Francis of Assisi

300   O my Jesus! I am not worthy to love thee! Yet because thou
biddest me love thee, and has told me that my soul was created
on purpose to love thee, I cheerfully resign my love and affection
to thee! I desire to love thee! I wish for nothing more than that I
may passionately love thee. Whom have I in heaven to love but
thee? And there is none on earth that I desire to love more than
thyself. For thou art altogether lovely, and thy love surpasses
all the love of friends, and the dearest relations I have.

O my blessed Redeemer! I desire to love thee with all my
heart, and with all my strength. Thou gavest me this heart
and this strength: And on whom can I bestow it better, than
on thee, the Author of it?

Anthony Horneck

301   We are the mediocre,
we are the half givers,
we are the half lovers,
we are the savourless salt.
Lord Jesus Christ,
restore us now,
to the primal splendour
of first love.
To the austere light
of the breaking day.
Let us hunger and thirst,
let us burn in the flame.
Break the hard crust
of complacency.
Quicken in us
the sharp grace of desire.

Caryll Houselander

302   O God, I love Thee, I love Thee –
       Not out of hope of heaven for me
       Nor fearing not to love and be
       In the everlasting burning.
       Thou, Thou, my Jesus, after me
       Didst reach Thine arms out dying,
       For my sake sufferedst nails and lance,
       Mocked and marred countenance,
       Sorrows passing number,
       Sweat and care and cumber,
       Yea and death, and this for me,
       And Thou couldst see me sinning:
       Then I, why should not I love Thee,
       Jesu, so much in love with me?
       Not for heaven's sake; not to be
       Out of hell by loving Thee;
       Not for any gains I see;
       But just the way that Thou didst me
       I do love and I will love Thee:
       What must I love Thee, Lord, for then?
       For being my king and God. Amen.

                                        Gerard Manley Hopkins

303   Set our hearts on fire with love of you, O Christ Our God,
       that in that flame we may love you with all our hearts, with
       all our mind, with all our soul, and with all our strength, and
       our neighbours as ourselves; so that, keeping your command-
       ments, we may glorify you, the giver of all good gifts.

                                                Orthodox prayer

304   O God, how patient you are!
           You make a world that develops over millions of years,
           slowly evolving new forms of life
           and still in growth today.
           How long you wait for the appearing of the children of light.
           You sent Jesus to us and men killed him.
        . We still disobey his word,
           wander far from his clear path,
           ignore his great promises,
           and tiptoe nervously into his new world.

O God, how patient you are!
  Your love for us goes on and on,
  never throwing us aside as worthless,
  always seeing what good may come out of evil.
  Help me to be more like that.
  May I stop prodding other people as though I were the
    shepherd and they the sheep.
  May I set my heart on great things and follow them steadily
    all my days.

O God, be patient still!
  The progress we make in this world is often two steps
    forward and then three steps back again.
  Do not let us go,
  but help us to grow,
  through every experience,
  towards your kingdom. Amen.

Bernard Thorogood

Love for Others

305 O God, who out of your great love for our world did reconcile
earth to heaven through your only-begotten Son; grant that
we, who by the darkness of our sins are turned aside from
brotherly love, may, by your light, shed forth in our souls your
own sweetness and embrace our friends in you, forgiving our
enemies, even as you forgive us for your Son's sake.

Mozarabic Sacramentary

306 Lord God of every place and time,
we are often lost in nostalgia.
We think that life in the past was simple,
that communities were more friendly,

and earning a living more straightforward.
Help us to recover from that backward look
and face the new realities of our neighbourhood,
the mixture of races, cultures and faiths,
the mobility of young people;
and to see right there opportunity and hope.
Enable us to create new communities
where mutual respect and support
give evidence of your gift of love. Amen.

Bernard Thorogood

307   O You who are love, and dwell in love, teach us to be children of
love in our actions, thoughts and words. May we never turn our
love away from those who are ignorant of your love. May we be
instruments of your mercy reaching out to those in distress and
need, giving such an example of your loving concern that all may
find unity in the discovery that they are your children. Amen.

James Martineau

308   Soften our hearts, O Lord, that we may be moved no less
at the necessities and griefs of our neighbours, than if they
concerned ourselves, or the cases that touched us nearest. Let
us pity them as ourselves, and, in their adversity, let us have
compassion upon them, that, as we would have pitied ourselves
for the like cause, so we may be moved with pity towards those
whom we see oppressed with the same adversities. Amen.

Johannes Ludovicus Vives

309   O God, perfect us in love, that we may conquer all selfishness
and hatred of others; fill our hearts with your joy, and shed
in them your peace which passes understanding; that so those
murmurings to which we are too prone may be overcome. Make
us long-suffering and gentle, and thus subdue our hastiness and
angry tempers, and grant that we may bring forth the blessed
fruits of the Spirit, to your praise and glory, through Jesus
Christ our Lord. Amen.

Henry Alford

310   O Lord, the author and persuader of peace, love and good will, soften our hard and steely hearts, warm our icy and frozen hearts, that we may wish well to one another, and may be the true disciples of Jesus Christ. And give us grace even now to begin to show forth that heavenly life, wherein there is no disagreement nor hatred, but peace and love on all hands, one towards another.

Johannes Ludovicus Vives

311 O Lord, give us more love, more self-denial, more likeness to you.
  Teach us to sacrifice our comforts to others, and our likings for the sake of doing good.
  Make us kindly in thought, gentle in word, generous in deed.
  Teach us that it is better to give than to receive; better to forget ourselves than to put ourselves forward; better to minister than to be ministered unto.
  And to you, the God of Love, be glory and praise for ever.

Henry Alford

312 Almighty and eternal God, who has revealed your nature in Christ Jesus your son as love, we humbly pray, give us your Holy Spirit to glorify you also in our hearts as pure love, and thus constrain us by your divine power to love you with our whole souls, and our brothers and sisters as ourselves; that so by your grace we may be fulfilled with love, and evermore abide in you and you in us, with all joyfulness, and free from fear or distrust; through Jesus Christ our Lord.

Christian K. J. Bunsen

313 O God, who has bound us together in this bundle of life, give us grace to understand how our lives depend on the courage, the industry, the honesty, and integrity of our fellow men; that we may be mindful of their needs, grateful for their faithfulness, and faithful in our responsibilities to them; through Jesus Christ our Lord.

Reinhold Niebuhr

314 Lord God, heavenly Father, who has bound us together in one

body through your Holy Spirit; help us, we pray you to serve
one another willingly and forgive one another from our hearts,
through Jesus Christ our Lord. Amen.

Thomas Bradwardine

315 Lord, save us from being self-centred in our prayers and teach
us to remember to pray for others. May we be so bound up
in love with those for whom we pray, that we may feel their
needs as acutely as our own, and intercede for them with
sensitivity, with understanding and with imagination. We ask
this in Christ's name.

John Calvin

316 Help me, Lord, to be more like you:
to draw a circle that includes rather than excludes.
Give me a genuine love for others,
both those I like and those I don't like.
Help me to overcome my fears and prejudices
and to see your image in all men.

Richard Harries

317 Almighty and most merciful Father, who has given us a new
commandment that we should love one another, give us also
grace that we may fulfil it. Make us gentle, courteous, and
forbearing. Direct our lives so that we may look each to the
good of others in word and deed. And hallow all our friendships by the blessing of thy spirit, for his sake, who loves us
and gave himself for us, Jesus Christ our Lord. Amen.

Brooke Foss Westcott

318 Bless me, O God, with the love of you, and of my neighbour.
Give me peace of conscience, the command of my affections;
and for the rest, your will be done! O King of peace, keep us
in love and charity. Amen.

Thomas Wilson

319 Heavenly Father, we thank you for our neighbours and for
the people around us with whom we share our daily lives.
We pray for those who are old and lonely;
those isolated because of ill-health;
and those who find it difficult to make friends.

Show us what we can do to help, and teach us to be good
     neighbours; for Jesus' sake.

Llewellyn Cumings

320   O God, fountain of love, pour your love into our souls, that
       we may love those whom you love with the love you give us,
       and think and speak of them tenderly, meekly, lovingly; and
       so loving our brothers and sisters for your sake, may grow
       in your love, and dwelling in love may dwell in you; for Jesus
       Christ's sake.

E. B. Pusey

321   Give us patience and fortitude to put self aside for you in the most
       unlikely people: to know that every man's and any man's suffering
       is our own first business, for which we must be willing to go out
       of our way and to leave our own interests.

Caryll Houselander

322   O God of love, who has given us a new commandment through
       your only begotten Son, that we should love one another even
       as you loved us, the unworthy and the wandering: We pray
       that you will give us, your servants, all our life on this earth, a
       mind forgetful of past injuries, a pure conscience and a heart of
       love for our brothers and sisters; for the sake of Jesus Christ
       our Lord.

Coptic Liturgy of St Cyril

Thanksgiving

323   Lord Jesus, I thank you
       not just with my lips and heart
       but with my spirit, with which I recognise
       and love you.
       You are my all, and everything is in you.
       In you I live, move and have being.

       You are my brother, my all.
       You are the true God, the true Son of God
       to whom all honour, glory and thanks
       are due.

Gallican Formularies

324   Almighty Giver of all good, may our hearts sing with gratitude
for the overwhelming number of blessings you have showered
upon us. Make us to sing your song of love and thanks in the
light and in the night feel the touch of your hand, and be at peace.
May you be our trusted Lord and King for evermore. Amen.
Henry W. Foote

325   Giver of all good things, we thank you: for health and vigour;
for the air that gives the breath of life, the sun that warms us,
and the good food that makes us strong; for happy homes and
for the friends we love; for all that makes it good to live. Make
us thankful and eager to repay, by cheerfulness and kindliness,
and by a readiness to help others. Freely we have received;
let us freely give, in the name of him who gave his life for us,
Jesus Christ our Lord.

Thomas Ken

326   O Infinite God, the brightness of whose face is often hidden
from my mortal gaze, I thank you that you sent your Son, Jesus
Christ, to be a light in a dark world.
       I thank you Christ, light of light, that in your most holy life
you pierced the eternal mystery as with a great shaft of light, so
that on seeing you we see him whom no one has ever seen.
John Baillie

327   We give you humble and hearty thanks, O most merciful Father,
for all your goodness and loving-kindness to us and to all men,
for the blessings of this life and for the promise of everlasting
happiness. And as we are bound, we specially thank you for the
mercies which we have received; for health and strength, for
outward prosperity and well-being, for the many enjoyments of
our daily life, and the hope of the future; for the opportunities of
learning, for the knowledge of your will, for the means of serving
you in your holy Church, for the love you have revealed to us in
your Son, our Saviour; for every blessing of soul and body, we
thank you, O God. Add this, O Lord, to your other mercies,
that we may praise you not with our lips only, but with our
lives, always looking to you as the author and giver of all good
things; for Jesus Christ's sake.

Brooke Foss Westcott

328   My God, from my heart I thank you for the many blessings you have given me. I thank you for having created and baptised me, for having placed me in your holy Church, and for having given me so many graces and mercies through the merits of Jesus Christ. I thank your Son Jesus, for having died upon the cross that I might receive pardon for my sins and obtain my eternal salvation. I thank you for all your other mercies you have given me through Jesus Christ, Our Lord.

Michael Buckley

329   We thank you, O Lord, for all those good things which are in our world and in our lives through your love. Save us from being ungrateful. Save us from magnifying our sorrows and forgetting our blessings. Give strength of spirit to rise into joyfulness of heart. By your help may we learn to live as those should who have trusted the promises of good which are incarnate in Jesus, and who know that in the end love must conquer all.

A. Herbert Gray

330   To the Spirit great and good,
Felt, although not understood,
By whose breath, and in whose eyes,
The green earth rolls in the blue skies,
Who we know, from things that bless,
Must delight in loveliness;
And who, therefore, we believe,
Means us well in things that grieve,
Gratitude! Gratitude!
Heav'n be praised as heavenly should
Not with slavery, or with fears,
But with a face as towards a friend,
And with thin sparkling tears.

Leigh Hunt

331   Father, may I never grow ungrateful for the life that you have given me, nor despairing of its possibilities. May I never grow cynical about the world in which you have set me. May each day be welcomed as a new opportunity and each person as the neighbour whom Christ has given me. Thank you for people,

for city streets and lonely mountains, for streams on a hillside
and rain on window panes, for the seasons, for sun and cloud,
for words, conversations, books, jokes, prayer, for music that
lifts me close to heaven and ordinary days that so often take
me by surprise.

Michael Walker

332   O Lord, my God, I cried to you in my trouble and you heard
me; I put my trust in you and have not been confounded.
You have turned my heaviness into joy, and guided me with
gladness. Therefore I praise you with all my heart, and give
thanks to your holy name for ever. Hear me and accept me,
for the sake of Jesus Christ our Lord.

Laurence R. Tuttiett

333   For eyes whereby I clearly see
The many lovely things there be;
For lungs to breathe the morning air,
For nose to smell its fragrance rare;
For tongue to taste the fruits that grow,
For birds that sing and flowers that blow;
For limbs to climb, and swing, and run,
For skin to feel the cheerful sun;
For sun and moon and stars in heaven,
Whose gracious light is freely given;
The river where the green weed floats,
And where I sail my little boats;
The sea, where I can bathe and play,
The sands where I can race all day,
The pigeons wheeling in the sun,
Who fly more quickly than I run;
The winds that sing as they rush by,
The clouds that race across the sky;
The shelter of the shady woods,
Where I may spend my lonely moods;
The gabled house that is my home,
The garden where I love to roam,
And bless my parents, every day,
Though they be very far away,
Take thou my thanks, O God above,
For all these tokens of thy love.

And when I am a man do thou
Make me as grateful then as now.

Richard Molesworth Dennis

334   Thanks be to thee,
      my joy and my glory
      and my hope and my God.
      Thanks be to thee for thy gifts;
      but do thou preserve them in me,
      thus thou wilt preserve me,
      and the things thou hast given me
      will increase and be made perfect,
      and I shall be with thee:
      because even that I exist is thy gift.

Augustine of Hippo

335   Thank you, God, for filling things:
      filling the world with people,
      filling words with meaning,
      filling life with happenings,
      filling our plates with food
      and our wallets with money.
      May we ask one more thing?
      Please fill our hearts with thankfulness,
      and, as our gratitude overflows
      in gifts to you and your Church,
      bless what we give
      and make it useful
      in the doing of what you want done,
      through Jesus Christ our Lord.

Jamie Wallace

336   Lord, we love to be independent, and we find it hard to give
      thanks for everything that happens to us, everything that comes
      our way.
          We want to feel that we have deserved success and a
      home and friends and honourable work; and so sometimes
      our thanksgivings ring false: just words that we take on our
      lips without meaning, without understanding.
          We are not ungrateful, but we expect our due. We feel we
      have earned our place in society, and that by our own labours,

our own thinking, our own vision, we have got where we are.
We accept our gifts as our right.

So we forget that the whole earth is yours, and you gave it
to us. We forget that the breath of life is your gift, and you made
us living souls. We forget that our best purposes are yours, and
that you have inspired us to achievement and strengthened us
for fulfilment.

Give us therefore a grateful heart, O Lord, that we may
offer our thanks with gladness and understanding, mindful that
all things come from you, and that without you we have nothing
and are nothing.

Stanley Pritchard

Forgiveness

337   O my Creator!
       Consume the thorns of all my offences.
       Make clean my soul, make holy my mind,
       Nail down my being in respect of your name,
       Ever keep watch, guard and protect me
       From every act and word that destroys the soul.
       Make me holy, make me clean, set me in order.
       Make me comely, give me understanding, give me light.
       Make me a worthy temple of your Spirit,
       No more a temple of sin,
       But a child of light.
       You alone are the shining brightness of souls,
       And to you, as God and Master,
       We give all glory every day of our lives.
       Simeon, the New Theologian

338   O Lord, the house of my soul is narrow;
       enlarge it, that you may enter in.
       It is in ruins, please repair it.
       It is displeasing to you; I know and acknowledge it.
       But to whom can I call for help, to clear and

repair it, but you?
Cleanse me from my secret faults, O Lord,
and spare your servant.

Augustine of Hippo

339 Stir up your power, Lord, and with great might come among
us; and, because we are sorely hindered by our sins, let your
bountiful grace and mercy speedily help and deliver us; through
Jesus Christ our Lord.

Gelasian Sacramentary

340 O Lord, because we often sin and have to ask for pardon, help
us to forgive as we would be forgiven; neither mentioning
old offences committed against us, nor dwelling upon them in
thought; but loving our brother freely as you freely love us; for
your name's sake.

Christina Rossetti

341 O God, though our sins be seven, though our sins be seventy
times seven, though our sins be more in number than the
hairs of our head, yet give us grace in loving penitence to cast
ourselves down into the depths of your Compassion.

Christina Rossetti

342 Forgive me my sins, O Lord; forgive me the sins of my youth
and the sins of my age, the sins of my soul and the sins of my
body, my secret and my whispering sins, my presumptuous and
my crying sins, the sins that I have done to please myself, and
the sins that I have done to please others. Forgive me those
sins which I know, and those which I know not; forgive them,
O Lord, forgive them all of your great goodness.

Lancelot Andrewes

343 Forgive us, O Lord,
For everything that has spoiled our home life:
For the moodiness and irritability which made us difficult to
    live with;

For the insensitiveness which made us careless of the feelings
   of others;
For selfishness which made life harder for others.

Forgive us, O Lord,
For everything that has spoiled our witness for you;
That so often men would never have known that we had been
   with Jesus and pledged ourselves to him:
That we have so often denied with our lives that which we said
   with our lips;
For the difference between our creed and our conduct, our
   profession and our practice;
For any example which made it easier for men to criticise your
   Church or for another to sin.

When we think of ourselves and of the meanness and ugliness
and weakness of our lives, we thank you for Jesus Christ our
Saviour. Grant us a true penitence for our sins. Grant that at
the foot of the Cross, we may find our burdens rolled away.
And so strengthen us by your Spirit that in the days to come,
we may live more nearly as we ought. Through Jesus Christ
our Lord. Amen.

William Barclay

344 The hatred which divides nation from nation,
race from race, class from class,
Father, forgive.
The covetous desires of men and nations to
possess what is not their own,
Father, forgive.
The greed which exploits the labours of men,
and lays waste the earth,
Father, forgive.
Our envy of the welfare and happiness of others,
Father, forgive.
Our indifference to the plight of the homeless
and the refugee,
Father, forgive.
The lust which uses for ignoble ends the
bodies of men and women,
Father, forgive.
The pride which leads to trust in ourselves

and not in God,
Father, forgive.

Coventry Cathedral prayer, 1964

345 If my soul has turned perversely to the dark;
If I have left some brother wounded by the way;
If I have preferred my aims to yours,
If I have been impatient and would not wait;
If I have marred the pattern drawn out for my life;
If I have cost tears to those I loved;
If my heart has murmured against your will,
O Lord, forgive.

F. B. Meyer

346 Jesus, I wish you would let me wash your feet, since it was
through walking about in me that you soiled them. I wish you
would give me the task of wiping the stains from your feet,
because it was my behaviour that put them there. But where
can I get the running water I need to wash your feet? If I
have no water, at least I have tears: let me wash your feet
with them, and wash myself at the same time.

Teach me to sympathise with sinners from the depths of my
heart. That is the supreme virtue, for Scripture says: 'You shall
not gloat over Judah's sons on the day of their downfall; you
shall not boast to them on the day of their discomfiture.'

May I show compassion whenever anyone falls and his sin
comes to my notice. Instead of reproving him, proudly, may I
grieve and lament with him. In weeping for others, may I weep
for myself.

Ambrose of Milan

347 Help us, Lord, to see ourselves as you see us, and, in shame for
what we are, to cast ourselves in trust upon your love; speak
to us the word of pardon, for our trust is not in any virtue or
wisdom of our own, but only in the mercy and love of God,
which you have shown us in your life and death, our Lord and
our God.

William Temple

348 O merciful God, full of compassion, longsuffering, and of great pity, who spares when we deserve punishment. Make me earnestly to repent, and to be heartily sorry for all my misdoings; make the remembrance so burdensome and painful, that I may flee to you with a troubled spirit and a contrite heart.

O merciful Lord, visit, comfort, and relieve me; cast me not out from your presence, and take not your Holy Spirit from me, but excite in me true repentance; give me in this world knowledge of your truth, and confidence in your mercy, and in the world to come life everlasting, for the sake of our Lord and Saviour, thy Son Jesus Christ. Amen.

Rev. Samuel Johnson

349 I have deceived myself, dear Christ, I confess it; I have fallen from the heights to the depths. O lift me up again, for well I know delusion came because I wanted it. If I presume again, I'll fall again, and fall to my undoing. Take me to you or I die. It cannot be that I alone shall find you hard and unresponsive.

Gregory of Nazianzus

350 O Searcher of hearts, You know us better than we know ourselves. You see the sins which our very sinfulness hides from our eyes. But our conscience does accuse us of failing; failing to watch against sin; failing to walk lovingly in one another's company; failing to offer ourselves completely, humbly to your will. Look upon our sorrow, lift us up from where we have fallen in our weakness. Let the dayspring still arise within our hearts bringing forgiveness, healing and strength. Amen.

James Martineau

351 Lord, I offer to you all the sins that I have committed from the moment when I could first offend you. Consume them, one and all, in the fire of your love, and burn away all their stains. Cleanse my conscience and restore me to your grace and favour.

I also offer to you all that is good within me, though it is small and imperfect, that the good may become more perfect and I may become more and more acceptable to you. Weak and lazy as I am, bring me finally to everlasting union with you. Amen.

Thomas à Kempis

352   When I look back upon my life nigh spent,
      Nigh spent, although the stream as yet flows on,
      I more of follies than of sins repent,
      Less of offence than Love's shortcomings moan,
      With self, O Father, leave me not alone –
      Leave not with the beguiler the beguiled;
      Besmirched and ragged, Lord, take back thine own:
      A fool I bring thee to be made a child.

                                        George Macdonald

353   O sweet Jesus, I grieve for my sins; vouchsafe to supply
      whatever is lacking to my true sorrow and to offer for me to
      God the Father all the grief which thou hast endured because
      of my sins and those of the whole world.

                                        Mechthild of Magdeburg

354   Almighty and everlasting God, who hatest nothing that thou hast
      made, and dost forgive the sins of all them that are penitent;
      Create and make in us new and contrite hearts, that we worthily
      lamenting our sins, and acknowledging our wretchedness, may
      obtain of thee, the God of all mercy, perfect remission and
      forgiveness; through Jesus Christ our Lord.

                                        Thomas Cranmer

355   O Lord Jesus Christ, look upon us with those eyes of yours, the
      eyes with which you looked upon Peter in the hall of judgement,
      that with Peter we may repent, and by your great love be
      forgiven and restored; for your mercy's sake.

                                        Lancelot Andrewes

356   Forgive my sins, O Lord - forgive me the sins of my present
      and the sins of my past, the sins of my soul and the sins of
      my body; the sins which I have done to please myself, and
      the sins which I have done to please others. Forgive me my
      wanton and idle sins, forgive me my serious and deliberate sins,
      forgive me those sins which I know and those sins which I know
      not, the sins which I have laboured so hard to hide from others
      that I have hid them from my own memory. Forgive them, O
      Lord, forgive them all. Of your great mercy let me be absolved,

and of your bountiful goodness let me be delivered from the
bonds of all that by my frailty I have committed. Grant this,
O heavenly Father, for the sake of Jesus Christ, our blessed
Lord and Saviour. Amen.

Thomas Wilson

357 Penetrate these murky corners where we hide memories, and
tendencies on which we do not care to look, but which we will
not yield freely up to you, that you may purify and transmute
them. The persistent buried grudge, the half-acknowledged
enmity which is still smouldering; the bitterness of that loss
we have not turned into sacrifice, the private comfort we cling
to, the secret fear of failure which saps our initiative and is
really inverted pride; the pessimism which is an insult to your
joy. Lord, we bring all these to you, and we review them with
shame and penitence in your steadfast light.

Evelyn Underhill

358 Forgive them all, O Lord:
    our sins of omission and our sins of commission;
    the sins of our youth and the sins of our riper years;
    the sins of our souls and the sins of our bodies;
    our secret and our more open sins;
    our sins of ignorance and surprise,
    and our more deliberate and presumptuous sin;
    the sins we have done to please ourselves
    and the sins we have done to please others;
    the sins we know and remember,
    and the sins we have forgotten;
    the sins we have striven to hide from others
    and the sins by which we have made others offend;
    forgive them, O Lord, forgive them all for his sake,
    who died for our sins and rose for our justification,
    and now stands at your right hand to make intercession
        for us,
Jesus Christ our Lord.

John Wesley

359 O God, our Judge and Saviour, set before us the vision of your
purity and let us see our sins in the light of your holiness. Pierce

our self-contentment with the shafts of your burning love, and let love consume in us all that hinders us from perfect service of your cause; for your holiness is our judgement, so are your wounds our salvation.

William Temple

360 Preserve me, Lord, from the sin which I fear so much: contempt for your love. May I never sin against the Holy Spirit who is love and union, harmony and peace. May I never be separated from your Spirit, from the unity of your peace, by committing the sin which can never be forgiven, neither here nor in the world to come. Keep me, O Lord, among my brothers and kinsfolk that I may proclaim your peace. Keep me among those who preserve the unity of the Spirit in the bond of peace.

Baldwin of Canterbury

361 You are rich in grace and mercy, you are willing to cleanse all sinners from their guilt. Cleanse me, have pity on me. In your mercy spare me, as you spared the publican and the sinful woman. You take the sinfulness from sinners, O Christ, and when we repent you make us welcome beside you. Redeemer of the human race, in your mercy save me.

Rabbula of Edessa

362 Almighty and merciful God, the fountain of all goodness, who knowest the thoughts of our hearts: We confess that we have sinned against thee, and done evil in thy sight. Wash us, we beseech thee, from the stains of our past sins, and give us grace and power to put away all hurtful things; that, being delivered from the bondage of sin, we may bring forth fruits worthy of repentance, and at last enter into thy promised joy; through the mercy of thy blessed Son Jesus Christ our Lord.

Alcuin

363 Don't tire of Your world, Master.
Don't wash Your hands of Your children,
shaking us off as hopeless,
worthless.

Give us one more chance,
and yet another,
and another.

How Your heart must sorrow as You see our need;
our selfishness and sinfulness,
cruelty and degradation,
indifference to Your commands,
contempt of Your love.

If our hearts sicken over the daily news,
what must You feel?
You who hold the world in Your cupped hands,
bending over it lovingly;
listening, yearning,
challenging to better ways.

Yet spiteful arrows pierce Your heart daily;
Your malicious children spit up in Your face:
that kind face bent over them in tender compassion.
Father-God, forgive Your world:
go on forgiving Your children.
Don't leave us to our own devices,
to our self-made hell,
don't cast us away,
flinging us like unwanted playthings into the chill of
outer space.

We have no merits to plead;
our very wickedness must speak for us.
We need You.

O God, forgive Your world:
give us one more chance.

Flora Larsson

364   Out of deep anguish I cry to you, Lord;
       Lord, can you hear me?
       To the groaning of my prayers
       please carefully listen.
       If you, Lord, keep a record of sins,
       then none of us dare face you.

But in you we find forgiveness,
therefore we can adore you.
I wait, with all my soul I want,
and hope for the word I need.
With all my soul I long for my Lord,
more than night-watchmen waiting for dawn.
Like the weary looking for sunrise,
let all God's people wait in hope.
For with the Lord there is pure love,
with him is abundant liberty.
He alone can set us free
from all our sins.

Bruce Prewer
(*version of Psalm 130*)

Reconciliation

365   Father, who formed the family of man to live in harmony and peace: we acknowledge before you our divisions, quarrels, hatreds, injustices and greed.

May your Church demonstrate before the world the power of the gospel to destroy divisions, so that in Christ Jesus there may be no barriers of wealth or class, age or intellect, race or colour, but all may be equally your children, members one of another and heirs together of your everlasting kingdom.

Timothy Dudley-Smith

366   Incarnate word of God, who in your flesh reconciled all men to the Father, and continue to reconcile all those who in heartfelt sorrow confess their sins, I thank you that your healing power has touched me, and cleansed me from the leprosy of sin. Mercifully direct all my thoughts, words and actions to the greater glory of the Father, and be my model and help for the rest of my life so that I may persevere in your service and love.

Michael Buckley

367 Let us pray for those who have fallen away,
that they may recover their footing.
Let us pray for those standing firm,
that they may not be tempted to their downfall.
Let us pray for those of whose fall we have been told,
that they may admit the gravity of their sin
and realise that it calls for a serious remedy.

Cyprian of Carthage

368 Peace to all men of evil will. Let vengeance cease and punishment and retribution. The crimes have gone beyond measure, our minds can no longer take them in. There are too many martyrs . . . Lord do not weigh their sufferings on your scales of justice, and let them not be written in their act of accusation and demand redress. Pay them otherwise. Credit the torturers, the informers and traitors with their courage and strength of spirit, their dignity and endurance, their smile, their love, their broken hearts which did not give in even in the face of death, even in times of greatest weakness . . . take all this into account, Lord, for the remission of the sins of their enemies, as the price of the triumph of justice. Take good and not evil into account. And let us remain in our enemies' thoughts not as their victims, not as a nightmare, but as those who helped them overcome their crimes. This is all we ask for them.

Concentration camp prayer, recorded by Anthony Bloom

369 God our Father, we praise you for the gospel of reconciliation. We thank you for the work of the Holy Spirit drawing the scattered flock of Christ into a deeper unity. May this be a sign of hope to our divided world. Enable us, who bear your name, to be instruments of your peace and ever to believe that the peace for which we pray is possible; through Jesus Christ our Lord. Amen.

Kenneth Greet

For Truth

370 God almighty, Father of our Lord Jesus Christ, by the gift of your Spirit establish and ground us in your truth. Reveal to us what we do not know; perfect in us what is lacking; strengthen in us what we know; and keep us in your service without fault; through the same Jesus Christ our Lord.

Clement of Rome

371 God of truth, who has guided men in knowledge throughout the ages, and from whom every good thought comes, help us in our study to use your gifts of wisdom and knowledge. Let us read good books carefully, and listen to wise teaching humbly, that we may be led into all truth, and strengthened in all goodness of life, to the praise of your holy Name.

Rowland Williams

372 Almighty God, who has sent the Spirit of truth to us to guide us into all truth, so rule our lives by your power, that we may be truthful in word, deed, and thought. O keep us, most merciful Saviour, with your gracious protection, that no fear or hope may ever make us false in act or speech. Cast out from us what makes for a lie, and bring us all to the perfect freedom of your truth; through Jesus Christ your Son our Lord.

Brooke Foss Westcott

373 Make our hearts to burn within us Jesus Christ, as we walk with you in the way and listen to your words; that we may go in the strength of your presence and your truth all our journey through, and at its end behold you, in the glory of the Eternal Trinity, God for ever and ever.

Eric Milner-White

For Freedom

374 Lord Jesus Christ, you came to set at liberty those who are oppressed; and we are oppressed by the tyranny of our guilt and of our fears. Lord, open our hearts to receive

your grace, the love that releases us from our bondage and
gives us freedom: freedom from cares and worries that stifle
our happiness; freedom from sins that cling to us, and to which
we cling; freedom from all that prevents our becoming what we
can be and ought to be. So bring us, O Lord, to the experience
of life more abundant, for your name's sake.

New Every Morning

375   From all my lame defeats and oh! much more
From all the victories that I seemed to score;
From cleverness shot forth on thy behalf,
At which, while angels weep, the audience laugh;
From all my proofs of thy divinity,
Thou, who wouldst give no sign, deliver me.
Thoughts are but coins. Let me not trust instead
Of thee, their thin-worn image of thy head.
From all my thoughts, even from my thoughts of thee,
O thou fair silence, fall, and set me free.
Lord of the narrow gate and needle's eye,
Take from me all my trumpery, lest I die.

C. S. Lewis

376   O my God, give me thy grace so that the things of this earth
and things more naturally pleasing to me, may not be as close
as thou art to me. Keep thou my eyes, my ears, my heart from
clinging to the things of this world. Break my bonds, raise my
heart. Keep my whole being fixed on thee. Let me never lose
sight of thee; and while I gaze on thee, let my love of thee
grow more and more every day.

John Henry Newman

377   Lord, people are always talking about freedom, about being
free, but I find it very difficult to understand what true freedom
is. Doing what I want the whole time doesn't seem to be true
freedom; if everyone did this life would be chaotic. Help me to
discover what freedom is. Does it come from forgetting myself
and serving you and others, since I am told that in serving you I
will have perfect freedom? Help me, Lord, to live in such a way
so that I can be freed of my own selfish desires which imprison
me more than most things I know.

I'm all caught up, Lord, in what I am. They tell me, the learned men, that everything is determined and I have no freedom. Sometimes, I feel this, but yet, deep down I know I can be free, with the freedom of the sons of God. Release me unto myself, Lord, release me unto the world. Let me be real, let me be free.

Michael Hollings

For Courage

378 Make us, O blessed Master, strong in heart, full of courage, fearless of danger, holding pain and danger cheap when they lie in the path of duty. May we be strengthened with all might by your Spirit in our hearts.

F. B. Meyer

379 God grant me the courage to change the things I can change, the serenity to accept those I cannot change, and the wisdom to know the difference – but God grant me the courage not to give up on what I think is right even though I think it is hopeless. Amen.

Chester W. Nimitz
(based upon Reinhold Niebuhr's prayer)

380 Almighty God, give us grace to contend always for what is true and right, and to be ready if need be to suffer for it. Give us not over to any death of the soul, but rather lift us into newness of life, and let us glorify and enjoy you for ever; through Jesus Christ our Lord.

Book of Prayers for Students

381 Take from us, O Lord God, all pride and vanity, all boasting and self-assertion, and give us the true courage that shows itself in gentleness; the true wisdom that shows itself in simplicity; and the true power that shows itself in modesty; through Jesus Christ our Lord.

Charles Kingsley

382 Lord Jesus Christ, light shining in our darkness; have mercy on our tired and doubting hearts. Renew in us the courage we need, to bring to completion the work your calling has begun in us.

Taizé prayer

383 Lord and King, we pray for courage to face unpopularity for the sake of truth; for courage to declare boldly our convictions, though they make us despised; for courage to break with evil custom and evil opinions. Give us strong hearts that will not fear what any man may do to us. Give us, O Lord, the spirit of boldness, that being delivered from all fears of our fellows, we may be strong in you, and very courageous.

John S. Hoyland

384 Help me, O Lord, so to strive and so to act, that those things which cloud my own way may not darken the path which others have to tread. Give me unselfish courage so that I am ready always to share my bread and wine yet able to hide my hunger and my thirst.

Leslie D. Weatherhead

For a Sense of Humour

385 Give us a sense of humour, Lord, and also things to laugh about. Give us the grace to take a joke against ourselves, and to see the funny side of the things we do. Save us from annoyance, bad temper, resentfulness against our friends. Help us to laugh even in the face of trouble. Fill our minds with the love of Jesus; for his name's sake.

A. G. Bullivant

386 Lord, I've been reading that people who are devoted to extreme

left- or right-wing causes are without humour. Somehow their
devotion doesn't allow them to relax, look at themselves and
the world and laugh; they are constantly serious! Lord, this can
easily happen to your followers. This is ridiculous, for loving
you should bring us joy and the ability to see the funny side
of life. You told us the story of the man who had such a large
plank in his eye that he couldn't see to take the speck of dust
out of his friend's eye! We read this with great seriousness and
can't realise what a comic picture it is! Then there is the camel
trying to get through the eye of a needle! I don't know but it
seems to me we are too serious about ourselves, and not full
of the self-forgiving joy which you offer us. So do help us to
laugh more, and particularly at ourselves, Lord!

Michael Hollings

387 Dear Lord, thank you for one of the greatest of all your many
gifts to us – a sense of humour. Teach us to value it and to use
it for the building up of your kingdom of joy and hope on earth;
for Jesus' sake.

Alan Warren

For Sincerity

388 Grant, Lord, that what we have said with our lips we may
believe in our hearts and practise in our lives; and of your
mercy keep us faithful to the end.

John Hunter

389 Lift up our hearts, O Lord, above the false show of things,
above fear, above laziness, above selfishness and covetousness, above custom and fashion, up to the everlasting truth
and order that you are; that so we may live joyfully and freely,
in faithful trust that you are our Saviour, our example, and our
friend, both now and for evermore.

Charles Kingsley

390 O Lord, the Lord whose ways are right, keep us in your mercy from lip-service and empty forms; from having a name that we live, but being dead.

Help us to worship you by good deeds and lives of holiness; that our prayer also may rise in your sight as incense, and the lifting up of our hands be as an evening sacrifice.

Christina Rossetti

For Patience and Perseverance

391 Grant me strength, merciful Father, that I may suffer and endure; patience alone I ask. Lord, give me this, and behold my heart is ready. O God, my heart is ready to receive whatever shall be laid upon me. Grant that in my patience I may possess my soul; to that end, may I often look upon the face of Christ your Son, that, as he has suffered such terrible things in the flesh, I may endeavour to be armed with the same mind. I commit my strength to you, O Lord; for you are my Strength and my Refuge. Amen.

Treasury of Devotion

392 When many are coming and going and there is little leisure, give us grace, O heavenly Father, to follow the example of our Lord Jesus Christ, who knew neither impatience of spirit nor confusion of work, but in the midst of his labours held communion with you, and even upon earth was still in heaven; where he now reigns with you and the Holy Spirit world without end.

Charles J. Vaughan

393 Help us this day, O God, to run with patience the race that is set before us. May neither opposition without nor discouragement within divert us from our goal. Inspire in us both strength of mind and steadfastness of purpose, that we may meet all fears and difficulties with unswerving courage, and may fulfil with quiet fidelity the tasks committed to our charge, through Jesus Christ our Lord.

H. Bisseker

394   Give us, O God, the power to go on,
To carry our share of Thy burden through to the end,
To live all the years of our life
Faithful to the highest we have seen,
With no pandering to the second best,
No leniency to our own lower selves;
No looking backward,
No cowardice. Give us the power to give ourselves,
To break the bread of our lives unto starving humanity;
In humble self-subjection to serve others,
As Thou, O God, dost serve Thy world. Amen.
John S. Hoyland

395   O God our Father, let us not be content to wait and see what
will happen, but give us the determination to make the right
things happen.
   While time is running out, save us from patience which is
akin to cowardice.
   Give us the courage to be either hot or cold, to stand for
something, lest we fall for anything. In Jesus' name. Amen.
Peter Marshall

396   O Lord, our God, grant us, we beseech you, patience in
troubles, humility in comforts, constancy in temptations, and
victory over all our spiritual foes. Grant us sorrow for our
sins, thankfulness for your benefits, fear of your judgement,
love of your mercies, and mindfulness of your presence; now
and for ever.
John Cosin

397   To me, Lord Jesus, you are the model of patience and its
reward. Urgently you ask it of me, and powerfully grant it.
Your own example strengthens me in every conflict, and the
reward of my endurance is the royal gift of your presence.
Either way, you, in a wonderful way, win me to yourself,
as it were, compelling me. Beckon me on, then; gladly will
I follow, and yet more gladly take joy in your presence; for
if you are so good to those who seek, what will you not be to
those who find?
Bernard of Clairvaux

398   O God, give me the gift of perseverance.

If I fail in something the first time, help me to try and try again,
   until I succeed.

If I have to do something difficult, help me not to get discour-
   aged, but to keep on trying.

If I find that results are slow to come, give me patience that I
   may learn to wait.

Help me to remember that the more difficult a thing is, the
   greater is the satisfaction in achieving it.

Help me to welcome every difficulty as a challenge and an
   opportunity for victory; through Jesus Christ my Lord.
   Amen.

William Barclay

399   O Holy Spirit,
      give me faith that will protect me
      from despair, from passions, and from vice;
      Give me such love for God and men
      as will blot out all hatred and bitterness;
      Give me the hope that will deliver me
      From fear and faint-heartedness.
      O holy and merciful God,
      my Creator and Redeemer,
      my Judge and Saviour,
      you know me and all that I do.
      You hate and punish evil without respect of persons
      in this world and the next;
      you forgive the sins of those
      who sincerely pray for forgiveness;
      you love goodness, and reward it on this earth
      with a clear conscience,
      and, in the world to come,
      with a crown of righteousness.
      I remember in your presence all my loved ones,
      my fellow-prisoners, and all who in this house
      perform their hard service;
      Lord, have mercy.
      Restore me to liberty
      and enable me to so live now

that I may answer before you and before men.
Lord, whatever this day may bring,
your name be praised. Amen.

Dietrich Bonhoeffer

For Help in Temptation

400 Lord, help us in times of temptation. May nothing induce us to distrust your care of us, nor use your gifts, denying knowledge of you as their Giver. May we never presume upon your protection, or be disloyal to your service. So support us, we pray, that when we have been tried and tested we may receive the crown of life, which you have prepared for those that love you. Amen.

Henry Alford

401 O Father, calm the turbulence of our passions; quiet the throbbing of our hopes; repress the waywardness of our wills; direct the motions of our affections; and sanctify the varieties of our lot.

Be Thou all in all to us; and may all things earthly, while we bend them to our growth in grace, and to the work of blessing, dwell lightly in our hearts, so that we may readily, or even joyfully, give up whatever Thou dost ask for.

May we seek first Thy kingdom and righteousness; resting assured that then all things needful shall be added unto us.

Father, pardon our past ingratitude and disobedience; and purify us, whether by Thy gentler or Thy sterner dealings, till we have done Thy will on earth, and Thou removest us to Thine own presence with the redeemed in heaven.

Mary Carpenter

402 O Lord, grant us grace never to parley with temptation, never to tamper with conscience; never to spare the right eye, or hand, or foot that is a snare to us; never to lose our souls, though in exchange we should gain the whole world.

Christina Rossetti

403   Let us beg the Lord with all our hearts that we may fight for
the truth body and soul to the very end. If circumstances arise
that put our faith to the test, and even if persecution breaks
out, may he find us ready. Otherwise, our houses might fall in
that winter; the building might be blown down by the storms,
as though it had been built on sand.

   When the Devil, the worst of the wicked spirits, blows with
his winds, may our conduct stand up to him, as it has until now
– unless it has been covertly undermined – and by preparing
ourselves for the campaign, may we show what love we have
for God and Christ Jesus, to whom glory and power belong and
will belong for ever and ever. Amen.

Origen

404   Lord God Almighty, strengthen me against the temptations of
the devil, and put far from me every unrighteousness. Shield
me against my foes, seen and unseen; and teach me to do Thy
will, that I may inwardly love Thee before all things with a clean
mind and a clean body. For Thou art my maker and redeemer,
my help, my comfort, my trust and my hope. Praise and glory
be to Thee, now, ever and ever, world without end. Amen.

King Alfred

405   Almighty and most merciful Father give us, we pray, the grace
to examine our inmost hearts and our secret thoughts. May we
never be drawn to do anything to dishonour your name; may
we, on the contrary, persevere in all good purposes, and in
your faithful service.

George Hickes

406   Lord Jesus, you were a man; you had my eyes, my ears, my
sense of touch and smell; you know my feelings of body and
heart; you were like me in everything – except sin. But, Lord,
were you never tempted by human beauty, the beauty you had
created? Surely, anyhow, you understand how I feel now. How
I long for what I should not have! Tempted as I am, help me
not to sin.

Michael Hollings

Dissatisfaction with Self

407 To you, O Jesus, peace of the troubled heart, I come! Save me from myself. Shine into my heart with your life and love. Melt away all cold distrust. Take away all sin; and make me like to yourself, for your love and kindness' sake, O Lord!

W. Boyd Carpenter

408 O Christ, my Lord, again and again I have said with Mary Magdalene, 'They have taken away my Lord and I know not where they have laid him.' I have been desolate and alone. And you have found me again, and I know that what has died is not you, my Lord, but only my idea of you, the image which I have made to preserve what I have found, and to be my security. I shall make another image, O Lord, better than the last. That too must go, and all successive images, until I come to the blessed vision of yourself, O Christ, my Lord.

George Appleton

409 O my Father, I have moments of deep unrest – moments when I know not what to ask by reason of the very excess of my wants. I have in these hours no words for you, no conscious prayers for you.

My cry seems purely worldly; I want only the wings of a dove that I may flee away. Yet all the time you have accepted my unrest as a prayer. You have interpreted its cry for a dove's wings as a cry for you, you have received the nameless longings of my heart as the intercessions of your Spirit.

They are not yet the intercessions of my spirit; I know not what I ask. But you know what I ask, O my God. You know the name of that need which lies beneath my speechless groan. You know that, because I am made in your image, I can find rest only in what gives rest to you; therefore you have counted my unrest as righteousness, and have called my groaning your Spirit's prayer.

George Matheson

410   I am tired, Lord,
       too tired to think,
       too tired to pray,
       too tired to do anything.
       Too tired,
       drained of resources,
       'labouring at the oars against a head wind',
       pressed down by a force as strong as the sea.
       Lord of all power and might,
       'your way was through the sea,
       your path through the great waters',
       calm my soul,
       take control,
       Lord of all power and might.

Rex Chapman

411   If I am to complain, let me complain to Jesus fastened on his cross. But in your presence, my Saviour, what have I to complain of? What are my sufferings compared with those you bore without complaining? I might perhaps convince my fellow-man that I am unjustly afflicted, but in your presence, Lord, I cannot, for my sins are known to you. You know my sufferings are far less than I deserve. And since all my afflictions proceed from you, reproach not my afflictions, not my wrongs, but myself and my own want of patience. To you I come; give me strength, and hearten me to suffer in silence; as once you did.

Claude de la Colombière

In Joy

412   Give us, Lord, a bit o' sun,
       a bit o' work and a bit o' fun;
       give us all in the struggle and sputter
       our daily bread and a bit o' butter;
       give us health, our keep to make,

an' a bit to spare for others' sake;
give us sense, for we're some of us duffers,
an' a heart to feel for all that suffers;
give us, too, a bit of a song
and a tale, and a book to help us along.
An' give us our share o' sorrow's lesson
that we may prove how grief's a blessin'.
Give us, Lord, a chance to be
our goodly best, brave, wise, and free,
our goodly best for ourself, and others,
till all men learn to live as brothers.

From the wall of an old inn, Lancaster

413   Lord, you have sent me joy! I leap . . . I skip . . . it is good to
be alive. You give life; you give the spirit of gladness to feed
it. I love you. My sins are forgiven. It is good to be alive . . .
and you have made it so.

Hubert van Zeller

414   Today my heart sings, Lord;
Everything within me rejoices.

Joy bubbles up in my soul,
overflows and cascades like a stream leaping all barriers;
the joy of knowing You,
the joy of union with You.
One with You, Creator of the world,
and my Creator,
one with You, Saviour of the world,
and my Saviour.
One with You, Spirit of the eternal God,
and my God,
one with You, almighty King of kings
and my Lord and King.

Joy, joy at the heart of living,
joy in doing, joy in being;
sing for joy, my heart,
for sheer joy, my soul.

The joy of loving You,

the joy of following You,
the joy of serving You;
all the way 'long it is glory.

Today my heart sings, Lord;
everything within me rejoices,
joy bubbles up in my soul,
glory . . . glory!

Flora Larsson

415   Thank you, Lord Jesus,
for all our happiness.
Thank you especially
for the happiness which takes us by surprise.
Above all we ask you
to lead us toward the surprising discovery
that what most pleases you
will bring the greatest joy to us.

Jamie Wallace

416   We rejoice in the pure things – a small baby, the unspoiled
      morning freshness, and kindnesses done with no thought
      of reward or self-interest.
      We rejoice in the lovely things – flowers and trees, small
      animals, and the happy faces of children and young
      people.
      We rejoice in the just things – the wisdom of our laws, and our
      nation's care for the widowed, the sick and the poor.
      We rejoice in the excellent things, good books, skilful paint-
      ings, radio and television programmes that increase our
      knowledge and enlighten our minds.
      But Lord, we rejoice most of all in You, who have given us all
      these things so that we may enjoy them. Amen.

Beryl Bye

417   Lord, there will be laughter in paradise,
      and the laughter has begun on earth:
      so save us from being humourless lest we be unprepared for
      heaven.
      May laughter put flight to the devil,

may humour lighten the darkness,
may our jokes be a way of learning your truth.
We do not pray for the grin of the Cheshire cat,
but for a light heart, a ready wit,
a blessed sense of humour.

Michael Walker

For the Imitation of Christ

418 Set before our minds and hearts, O heavenly Father, the
example of our Lord Jesus Christ, who, when he was upon
earth, found his refreshment in doing the will of him that sent
him, and in finishing his work. When many are coming and going,
and there is little leisure, give us grace to remember him who
knew neither impatience of spirit nor confusion of work, but in
the midst of all his labours held communion with you, and even
upon earth was still in heaven; where now he reigns with you
and the Holy Spirit world without end.

Charles J. Vaughan

419 Give me, O Christ, the courage of faith. Pierce the hidden
depths of my spirit like a two-edged sword. Give me your
clear light to guide my conscience. Give me that love which
delights me in the seclusion of my timid heart and without
which I cannot know you as the Lord of all things, of atoms
and stars, of human bodies and spiritual worlds. Then shall I
be truly blessed in you, then shall I have my heart's desire and
the purpose of my existence.

Hugo Rahner

420 If I were not yours, my Christ,
I would feel a finite creature.
I have been born and my life is dissolving away,
I eat, sleep, rest and walk,
sicken and am healed;

numberless are the desires and torments that assail me.
I enjoy the sunlight and the fruit of the earth;
but I die and my flesh will crumble into dust,
like that of the animals who have not sinned.
What more have I than they?
Nothing more, if not God.
If I were not yours, my Christ,
I would feel a dead creature.

Gregory of Nazianzus

421   Lord Jesus Christ, pierce my soul with your love so that I may always long for you alone, who are the bread of angels and the fulfilment of the soul's deepest desires. May my heart always hunger and feed upon you, so that my soul may be filled with the sweetness of your presence. May my soul thirst for you, who are the source of life, wisdom, knowledge, light and all the riches of God our Father. May I always seek and find you, think upon you, speak to you and do all things for the honour and glory of your holy name. Be always my only hope, my peace, my refuge and my help in whom my heart is rooted so that I may never be separated from you.

Bonaventure

422   Lord Jesus, let me know myself; let me know thee,
And desire nothing else but thee.
Let me love myself only if I love thee,
And do all things for thy sake.
Let me humble myself and exalt thee,
And think of nothing else but thee.
Let me die to myself and live in thee,
And take whatever happens as coming from thee.
Let me forsake myself and walk after thee,
And ever desire to follow thee.
Let me flee from myself and turn to thee,
So that I may merit to be defended by thee.
Let me fear for myself, let me fear thee,
And be among those that are chosen by thee.
Let me distrust myself and trust in thee,
And ever obey for the love of thee.
Let me cleave to nothing but thee,

And ever be poor because of thee.
Look upon me that I may love thee,
Call me, that I may see thee,
And forever possess thee, for all eternity.

Augustine of Hippo

423　May the strength of God guide me this day, and may his power
　　　preserve me.
　　　May the wisdom of God instruct me; the eye of God watch over
　　　me; the ear of God hear me; the word of God give sweetness
　　　to my speech; the hand of God defend me; and may I follow
　　　the way of God.
　　　Christ be with me, Christ before me,
　　　Christ be after me, Christ within me,
　　　Christ beneath me, Christ above me,
　　　Christ at my right hand, Christ at my left,
　　　Christ in the fort, Christ in the chariot,
　　　Christ in the ship.
　　　Christ in the heart of every man who thinks of me,
　　　Christ in the mouth of every man who speaks to me.
　　　Christ in every eye that sees me.
　　　Christ in every ear that hears me.

Attributed to St Patrick

424　I come to you, O Lord, not only because I am unhappy without
　　　you; not only because I feel I need you, but because your grace
　　　draws me on to seek you for your own sake, because you are
　　　so glorious and beautiful. I come in great fear, but in greater
　　　love. Oh may I never lose, as years pass away, and the heart
　　　shuts up, and all things are a burden, let me never lose this
　　　youthful, eager, elastic love of you. Make your grace supply
　　　the failure of nature. Do the more for me, the less I can do for
　　　myself.

John Henry Newman

425　Sever me from myself that I may be grateful to you;
　　　may I perish to myself that I may be safe in you;
　　　may I die to myself that I may live in you;
　　　may I wither to myself that I may blossom in you;
　　　may I be emptied of myself that I may abound in you;

may I be nothing to myself that I may be all to you.

Erasmus

426 I need you to teach me day by day, according to each day's opportunities and needs. Give me, O my Lord, that purity of conscience which alone can receive, which alone can improve your inspirations.

My ears are dull, so that I cannot hear your voice. My eyes are dim, so that I cannot see your tokens of love. You alone can quicken my hearing, and purge my sight, and cleanse and renew my heart.

Teach me to sit at your feet, and to hear your word.

John Henry Newman

427 O Holy and ever-blessed Jesus, who being the eternal Son of God and most high in the glory of the Father, didst vouchsafe in love for us sinners to be born of a pure virgin, and didst humble thyself unto death, even the death of the cross: Deepen within us, we beseech thee, a due sense of thy infinite love; that adoring and believing in thee as our Lord and Saviour, we may trust in thy infinite merits, imitate thy holy example, obey thy commands, and finally enjoy thy promises; who with the Father and the Holy Ghost livest and reignest, one God, world without end.

John Wesley

428 May Christ give us all the courage that we need to go the way he shepherds us, that when he calls we may go unfrightened. If he bids us come to him across the waters, that unfrightened we may go. And if he bids us climb the hill, may we not notice that it is a hill, mindful only of the happiness of his company. He made us for himself, that we should travel with him and see him at last in his unveiled beauty in the abiding city, where he is light and happiness and endless home.

Bede Jarrett

Indwelling God

429 Help me, O Lord, to descend into the depths of my being, below my conscious and sub-conscious life until I discover my real self, that which is given me from you, the divine likeness in which I am made and into which I am to grow, the place where your Spirit communes with mine, the spring from which all my life rises.

George Appleton

430 Grant me, O Lord, the royalty of inward happiness and the serenity which comes from living close to you. Daily renew the sense of joy, and let the eternal spirit of the Father dwell in my soul and body, filling every corner of my heart with light and grace, so that bearing about with me the infection of a good courage, I may be a diffuser of life and may meet all ills and crosses with gallant and high-hearted happiness, giving you thanks always for all things.

Robert Louis Stevenson

431 Work within me, within us, within the Church.
Be at the centre of our lives.
Mould us in your image.
Bring about our transformation.
Make us fruitful, Lord,
Now,
Here as well as there,
Me as well as the others.

Rex Chapman

432 And if still I cannot find you, O God, then let me search my heart and know whether it is not rather I who am blind than you who are obscure, and I who am fleeing from you rather than you from me; and let me confess these my sins before you and seek your pardon in Jesus Christ my Lord.

John Baillie

433   It is not far to go
        for you are near.
        It is not far to go,
        for you are here.
        And not by travelling, Lord,
        men come to you,
        but by the way of love,
        and we love you.

Amy Carmichael

434   Most Holy Spirit, Comforter Divine,
        through you the life of prayer is made complete,
        through you the suffering pilgrimage is made joyful,
        through you the darkness is made light:
        illumine my life, inspire my prayer,
        be the unity that makes me one,
        that I may be all prayer,
        one coinherence with my Source and End,
        one coinherence with the world of men and nature's order,
        one wholeness in myself;
        purged, restored, reunited in the life
        from which man fell
        and which the passion of the Lord restored
        a temple for your majesty.

Gilbert Shaw

435   Open wide the window of our spirits and fill us full of light; open
        wide the door of our hearts, that we may receive and entertain
        you with all our powers of adoration and love.

Christina Rossetti

436   O Lord, I rejoice and am exceeding glad;
        Because of thy goodness,
        In creating the world.
        But much more abundantly,
        For the glory of my soul;
        Which cut out of nothing thou hast builded
        To be a temple unto God,
        A living temple of thine omnipresence,
        An understanding eye,
        A temple of eternity,

A temple of thy wisdom, blessedness, and glory.
O ye powers of mine immortal Soul, bless ye the Lord,
praise him and magnify him for ever.
He hath made you greater,
More glorious, brighter,
Better than the heavens,
A meeter dwelling place for his eternal Godhead
Than the heaven of heavens.
The heaven of heavens,
And all the spaces above the heavens,
Are not able to contain him.
Being but dead and silent place,
They feel not themselves.
They know nothing,
See no immensity nor wideness at all.
But in thee, my soul, there is a perceptive power
To measure all spaces beyond the heavens
And those spaces
By him into thee
To feel and see the heaven of heavens
All things contained in them,
And his presence in thee.
Nor canst thou only feel his omnipresence in thee,
But adore his goodness,
Dread his power,
Reverence his majesty,
See his wisdom,
Rejoice in his bounty,
Conceive his eternity,
Praise his glory.
Which being things transcendent unto place,
Cannot by the heavens at all be apprehended.
With reverence, O God, and dread mixed with joy,
I come before thee.
To consider thy glory in the perfection of my soul
The workmanship of the Lord.

Thomas Traherne

437   God be in my head
        And in my understanding.
        God be in mine eyes

And in my looking.
God be in my mouth
And in my speaking.
God be in my heart
And in my thinking.
God be at mine end
And at my departing.

Sarum Primer

438 O eternal God, who has taught us by your holy word that our
bodies are the temples of your Spirit, keep us we most humbly
beseech you temperate and holy in thought, word, and deed, that
at the last we, with all the pure in heart, may see you, and be
made like unto you in your heavenly kingdom, through Christ
our Lord.

Brooke Foss Westcott

439 I adore you, Lord Jesus, dwelling in my heart. I implore you, live
in me, in all the tranquillity of your power, in all the perfection of
your ways, in all the brightness of your presence and in all the
holiness of your Spirit; that I may know the breadth and length
and depth and height of your love; and do you trample down in
me all power of evil in the might of your Spirit to the glory of
God the Father.

Jean-Jacques Olier

440 Be born in us
Incarnate Love.
Take our flesh and blood and
give us Your humanity;
take our eyes and
give us Your vision;
take our minds and
give us Your pure thought;
take our feet and
set them in Your path;
take our hands and
fold them in Your prayer;
take our hearts and
give them Your will
to Love.

Caryll Houselander

Abandonment into God's Hands

441   Teach us, O Father, to trust you with life and with death,
       And (though this is harder by far)
       With the life and the death of those that are dearer to us than
       our life.

       Teach us stillness and confident peace
       In your perfect will,
       Deep calm of soul, and content
       In what you will do with these lives you have given.

       Teach us to wait and be still,
       To rest in yourself,
       To hush this clamorous anxiety,
       To lay in your arms all this wealth you have given.

       You love these souls that we love
       With a love as far surpassing our own
       As the glory of noon surpasses the gleam of a candle.

       Therefore will we be still,
       And trust in you.

                                                    John S. Hoyland

442   Eternal Father, even as your divine Son, Our Lord Jesus Christ,
       offers himself to your majesty as holocaust and victim for the
       human race, even so do I offer myself body and soul to you;
       do with me what you will; to this end I accept all troubles,
       mortifications, afflictions, which it shall please you to send me
       this day. I accept all from your divine will; O my God, may my
       will ever be conformed to yours!

                                                    Columba Marmion

443   O Lord God, make my religion to be my love, my deepest love,

my delight, the love of my life.

Let me never be content with giving you less than my whole heart; and that, with no motive which is not pure, no mind which is not joyful.

Make all my days a looking up and a going forth to greet and meet that majesty of love which has visited and redeemed your people: the love that would save to the uttermost and is the glory of your glory, illimitable, inexhaustible, world without end.

Eric Milner-White

444 Father,
I abandon myself into your hands;
do with me what you will.
Whatever you may do I thank you:
I am ready for all, I accept all.

Let only your will be done in me,
and in all your creatures.
I wish no more than this, O Lord.

Into your hands I commend my soul:
I offer it to you
with all the love of my heart,
for I love you, Lord,
and so need to give myself,
to surrender myself into your hands,
without reserve,
and with boundless confidence,
for you are my Father.

Charles-Eugène de Foucauld

445 Into your hands we commit our spirit.
Into your hands, the open and defenceless hands of love,
into your hands, the accepting and welcoming hands of love,
into your hands, the firm and reliable hands of love,
we commit our spirit.

Rex Chapman

446 O Lord Jesu, our only health and our everlasting life, I give myself wholly unto Thy will; being sure that the thing cannot perish which is committed unto Thy mercy.

Thou, merciful Lord, wast born for my sake: Thou didst suffer both hunger and thirst for my sake; Thou didst preach and teach, didst pray and fast, for my sake: and finally Thou gavest Thy most precious body to die and Thy blood to be shed on the cross, for my sake. Most merciful Saviour, let all these things profit me which Thou freely hast given me. O Lord, into Thy hands I commit my soul.

Primer of 1559

447 God, of your goodness, give me yourself; for you are sufficient for me. I cannot properly ask anything less, to be worthy of you. If I were to ask less, I should always be in want. In you alone do I have all.

Julian of Norwich

448 Deign, Lord, to fulfil your high purposes in me, whatever they be. Work in and through me. I am born to serve you, to be yours, to be your instrument. Let me be your blind instrument; I ask not to see; I ask not to know; I ask simply to be used.

John Henry Newman

Gift of One's Self

449 O Bounteous God, from your hand I have received everything. All that I am and have; life itself, the love of family and friends, and the precious gift of faith. How can I ever thank you, for all I have is yours? You so loved the world that you gave us your son. I can do no less than offer you myself, body and soul, to you and your service. Take all that I am and have, and keep me for ever faithful to you.

Michael Buckley

450   O God, our heavenly Father, who so loved the world that you
gave your only Son to die upon the cross: Pour your love into
our hearts, we humbly beseech you; that we loving you above
all things, may give up ourselves, our time, our money, our
talents, to your service; for the sake of him who loved us and
gave himself for us, Jesus Christ your Son our Lord.

John R. W. Stott

451   O God, you made me for yourself, to show forth your goodness
through me. Show forth, I humbly pray, the life-giving power
of your nature; help me to such a true and lively faith, such a
thirst after the life and spirit of your Son, Jesus, in my soul that
all that is within me may be turned from every inward thought
or outward action that is not you.

William Law

452   Lord Jesus Christ, no matter where we are, far away or near at
hand, off involved in the hurly-burly of life, immersed in human
cares or joys, light-hearted or down in the dumps, draw us to
yourself, draw us so that we become totally yours.

Søren Kierkegaard

453   I vow and consecrate to God all that is in me: my memory and
my actions to God the Father; my understanding and my words
to God the Son; my will and my thoughts to God the Holy Ghost;
my heart, my body, my tongue, my senses and all my sorrows to
the sacred Humanity of Jesus Christ, 'who was contented to be
betrayed into the hands of wicked men and to suffer the torment
of the Cross'.

Francis of Sales

454   O Lord, in the simplicity of my heart, I offer myself to you
today, to be your servant for ever, to obey you, and to be a
sacrifice of perpetual praise. Amen.

Thomas à Kempis

455   Lord, teach us to understand that your Son died to save us, not
from suffering, but from ourselves; not from injustice, far less
from justice, but from being unjust. He died that we might live –
but live as he lives, by dying as he died who died to himself.

George Macdonald

456 Lord, bestow on me two gifts,
– to forget myself
– never to forget you.
Keep me from self-love, self-pity, self-will
in every guise and disguise
nor ever let me measure myself by myself.
Save me from self,
my tempter, seducer, jailer;
corrupting desire at the spring,
closing the avenues of grace,
leading me down the streets of death.
Rather, let my soul devote to you
its aspirations, affections, resolutions.
Let my mind look unto you
in all its searchings, shinings, certitudes.
Let my body work for you
with its full health and abilities.
Let your love pass
into the depth of my heart,
into the heart of my prayer,
into the heart of my whole being;
So that I desert myself
and dwell and move in you
in peace, now and evermore.

Eric Milner-White

457 My Lord and my God,
take me from all that keeps me from you.
My Lord and my God,
grant me all that leads me to you.
My Lord and my God,
take me from myself and give me completely to you.

Nicholas of Flue

458 Help me, O God, to put off all pretence and to find my true self.
Help me, O God, to discard all false pictures of you, whatever the cost to my comfort.
Help me, O God, to let go all my problems, and fix my mind on you.

Help me, O God, to see my own sins, never to judge my
    neighbour, and may the glory be all yours.
Into your hands I commend my spirit,
Your will, not mine, be done.

Anthony Bloom

459   Lord, I believe, but would believe more firmly; O Lord, I
        love, but yet would love more warmly. I offer unto you my
        thoughts, that they may dwell on you; my deeds, that they
        may be according to you; my sufferings, that they may be for
        you. Amen.

Treasury of Devotion

460   Lord Jesus,
        I give you my hands to do your work.
        I give you my feet to go your way.
        I give you my eyes to see as you do.
        I give you my tongue to speak your words.
        I give you my mind that you may think in me.
        I give you my spirit that you may pray in me.
        Above all, I give you my heart that you may love in me your
            Father and all mankind.
        I give you my whole self that you may grow in me, so that it
            is you, Lord Jesus
        Who live and work and pray in me.

The Grail prayer

461   O Lord, help us to go out of ourselves, so that we may give
        ourselves over to you, with all our powers, with all that we are
        and all that we have.

Jacob Boehme

462   We offer you the material of our daily life, believing that you
        can make it a stepping-stone to heaven.
            Free us from fuss and worry and fret, with the thoughts of
        your eternal love.
            Help us to laugh at our petty discontent and jealousies and
        give us that divine discontent that reaches always for you and
        sees your goodness everywhere.

Help us to live now in the kingdom prepared for those who love you.

Elsie Chamberlain

463 Lord, my thoughts turn in upon myself. Turn them upward to you and outward to your other children, that I may forget myself, and lose all fear and anxiety, all self-seeking and self-consciousness, in worship of you and in love of others. O save me from myself to worship, love and serve in perfect freedom.

George Appleton

464 O God, grant that at all times you may find me as you desire me and where you would have me be, that you may lay hold on me fully, both by the Within and the Without of myself, grant that I may never break this double thread of my life.

Teilhard de Chardin

465 Lord Jesus Christ,
take all my freedom,
my memory, my understanding, and my will.
All that I have and cherish,
you have given me.
I surrender it all to be guided by your will.
Your grace and your love are wealth enough for me.
Give me these, Lord Jesus,
and I ask for nothing more.

Ignatius of Loyola

Seeking God's Will

466 O Heavenly Father, subdue in me whatever is contrary to your holy will. Grant that I may ever study to know your will, that I may know how to please you.
Grant, O God, that I may never run into those temptations, which in my prayers I desire to avoid.
Lord, never permit my trials to be above my strength. Amen.

Thomas Wilson

467 Grant me, O Lord, the single eye, that I may see the one thing needful, the thing that you want done. Don't let my vision be blurred by looking at too many things, or longing to please anyone but you. Give me simplicity of heart, quiet confidence in you, and eagerness to know and do your will.

George Appleton

468 We let the world overcome us; we live too much in continual fear of the chances and changes of mortal life. We let things go too much their own way. We try too much to get what we can by our own selfish wits, without considering our neighbours. We follow too much the ways and fashions of the day, doing and saying and thinking anything that comes uppermost, just because there is so much around us. Free us from our selfish interests, and guide us, good Lord, to see your way, and to do your will.

Charles Kingsley

469 O Lord, you know what is best for me. Let this or that be done, as you please. Give what you will, how much you will and when you will.

Thomas à Kempis

470 Most dear and tender Father, our defender and nourisher, fill us with your grace that we may cast aside our blindness and attraction to material things; and may instead put all our efforts into discovering your will and obeying your law. Let us work, like the birds and the flowers, for what gives you glory, leaving all care in your hands. Amen

Henry VIII's Primer

471 O Lord, let me not henceforth desire health or life, except to spend them for you, with you and in you. You alone know what is good for me; do therefore what seems best to you. Give to me or take from me; conform my will to yours; and grant that with humble and perfect submission and in holy confidence I may receive the orders of your eternal providence, and may equally adore all that comes to me from you.

Blaise Pascal

472   Grant, gracious Father, that I may never dispute the reason-
       ableness of your will, but ever close with it, as the best that
       can happen. Prepare me always for what your providence shall
       bring forth. Let me never murmur, be dejected, or impatient,
       under any of the troubles of this life, but ever find rest and
       comfort in this, the will of my Father, and of my God; grant
       this for Jesus Christ's sake. Amen.

                                                      Thomas Wilson

473   O my God, bestow upon us such confidence, such peace, such
       happiness in you, that your will may always be dearer to us
       than our own will, and your pleasure than our own pleasure.
       All that you give is your free gift to us, all that you take away
       your grace to us. May you be thanked for all, praised for all,
       loved for all; through Jesus Christ our Lord. Amen.

                                                   Christina Rossetti

474   Grant me, O Lord, to know what I ought to know, to love what
       I ought to love, to praise what delights you most, to value what
       is precious in your sight, to hate what is offensive to you.
          Do not suffer me to judge according to the sight of my eyes,
       but to discern with a true judgement between things visible and
       spiritual, and above all things always to inquire what is the good
       pleasure of your will.

                                                   Thomas à Kempis

475   O most merciful Lord, grant me your grace. May it work within
       me and help me to persevere to the end. Grant that I may
       always will what is most pleasing to you. Let your will be mine
       and my will yours. Grant that my heart may find complete peace
       in you, its true resting place. Amen.

                                                   Thomas à Kempis

476   You have placed the honour of your will in my hands. Each word
       of your revelation says that you respect and trust me, that you
       give me dignity and responsibility. Teach me to understand that.
       Give me that holy maturity that is capable of receiving the light
       you grant and of assuming the responsibility that you entrust.
       Keep my heart awake that at all times it may be before you, and
       let what I do become one with the command and the obedience
       to which you have called me.

                                                   Romano Guardini

477   Almighty God, in whom we live and move and have our being,
       you have made us for yourself, so that our hearts are restless
       until they rest in you; grant us purity of heart and strength of
       purpose, that no selfish passion may hinder us from knowing
       your will, no weakness from doing it; but that in your light
       we may see light clearly, and in your service find our perfect
       freedom; through Jesus Christ our Lord.

                                                  Augustine of Hippo

478   Dear Lord, quieten my spirit and fix my thoughts on your will,
       that I may see what you would have done, and contemplate its
       doing without self-consciousness or inner excitement, without
       haste and without delay, without fear of other people's judge-
       ments or anxiety about success, knowing only that it is your
       will and therefore must be done quietly, faithfully and lovingly,
       for in your will alone is our peace.

                                                   George Appleton

479   We beseech you, Lord, to enlighten our minds and to strengthen
       our wills, that we may know what we ought to do, and be enabled
       to do it, through the grace of your most Holy Spirit, and for the
       merits of your Son, Jesus Christ our Lord.

                                                    William Bright

480   O Lord
       you have honoured us with your own image
       and given us free will,
       so deliver us from all afflictions that oppress us;
       keep us in faith and righteousness
       all the days of our life
       and let us do all things
       in accordance with your will.

       For yours is the greatness,
       the majesty, the power and the glory,
       Father, Son and Holy Spirit,
       now and for ever,
       to the ages of ages. Amen.

                                                   Orthodox Liturgy

481   Lord Jesus Christ, give me obedience like yours, so that even
      when I am faced with a path I fear and dislike to tread, I may
      say, as you said in the garden of Gethsemane: 'Take this cup of
      suffering from me. Yet not what I want, but what you want.'

      Give me also, I pray, faithfulness, loyalty and obedience, not
      merely in the supreme, dramatic moments of my life when I
      am keyed up to accept whatever in your mercy may be in
      store for me, but in the little things of everyday life when I
      find it so much easier to please myself, seek my own comfort,
      find the easy way. Help me to discover what it means to take
      upon myself with joy the yoke of obedience.

                                                    Allen Birtwhistle

Seeking Unity with God

482   Give me, O Lord, a tender conscience; a conversation discreet
      and affable, modest and patient, liberal and obliging; a body
      chaste and healthful, competency of living according to my
      condition, contentedness in all estates, a resigned will and
      mortified affections: that I may be as you would have me, and
      my portion may be in the lot of the righteous, in the brightness
      of your countenance, and the glories of eternity.

                                                     Jeremy Taylor

483   O Lord seek us, O Lord find us
      In Thy patient care,
      Be Thy love before, behind us,
      Round us everywhere.
      Lest the god of this world blind us,
      Lest he bait a snare,
      Lest he forge a chain to bind us,
      Lest he speak us fair,
      Turn not from us, call to mind us,
      Find, embrace us, hear.
      Be Thy love before, behind us,

Round us everywhere.

Christina Rossetti

484 Holy the God who from my youth
has shown me life and light.
Stoop to me, make me strong,
that I may transmit that grace, as love bids,
to my brothers, your sons.
My spirit is the Holy Spirit's.
Therefore I believe and confess my faith,
which is the source of light and life to me.
Blessed Father,
man, your creature,
would have you make him holy like yourself,
for you have given him every means to become so.
Glory is yours, now and always,
age after age. Amen.

From a second-century papyrus

485 Almighty Father, teach me to do everything with the utmost
sincerity. Save me from posing even to myself. Make my life
unaffected, simple and sincere. Cleanse me from selfishness;
let my gaze be outward rather than inward. Teach me to think
more of others than of myself. Forbid that my own interests
should be paramount. Pardon, I implore you, all that is and has
been wrong in my life and character. Had I always sought your
will I should now have been strong in the Lord, instead of being
the weak, slothful, vacillating creature that I am. But it is never
too late. Help me to remedy the evil and henceforth to build
with honesty and prayer.

Walter James

486 Guide me, teach me, strengthen me, till I become such a person
as thou wouldst have me be; pure and gentle, truthful and
high-minded, brave and able, courteous and generous, dutiful
and useful.

Charles Kingsley

487 O God, in whose strong hands are the threads of every man's life, into your hands we would commit our lives with all their details and desires.

May we be able, in your strength, so to react to all those experiences which befall us, that we may wring from them victory in our souls and spiritual gain for the world.

May we love you enough to make all things work together for good.

Leslie D. Weatherhead

488 Set me free, Lord, from faith and hope in lesser things.
Set me free from commitment to my own blueprints for my own future.
Set me free for faith and hope in you.
Set me free for commitment to your plans for my future.
Set me free to live and work and serve, building your future.
Set me free, Lord, to be a man.

Rex Chapman

489 O God, we are one with you.
You have made us one with you.
You have taught us that if we are open to one another,
     you dwell in us.
Help us to preserve this openness and to fight for it with all our hearts.
Help us to realise that there can be no understanding
     where there is mutual rejection.
O God, in accepting one another wholeheartedly, fully, completely,
we accept you, and we thank you, and we adore you;
and we love you with our whole being,
     because our being is in your being,
     our spirit is rooted in your spirit.
Fill us then with love,
and let us be bound together with love as we go our
     diverse ways,
united in this one spirit which makes you present to
     the world,
and which makes you witness to the ultimate reality
     that is love.
Love has overcome.

Love is victorious.
Amen.

Thomas Merton

The Work of Prayer

490　My God and Father,
help me to pray
as my first work,
my unremitting work,
my highest, finest, and dearest work;
as the work I do for you, and by you,
and with you,
for your other children and for the whole world.
Infuse and influence it with your blessed Spirit,
that it be not unwilling, nor unworthy, nor in vain;
that it be not occupied with my own concerns,
nor dwell in the interests dear to myself;
but seek your purposes, your glory only;
that it be holy and more holy to the Holiest,
and ever and all through your Son,
my Saviour Jesus Christ.

Eric Milner-White

491　Lord, we know not what we ought to ask of you; you only know
what we need; you love us better than we know how to love
ourselves.

O Father! give to us, your children, that which we ourselves
know not how to ask. We would have no other desire than to
accomplish your will.

Teach us to pray. Pray in us yourself, for Christ's sake.

François Fénelon

492　Still am I haunting
Thy door with my prayers;
Still they are panting
Up thy steep stairs!
Wouldst thou not rather
Come down to my heart,

And there, O my Father,
Be what thou art?

George Macdonald

493   My prayers, my God, flow from what I am not,
I think thy answers make me what I am.
Like weary waves thought flows upon thought,
But the still depth beneath is all thine own,
And there thou mov'st in paths to us unknown.
Out of strange strife thy peace is strangely wrought.
If the lion in us pray – thou answerest the lamb.

George Macdonald

494   Good God, say amen to my prayers, if it be your gracious
will; but if in anything I have asked or done amiss, pardon
my infirmities, and answer my necessities, for Jesus and His
mercies' sake. Amen.

Thomas Wilson

495   O Lord our God! You know who we are; men with good
consciences and with bad, persons who are content and those
who are discontent, the certain and the uncertain, Christians
by conviction and Christians by convention, those who believe,
those who half-believe, those who disbelieve.

And you know where we have come from: from the circle of
relatives, acquaintances and friends or from the greatest loneliness, from a life of quiet prosperity or from manifold confusion
and distress, from family relationships that are well ordered or
from those disordered or under stress, from the inner circle of
the Christian community or from its outer edge.

But now we all stand before you, in all our differences, yet
alike in that we are all in the wrong with you and with one
another, that we must all one day die, that we would all be lost
without your grace, but also in that your grace is promised and
made available to us all in your dear Son Jesus Christ. We are
here together in order to praise you through letting you speak
to us. We beseech you to grant that this may take place in this
hour, in the name of your Son our Lord.

Karl Barth

496 O Lord, take away all coldness, all wanderings of the thoughts, and fix our souls upon you and your love, O merciful Lord and Saviour, in this our hour of prayer.

Edward W. Benson

497 Lift up our souls, O Lord, to the pure, serene light of your presence; that there we may breathe freely, there repose in your love, there may be at rest from ourselves, and from thence return, arrayed in your peace, to do and bear what shall please you; for your holy name's sake.

E. B. Pusey

498 Holy Jesus, give me the gift and spirit of prayer; supply my ignorances, passionate desires and imperfect choices with your grace, that my needs may be fulfilled.

Jeremy Taylor

499 Look graciously upon us, O Holy Spirit, and give us, for our hallowing, thoughts which pass into prayer, prayers which pass into love, and love which passes into life with you for ever.

New Every Morning

500 Lord, you know what I want, if it be your will that I have it, and if it be not your will, good Lord, do not be displeased, for I want nothing which you do not want.

Julian of Norwich

501 He prayeth well who loveth well
Both man and bird and beast;
He prayeth best who loveth best
All things both great and small,
For the dear God who loveth us
He made and loveth all.

William Blake

502 Be present with us as we pray, O Lord, that our prayers may reach you the quicker; and may our Saviour, who is seated in your presence, continually accompany us through the dangers of this life; through the same Jesus Christ, our Lord.

Leonine Sacramentary

503 Almighty God, who has given us the desire to join with one
another in our common prayer. We remember your promise
that when two or three are gathered together in your name you
will grant our requests; hear our prayers and fulfil our desires,
granting us, above all else, a knowledge of your truth in this
world and everlasting life with you in the next.

John Chrysostom

504 Teach us, O Spirit of God, that silent language which says all
things. Teach our souls to remain silent in your presence: that
we may adore you in the depths of our being and await all things
from you, whilst asking of you nothing but the accomplishment
of your will. Teach us to remain quiet under your action and
produce in our soul that deep and simple prayer which says
nothing and expresses everything, which specifies nothing and
expresses everything.

John Nicholas Grou

505 Why, O Lord, is it so hard for me to keep my heart directed
toward you? Why do the many little things I want to do, and
the many people I know, keep crowding into my mind, even
during the hours that I am totally free to be with you and you
alone? Why does my mind wander off in so many directions, and
why does my heart desire the things that lead me astray? Are
you not enough for me? Do I keep doubting your love and care,
your mercy and grace? Do I keep wondering, in the centre of
my being, whether you will give me all I need if I just keep my
eyes on you?

Please accept my distractions, my fatigue, my irritations,
and my faithless wanderings. You know me more deeply and
fully than I know myself. You love me with a greater love than
I can love myself. You even offer me more than I can desire.
Look at me, see me in all my misery and inner confusion, and
let me sense your presence in the midst of my turmoil. All
I can do is show myself to you. Yet, I am afraid to do so.
I am afraid that you will reject me. But I know – with the
knowledge of faith – that you desire to give me your love.
The only thing you ask of me is not to hide from you, not
to run away in despair, not to act as if you were a relentless
despot.

Take my tired body, my confused mind, and my restless soul
into your arms and give me rest, simple quiet rest. Do I ask too
much too soon? I should not worry about that. You will let me
know. Come, Lord Jesus, come. Amen.

Henri Nouwen

506 O Lord our God, grant us grace to desire you with a whole
heart, so that desiring you we may seek and find you; and so
finding you, may love you; and loving you, may hate those sins
which separate us from you, for the sake of Jesus Christ.

Anselm of Canterbury

507 O Lord, hear our prayers,
not according to the poverty of our asking
but according to the richness of your grace,
so that our lives may conform to those desires
which accord with your will;
through Jesus Christ our Lord.

Reinhold Niebuhr

That God May Use Us

508 Use me, my Saviour, for whatever purpose and in whatever way
your may require. Here is my poor heart, an empty vessel; fill it
with your grace. Here is my sinful, troubled soul; quicken it and
refresh it with your love. Take my heart for your own abode;
my mouth to spread abroad the glory of your name; my love and
all my powers for the advancement of your believing people,
and never suffer the steadfastness and confidence of my faith
to abate.

Dwight L. Moody

509 O Lord, you order and arrange all things for us in your infinite
wisdom and love. You know my weakness and every beat and
ache of my heart is known to you. Blindly I give myself to your
tender loving heart. Only give me grace to think, speak, act,
feel according to your loving purposes. Amen.

E. B. Pusey

510   Lord Jesus,
        I give you my hands to do your work.
        I give you my feet to go your way.
        I give you my eyes to see as you do.
        I give you my tongue to speak your words.
        I give you my mind that you may think in me.
        I give you my spirit that you may pray in me.

        Above all,
        I give you my heart that you may love in me,
        your Father, and all mankind.
        I give you my whole self that you may grow in me,
        so that it is you, Lord Jesus,
        who live and work and pray in me.
        I hand over to your care, Lord,
        my soul and body,
        my mind and thoughts,
        my prayers and my hopes,
        my health and my work,
        my life and my death,
        my parents and my family,
        my friends and my neighbours,
        my country and all men.
        Today
        and always.

Lancelot Andrewes

511   Sever me from myself that I may be grateful unto thee;
        May I perish to myself that I may be safe in thee;
        May I die to myself that I may live in thee;
        May I wither to myself that I may blossom in thee;
        May I be emptied of myself that I may abound in thee;
        May I be nothing to myself that I may be all to thee.

Erasmus

In Sickness

512   Grant, Lord, that as you sent this sickness to me, you will also

send your Holy Spirit into my heart so that my present illness may be sanctified and used as a school in which I may learn to know the greatness of my misery and the riches of your mercy. May I be so humbled at my misery that I despair not of your mercy and thus renounce all confidence in myself and every other creature so that I may put the whole of my salvation in your all-sufficient merits.

Lewis Bayley

513   Lord, let this sickness, like that of Lazarus, be unto the Father's glory and for the good of those who stand by. I must see to it that whatever I have to suffer is not wasted but is offered to the Father, and also that I do not give cause for disedification to those who have to wait on me. Inspire me during my illness at least to think of you occasionally: I do not want to make this time, so far as prayer is concerned, a blank. If my regular practices have to be abandoned, show me what new ones I may substitute. Give me, I pray you, a more vivid awareness of your presence, so as to make up for the kind of willed recollection which I try to maintain when I am well.

Hubert van Zeller

514   My strength fails; I feel only weakness, irritation and depression. I am tempted to complain and to despair. What has become of the courage I was so proud of, and that gave me so much self-confidence? In addition to my pain, I have to bear the shame of my fretful feebleness. Lord, destroy my pride; leave it no resource. How happy I shall be if you can teach me by these terrible trials, that I am nothing, that I can do nothing, and that you are all!

François Fénelon

515   I cannot tell why this day I am ill:
But I am unwell because it is thy will –
Which is to make me pure and right like thee.
Not yet I need escape – 'tis bearable
Because thou knowest. And when harder things
Shall rise and gather, and overshadow me,
I shall have comfort in thy strengthenings.

George Macdonald

516   Lord, bless all means that are used for my recovery, and
restore me to my health in your good time; but if otherwise
you have appointed for me, your blessed will be done. O draw
me away from an affection for things below, and fill me with
an ardent desire after heaven. Lord, fit me for yourself, and
then call me to those joys unspeakable and full of glory, when
it pleases you, and that for the sake of your only Son, Jesus,
my Saviour. Amen.

Thomas Ken

517   Lord Jesus,
You know what pain is like.
You know
the torture of the scourge upon your back,
the sting of the thorns upon your brow,
the agony of the nails in your hands.
You know what I'm going through just now.
Help me
to bear my pain
gallantly, cheerfully and patiently,
And help me to remember
that I will never be tried
above what I am able to bear,
and that you are with me,
even in this valley of the deep dark shadow.
In ev'ry pang that rends the heart,
The Man of Sorrows had a part;
He sympathises with our grief,
And to the suff'rer sends relief.

William Barclay

518   The worst of pain, O Lord, is that it makes it difficult to pray.
Yet, O Lord, I desire to pray, to have communion with you, to
draw strength and healing from you, to link to you those I love
and those who need your love, to thank you for those who look
after me, and those who wish me well.

George Appleton

519   Lord, a whole long day of pain now, at last is o'er!
Ah, how much we can sustain, I have felt once more!

Felt how frail are all our powers, and how weak our trust;
If Thou help not, these dark hours crush us to the dust.
Could I face the coming night if Thou wert not near?
Nay, without Thy love and might I must sink with fear:
Round me falls the evening gloom, sights and sounds all
    cease,
But within this narrow room, Night will bring no peace!
O Lord, my God, do Thou Thy holy Will!
I will lie still!
I will not stir lest I forsake Thine arm,
And break the charm,
Which lulls me, clinging to my Father's breast
In perfect rest!

John Keble

520   Lord, I thank you that in your love you have taken from me all
       earthly riches, and that you now clothe and feed me through
       the kindness of others. Lord, I thank you, that since you have
       taken from me the sight of my eyes, you serve me now with
       the eyes of others.

       Lord I thank you that since you have taken away the power
       of my hands and my heart, you serve me by the hands and
       hearts of others. Lord, I pray for them. Reward them for it in
       your heavenly love, that they may faithfully serve and please
       you till they reach a happy end.

Mechthild of Magdeburg

521   Lord, suddenly my body feels different, as if it doesn't belong
       to me any more. I'm used to being in control, but now the
       illness has taken over. Help me to accept this time of illness
       and to learn something from it. Help me to learn from my
       dependence upon others. Help me to accept what they do
       for me with gratitude but not to make my weakness an
       excuse for demanding so much that I drain their resources.
       Help me to accept the fact that I am not as brave as I
       thought I was. Above all, surround me with your peace and
       assurance that I may grow closer to you than I have ever been
       before.

Michael Walker

522   Lord, you gave me health and I forgot you. You take it away and I come back to you. What infinite compassion that God, in order to give himself to me, takes away his gifts which I allowed to come between me and him. Lord, take away everything that is not you. All is yours. You are the Lord. Dispose everything, comforts, success, health. Take all the things that possess me instead of you that I may be wholly yours.

François Fénelon

523   Father, the world is full of pain; each of us has a share; for some it is a slight burden, for others it is crushing. But every Christian can turn it into a blessing if he will seek the companionship of Christ in his sufferings; then the pain becomes a new point of fellowship with Christ; and even our suffering becomes part of the price of the world's redemption as we fill up what is left over of the suffering of Christ.

    Pain does not then cease to be pain; but it ceases to be barren pain; and with fellowship with Christ upon the cross we find new strength for bearing it and even making it the means by which our hearts are more fully cleansed of selfishness and grow towards perfect love. Accomplish this in us through Christ our Lord.

William Temple

Preparing for Death

524   Jesus, Mary and Joseph I give you my heart, my soul and my life.
    Jesus, Mary and Joseph assist me in my last agony.
    Jesus, Mary and Joseph may I breathe forth my soul in peace with you. Amen.

Traditional prayer

525   Grant, Lord, that we may live in your fear, die in your favour, rest in your peace, rise in your power and reign in your glory; for your own beloved Son's sake, Jesus Christ our Lord.

William Laud

526   Lord, I am coming as fast as I can. I know I must pass through the shadow of death, before I can come to you. But it is but a mere shadow, a little darkness upon nature: but you, by your merits and passion, have broken through the jaws of death. So, Lord, receive my soul, and have mercy upon me; and bless this kingdom with peace and plenty, and with brotherly love and charity, for Jesus Christ His sake, if it be your will.

William Laud
(before execution)

527   O Lord, support us all the day long, until the shadows lengthen and the evening comes, and the busy world is hushed, and the fever of life is over, and our work is done. Then, Lord, in your mercy grant us a safe lodging, and a holy rest, and peace at the last; through Jesus Christ our Lord.

Attributed to John Henry Newman,
although probably earlier in origin

528   Lord Jesus, today we accept from your merciful hands what is to come. The times of trial in this world, the suffering of our death, the sorrow and loneliness of our last hours upon earth, the purifying, unknown pains of our purgatory. Into your hands, O Lord, into your hands, we commit our living and dying, knowing that you are the dawn of eternal day, the burning light of the morning star.

Caryll Houselander

529   My Lord, give me to know you, to believe in you, to love you, to serve you, to live to and for you. Give me to die just at that time and in that way which is most for your glory.

John Henry Newman

530   Heavenly and eternal Father, source of all being, from whom I spring, unto whom I shall return, thine I shall ever be. Thou wilt call me unto thyself when my hour comes. Blessed shall I then be if I can say: 'I have fought a good fight.' I fear not death, O Father of life; for death is not eternal sleep; it is the transition to a new life, a moment of glorious transformation, an ascension towards thee. How could that be an evil that cometh from thy hand, when thou art the all-good! Lord of life and death, I am in thy hand; do unto me as thou deemest fit; for what thou dost is well done. When thou didst call me from nothing into life, thou didst will my happiness; when thou callest me away from life, will my happiness be less thy care? No, no, thou art love, and whosoever dwells in love, dwells in thee, O Lord, and thou in him. Amen.

Heinrich Tschokke

531 Before the beginning Thou hast foreknown the end,
Before the birthday the death-bed was seen of Thee:
Cleanse what I cannot cleanse, mend what I cannot mend,
O Lord All-Merciful, be merciful to me.

While the end is drawing near I know not mine end;
Birth I recall not, my death I cannot foresee:
O God, wise to defend, wise to befriend,
O Lord All-Merciful, be merciful to me.

Christina Rossetti

532 Bring us, O Lord God, at our last awakening into the house and gate of heaven, to enter into that gate and dwell in that house, where there shall be no darkness nor dazzling, but one equal light; no noise nor silence, but one equal music; no fears nor hopes, but one equal possession; no ends nor beginnings, but one equal eternity; in the habitations of your glory and dominion world without end.

John Donne

533 Lord God,
you have made us mortal and we must die.
Do not, we beseech you,
take our lives away for ever,
you who are a God of the living.
We ask you this for Jesus' sake,
today and every day,
for ever and ever.

Huub Oosterhuis

534 Hold thou my hands!
    In grief and joy, in hope and fear,
Lord, let me *feel* that thou art near,
    Hold thou my hands.

If e'er by doubts
Of thy good fatherhood depressed,
I cannot find in thee my rest,
  Hold thou my hands.

Hold thou my hands,
These passionate hands too quick to smite,
These hands so eager for delight,
  Hold thou my hands.

And when at length,
With darkened eyes and fingers cold,
I seek some last loved hand to hold,
  Hold thou my hands.

William Canton

535 Lord, who said that at midnight, at an hour we least expect,
the Bridegroom shall come; grant that the cry, 'the Bridegroom
cometh', may sound continually in all ears so that we may never
be unprepared to go out and meet our Lord and Saviour,
Jesus Christ.

Lancelot Andrewes

536 Father, there will come a day when I must die. I don't know
how I shall feel when that day comes, as life drains from my
body and I feel the only world I know drifting away from me.
I can only begin to imagine what it feels like to die.
Father, when that day comes I ask that I may know you near
me. As my strength leaves me may your love penetrate me. As
this world passes from my sight may I see ever more clearly the
world that awaits me at my death.
Father, may my death be resurrection in Christ.

Michael Walker

In Times of Trouble

537 Dear God, it is so hard for us not to be anxious,
we worry about work and money,
about food and health,

about weather and crops,
about war and politics,
about loving and being loved.
Show us how perfect love casts out fear.

Monica Furlong

538   Lord give us grace
       to hold to you
       when all is weariness and fear
       and sin abounds within, without,
       when that which I would do I cannot do
       and that I do I would not do,
       when love itself is tested by the doubt
       that love is false, or dead within the soul,
       when every act brings new confusion, new distress,
       new opportunities, new misunderstandings,
       and every thought new accusation.

       Lord give us grace
       that we may know that in the darkness pressing round
       it is the mist of sin that hides your face
       that you are there
       and you know we love you still . . .

Gilbert Shaw

539   Jesus, Deliverer!
       Come to me:
       Soothe my voyaging
       Over Life's sea.
       When the storm of Death
       Roars, sweeping by,
       Whisper, O Truth of Truth –
       'Peace! It is I.'

Anatolius

540   O God, by your mercy strengthen us who lie exposed to the
       rough storms of troubles and temptations. Help us against
       our own negligence and cowardice, and defend us from the
       treachery of our unfaithful hearts. Help us, we implore you,
       and bring us to your safe haven of peace and happiness.

Augustine of Hippo

541   O God, Creator of mankind, I do not aspire to comprehend You or Your creation, nor to understand pain or suffering. I aspire only to relieve the pain and suffering of others, and I trust in doing so, I may understand more clearly Your nature, that You are the Father of all mankind, and that the hairs of my head are numbered.

Francis of Assisi

542   Father, you do not protect us against catastrophes but in them you come to our aid. It is in the very midst of the tempest and misfortune that a wonderful zone of peace, serenity and joy bursts in us if we dwell in your grace. You do not help us before we have helped ourselves, but when we are at the end of our resources you manifest yourself, and we begin to know that you have been there all the time.

Louis Evely

543   I am silent, Lord, in my affliction. I am silent. In the stillness of a contrite and humble heart, I listen to you. Lord, see my wounds; you have made them. You have smitten me. I am silent; I suffer, I worship silently. Yet you hear my sighs, and the lamentations of my heart are not hidden from you. Let me not listen to myself. I long to hear your voice and to follow you.

François Fénelon

544   Lord, ease my great affliction, or increase my patience; but, Lord, I do not complain, I am dumb, Lord, before You, because You permit it.

George Herbert

545   To all who are tossed by the sea; you are the calm of the harbour; you are the hope of the hopeful.
You are the health of the sick, the relief of the needy; the guide of the blind.
To those exposed to punishment on every count you are merciful, to the weary a wall, in darkness light.
You created the land, you rule the sea, you set every element in its place; a word from you and the heavens, the stars and all else was made, and made perfect.
You kept Noah safe and gave wealth to Abraham,
let Isaac go free and provided a victim in his place,

wrestled with Jacob, to his sweet confusion,
took Lot away from the accursed land of Sodom.
Moses you showed yourself to; to Jesus, son of Nun, you gave
prudence.
In your mercy you went with Joseph on his way and brought
your people out of the land of Egypt, leading them to the land
they had been promised.
You protected the three children in the furnace.
You closed the lions' mouths, gave life to Daniel.
You did not allow Jonah to perish in the depths of the sea.
You gave Judith the weapons she needed; Susanna you saved
from the unjust judges.
Esther had her triumph from you; you procured the downfall
of Aman.
You brought us from darkness to eternal light, Father of our
Lord and Saviour, Jesus Christ, light unquenchable, you who
gave me the sign of the cross, the sign of Christ.
I beg you not to decide, Lord, that I am unworthy of these
sufferings that my brothers and sisters have been allowed to
undergo. Let me share the crown with them; let me be with
them in glory.

Severus of Thrace

546 Lord, my God! the amazing horrors of darkness were gathered
round me, and covered me all over, and I saw no way to go forth;
I felt the depth and extent of the misery of my fellow-creatures
separated from the Divine harmony, and it was heavier than I
could bear, and I was crushed down under it; I lifted up my
hand, I stretched out my arm, but there was none to help me;
I looked round about, and was amazed.

In the depths of misery, O Lord, I remembered that you
are omnipotent; that I had called you Father; and I felt that
I loved you, and I was made quiet in my will, and I waited
for deliverance from you. You had pity upon me, when no
man could help me; I saw that meekness under suffering was
showed to us in the most affecting example of your Son, and
you taught me to follow him, and I said: 'Thy will, O Father,
be done!'

John Woolman

547 O God, the refuge of the poor, the strength of those who toil, and the Comforter of all who sorrow, we commend to your mercy the unfortunate and needy in whatever land they may be. You alone know the number and extent of their sufferings and trials. Look down, Father of mercies, at those unhappy families suffering from war and slaughter, from hunger and disease, and other severe trials. Spare them, O Lord, for it is truly a time for mercy.

Peter Canisius

548 O crucified Jesus, in giving me your cross give me too your spirit of love and self-abandonment; grant that I may think less of my suffering than of the happiness of suffering with you. What do I suffer that you have not suffered? Or rather what do I suffer at all, if I dare to compare myself with you? O Lord, grant that I may love you and then I shall no longer fear the cross.

François Fénelon

549 O my Lord Jesus, I believe, and by your grace will ever believe and hold, and I know that it is true, and will be true to the end of the world, that nothing great is done without suffering, without humiliation, and that all things are possible by means of it.

O my dear Lord, though I am so very weak that I am not fit to ask you for suffering as a gift, and have not strength to do so, at least I will beg of you grace to meet suffering well, when you in your love and wisdom bring it upon me. Let me bear pain, reproach, disappointment, slander, anxiety, suspense, as you would have me, O my Jesu, and, as you by your own suffering have taught me, when it comes.

I wish to bear insult meekly, and to return good for evil. I wish to humble myself in all things, and to be silent when I am ill-used, and to be patient when sorrow or pain is prolonged, and all for the love of you and your cross.

John Henry Newman

550 O God, animate us to cheerfulness. May we have a joyful sense of our blessings, learn to look on the bright circumstances of our lot, and maintain a perpetual contentedness. Preserve us from despondency and from yielding to dejection. Teach us that nothing can hurt us if, with true loyalty of affection, we keep your commandments and take refuge in you.

William E. Channing

551   Grant us peace and establish your truth in us. Remember every faithful soul in trial; and comfort, if it be possible, everyone in sorrow and distress.

O Helper of the helpless, bring the wanderer home, and give health to the sick, and deliverance to the captive.

Sustain the aged, comfort the weak-hearted, set free those whose souls are bound in misery, remember all those who are in affliction, necessity, and emergency everywhere.

Let us dwell with you in peace, as children of light; and in your light, Lord, let us see the light. Amen.

Rowland Williams

552   Teach us to know you, our God, and enable us to do your will as we ought to do. Give us hearts full of love for you, full of trust, full of faithfulness. May no temptations rock us, no tribulations drive us from you. May all that befalls us draw us closer in love and trust and fit us for your heavenly kingdom. Amen.

Benjamin Jenks

553   Save me from being altogether selfish in my prayers, and help me to remember others who are in trouble.

The sick and those who must lie in bed throughout the sunlit hours, especially young folk laid aside too soon in the morning of their day;

Those who are sad and sorry because someone they loved has died;

Those who are disappointed because something they wanted very much has passed them by;

The discontented, those who live with a chip on their shoulder, who are their own worst enemies;

Those who have done something wrong and who are in disgrace, that they may redeem themselves;

Those who are underrated and undervalued, and who have never been appreciated as they ought to have been;

Those who have been passed over for some office they had expected to receive;

All those in pain, in sorrow, in misfortune, in disgrace:

Bless all such. For your love's sake I ask it. Amen.

William Barclay

554   Lord, there are shadows at the edge of my heart,
     the darkness creeps nearer,
     enemies lurk there, too vague to be resisted,
     I can't think straight, logic has deserted me,
     I fear my dreams, and dread waking early:
     help me, Lord.
May I feel your strength beneath me when I fear that I am
sinking.
May your light scatter the darkness where fear hides. Bring
me out to daylight and resurrection.

Michael Walker

555   Lord, if we are bitter, sweeten us;
     if we are rebellious, reason with us;
     if we are resentful, be understanding with us;
     if we are sad, comfort us;
     if we are downcast, lift us up;
     if we are doubtful, reassure us.
Lord, we need You.
Meet our need, we pray You. Amen.

Beryl Bye

556   When the heart is hard and parched up, come upon me with a
shower of mercy.
    When grace is lost from life, come with a burst of song.
    When tumultuous work raises its din on all sides shutting me
out from beyond, come to me, my Lord of silence, with your
peace and rest.
    When my beggarly heart sits crouched, shut up in a corner,
break open the door, my king, and come with the ceremony
of a king.
    When desire blinds the mind with delusion and dust, O
you holy one, you wakeful, come with your light and your
thunder.

Rabindranath Tagore

557   O God, early in the morning I cry to you.
Help me to pray,
     and to concentrate my thoughts on you:
I cannot do this alone.

In me there is darkness,
But with you there is light;
I am lonely,
    but you do not leave me;
I am feeble in heart,
    but with you there is help;
I am restless,
    but with you there is peace.
In me there is bitterness,
    but with you there is patience;
I do not understand your ways,
    but you know the way for me . . .

Restore me to liberty,
And enable me so to live now
    that I may answer before you and before me.
Lord, whatever this day may bring,
Your name be praised.

Dietrich Bonhoeffer

Through Life's Journey

558 My Lord God,
I have no idea where I am going.
I do not see the road ahead of me.
I cannot know for certain where it will end.
Nor do I really know myself,
and the fact that I think that I am following
your will does not mean that I am
actually doing so.
But I believe that the desire to please you
does in fact please you.
And I hope I have that desire in all that I am doing.
I hope that I will never do anything apart from that desire.
And I know that if I do this,
you will lead me by the right road though I
may know nothing about it.
Therefore will I trust you always though I

may seem lost and in the shadow of death.
I will not fear, for you are ever with me,
and you will never leave me to face my perils alone.

Thomas Merton

559   O God
    my God
       keep me from flinching/waning
          slumbering into that timeless rest
            that never is
     keep me from falling into a prison
         of egotistical habits
           where the bars
           are superficial friends
             and drinks
             and stupid laughter
             kisses without love
             business and organisation
              without heart
             and gifts for self-flattery
        these bars that prevent life evolving
         towards that taste of the infinite
           open to your call . . .
      break down those barriers
        that prevent me living, my God.

Jean Vanier

560   Teach us, good Lord, to serve you as you deserve; to give and
not to count the cost; to fight and not to heed the wounds; to toil
and not to seek for rest; to labour and not to ask for any reward,
save that of knowing that we do your will; through Jesus Christ
our Lord.

Ignatius of Loyola

561   Lord Jesus, our Saviour, let us now come to you:
Our hearts are cold; Lord, warm them with your selfless
   love.
Our hearts are sinful; cleanse them with your precious blood.
Our hearts are weak; strengthen them with your joyous
   Spirit.
Our hearts are empty; fill them with your divine presence.

Lord Jesus, our hearts are yours; possess them always and only for yourself.

Augustine of Hippo

562 Fix our steps, O Lord, that we stagger not at the uneven motions of the world, but steadily go on to our glorious home; neither censuring our journey by the weather we meet with, nor turning out of the way for anything that befalls us.

The winds are often rough, and our own weight presses us downwards. Reach forth, O Lord, your hand, your saving hand, and speedily deliver us.

Teach us, O Lord, to use this transitory life as pilgrims returning to their beloved home; that we may take what our journey requires, and not think of settling in a foreign country.

John Wesley

563 Dear God, make me think about what I'm doing
with my mind
with my body
with my habits
with my study
with my friends
with my hopes
with my parents
with my faith
with life.

Carl Burke

564 Lord, be with my spirit and dwell by faith in my heart. Oh make me as you would have me to be. Be with me everywhere and at all times, in all the events and circumstances of my life. Never leave me in my earthly pilgrimage, but bring me safe through all trials and dangers to be with you forever. Amen

Benjamin Jenks

565 We trust that you will bear us up, as tiny children and on to old age. When you are our strength it is strength indeed, but when our strength is our own it is only weakness. The good in us only grows and develops if you nourish it. Be our hope and our strength unto eternity.

Augustine of Hippo

566 O God, our Father, we are exceedingly frail, and indisposed to every virtuous and gallant undertaking: Strengthen our weakness, we implore you, that we may do valiantly in this spiritual war; help us against our own negligence and cowardice, and defend us from the treachery of our unfaithful hearts; for the sake of Jesus Christ our Lord.

Augustine of Hippo

567 Father, I look at Jesus and see what I long to be.
I am tired and I see in him your creative energy;
I care what people think of me, but Jesus went on his way,
   ready to be laughed at;
I miss so often the real longing in the words of my friends,
   but Jesus knows the heart;
I fear the future, but I see Jesus setting his face to go
   up to Jerusalem.
Thank you, Father, for Jesus our brother,
revealing human nature as you created it to be,
and staying with us in all our days.

Bernard Thorogood

PRAYERS OF INTERCESSION

For the Church

568 O God, our Shepherd, give to the Church a new vision and a new charity, new wisdom and fresh understanding, the revival of her brightness and the renewal of her unity; that the eternal message of Thy Son, undefiled by the traditions of men, may be hailed as the good news of the new age; through him who maketh all things new, Jesus Christ our Lord. Amen.

Percy Dearmer

569 We pray you, Lord, to direct and guide your Church with your unfailing care, that it may be vigilant in times of quiet, and daring in times of trouble; through Jesus Christ our Lord.

Franciscan Breviary

570 O most gracious Father, we most humbly beseech you for your holy Catholic church. Fill it with all truth; in all truth with all peace. Where it is corrupt, purge it; where it is in error, direct it; where anything is amiss, reform it; where it is right, strengthen and confirm it; where it is in want, furnish it; where it is divided, heal it and unite it in your love; through Jesus Christ our Lord.

William Laud

571   What a wonderful experience they had, Lord,
in those first days of the Church!
It was a shattering discovery
that you have no favourites,
and that all may come to your presence
in and through the Lord, Jesus Christ.
May we know this joy, as we meet people
of all colours and languages, and discover
that you make us one family.

Lord, open out our heart and mind
   to glimpse what still the Church could be –
   a source of hope and unity,
a prototype for all mankind.
Help us to honour, trust and serve
   each unknown friend that Christ has made.
   Give us a hope that does not fade,
to build a world of peace and love.

Brian Wren

572   Lord God, our heavenly Father,
grant to your Church today
   the faith of her apostles
   the hope of her martyrs
   and the love of her Lord,
even Jesus Christ, in whose name we pray.

Christopher Idle

573   Lord, how can you expect me to belong to your Church when
I see how often it has persecuted Christians who were trying
to follow Jesus in simple faith? Every historical series on TV
shows Christians of different kinds being killed by the Church
of the time. How can these persecutors be followers of Jesus?
It is impossible to see that they were showing forth your love
to the world. .

Lord, it undermines my belief in the institutional churches,
yet I love you and want to follow you. I don't know what to do;
I can't see how it could be your will that I should belong to an
institutional church which has grown from so much hate, fear
and bloodshed. Lord, what am I to do and how can I 'show forth'
your love in the world? But first take this bitterness and hate

of the persecuting church out of my heart, and help me to say
'Forgive them, for they did not know what they were doing!'

Michael Hollings

574 Lord God, we thank you
For calling us into the company of those
Who trust in Christ and seek to do his will.
May your Spirit guide and strengthen us
In mission and service to your world;
For we are strangers no longer
But pilgrims together on the way to your kingdom.

Prayer of the Inter-Church Process

575 Almighty God and merciful Father,
pour out on your church
the Spirit of your Son Jesus
so that dreams may be dreamt
and visions seen.

Open our eyes for his work among people,
so that we may join all those
who with persistence and humility
pursue his will for our world.

Holy Spirit of God,
who brooded over the waters
long before we were born;

Who inspired the people of God
to praise and trust;

Who lit the fire of the prophets
and sustained their faith
among unbelief;

Who fulfilled through our brother Jesus
the hope of the generations,
and revealed the dimensions of God;

Holy Spirit of God,
fill us with confidence

and make us available;

Teach us to pray
and to hear the cries
of God's children;

Help us interpret
the signs of the times;

And prepare us
for the kingdom of God
each day and for ever.
Amen.

Let's Worship

For the Work of Evangelisation

576   O Lord, you have warned us that you will require much of those
to whom much is given. Grant that we, who have received so
much, may strive together, by our prayers, hard work and gifts
to extend to those who know you not, what we so richly enjoy.
So may your will be fulfilled with the salvation of all mankind.
Fifth-century prayer

577   Almighty and everlasting God, whose beloved Son became man
for us men and for our salvation, and gave commandment to his
disciples that they should go and teach all nations, and baptise
them in the name of the Father and of the Son and of the Holy
Ghost: Give us grace to be obedient to his command, and grant
that all men may have new birth in him, and, being delivered out
of the power of darkness, may be received into the kingdom of
your love: through the same Jesus Christ our Lord.
George Appleton

578   Almighty God, help us to be missionaries in the place in which
we live; to our families, living out day by day the faith we

profess; to our neighbours, always ready to listen to their
troubles and to offer our help; to our tradesmen, showing
by our patience and courtesy the grace of Christ; to our
friends, sharing their joys and respecting their confidences
with unfailing love and loyalty.
Father, we know we're not really worthy – but please use
us just the same. Amen.

Beryl Bye

579 You desire, O God, that all people should come to know your
truth and all be saved. Send then, we pray, workers into
your harvest field, and give them power boldly to proclaim
your word. Thus may your gospel be received and honoured
throughout the world, and every people know you, the one
true God, and your Son whom you have sent, our Lord
Jesus Christ.

Michael Buckley

For New Christians

580 Lord God, by our baptism into the death and resurrection of
your Son Jesus Christ we have been born again to be your
children and heirs of eternal life; strengthen us by your Spirit
to live in newness of life all our days; through the same Christ
our Lord.

David Silk

581 Lord God, you give us Jesus,
    you come to the world in the form we understand,
    you travel with us the journey from birth to death.
    Help us to know and trust in Jesus our brother
    that we may enter into his way of obedience
    and, having passed through the tests of life,
    join in your feast of joy at the end. Amen.

Bernard Thorogood

582   Bless, O Lord,
your servants these catechumens
whom you have brought through a holy calling
to the wonderful light of knowing you:
help them to know
the sure foundation of your word
on which their instruction rests.
Pour your Holy Spirit upon them
that they too may become
the little sheep of the one true shepherd,
signed with the seal of the Holy Spirit
and precious members
of the body of your Church;
and in the world to come
make them worthy
of the real and blessed hope
of the kingdom of heaven.

That with us
they too may glorify your Name
which is worthy of all honour and majesty,
Father, Son and Holy Spirit,
now and for ever,
to the ages of ages. Amen.

Orthodox Liturgy

583   God the all-powerful, Father of Christ, who is your only Son,
give me a clean body, a pure heart, a watchful mind and
knowledge free from error. May your Holy Spirit come to
me and bring me truth, yes and the fullness of truth, through
your Christ.
    Through him may glory be yours, in the Holy Spirit,
throughout the ages. Amen.

Third-century prayer

584   Keep us, O Lord, from the vain strife of words, and grant us
a constant profession of our faith. Preserve us in the way of
truth, so that we may ever hold fast that which we professed
when we were baptised into the name of the Father, and of the
Son, and of the Holy Ghost, and may give glory to you, our

Creator, Redeemer and Sanctifier, now and for evermore.

Hilary of Poitiers

585 O Lord our God,
     look mercifully on us
     and on those who are preparing
     for Holy Baptism,
     and have their heads bowed before you now:
     make the light of your Gospel
     shine upon them;
     send an angel of light
     to deliver them from all powers of the enemy,
     that when they are fit to receive your immortal gift
     and are brought into a life
     of obedience to your commandments,
     they may know the joys of heaven.

     For you are their light
     and we glorify you,
     Father, Son and Holy Spirit,
     now and for ever,
     to the ages of ages. Amen.

Orthodox Liturgy

For Christian Unity

586 O Lord Jesus Christ, who on the eve of your Passion prayed
     that all your disciples might be one, as you are in the Father,
     and the Father in you, grant that we may suffer keenly on
     account of the unfaithfulness of our disunity. Grant us the
     loyalty to recognise and the courage to reject all our hidden
     indifference and mistrust, and our mutual hostility.

     Grant that we may find each other in you, so that from our
     hearts and from our lips may ceaselessly arise your prayer for
     the Unity of Christians, such as you willed and by the means
     that you willed. Grant that in you, who are perfect love, we

may find the way that leads to Unity, in obedience to your love
and to your truth.

Abbé Paul Couturier and Père Michalon

587 Lord, I feel very deeply my separation from other Christians
when I attend their Eucharist and cannot receive Communion.
Why must we be so cut off from each other at the moment
when we should be sharing you? This should be the time when
we are closest together, but it is now that I know most deeply
the agony of separation. Lord, if it breaks my heart in this way,
how much more must it break yours? We love each other and
we love you, why must we be separated at this feast of love
and union? Lord, make it possible for us to worship together
in complete union and fellowship, and show us what we must
do to bring this about!

Michael Hollings and Etta Gullick
(See also Week of Prayer for Christian Unity, 93–100)

For the Nation

588 Lord God of our fathers, we thank you for your mercy towards
our nation throughout its long history.

Hear us as we seek your continuing mercy in this our day.

Deliver us from the sins of affluence, from pride, from
materialism, and from indifference to the needs of the
developing world.

Inspire your Church to be the nation's conscience.

Give to our leaders soundness of judgement and courage of
decision; and unite us all in a common zeal to honour you and
serve mankind; through Jesus Christ our Lord.

John R. W. Stott

589 Almighty God, I thank you that there is much in our national
history to recall with justifiable pride. So with joy and dignity
I honour:

those who have given themselves to raise the standard of
   life in other lands;

missionaries who have taught in schools and colleges, doctors
   and nurses who have risked their own health and lives to
   bring healing to the sick and comfort to the dying, evangelists
   who have brought hope and confidence by telling of your
   love for all mankind;

those government officials and traders who have brought
   peace, prosperity and hope in place of superstition, cruelty
   and poverty.

For the great company of those who have shown, by lives of
integrity, compassion and dedication, something of your nature
to people all over the world, I give you thanks.

Allen Birtwhistle

590 God our Father,
   you guide everything in wisdom and love.
   Accept the prayers we offer for our nation;
   by the wisdom of our leaders and integrity
      of our citizens,
   may harmony and justice be secured
   and may there be lasting prosperity and peace.

Roman Liturgy

591 Most merciful God, we ask for our nation
      not material prosperity
      or a higher standard of living,
   but what is most for its true welfare:
      a renewal of Christian faith,
      a recovery of spiritual values,
      a return to the paths of righteousness;
   and this we pray in the name of Christ our Lord.

Frank Colquhoun

For the Queen and the Royal Family

592   Pour your blessing, O God, we pray you,
        upon Elizabeth our Queen, that she may fulfil her
            calling as a Christian ruler.
        Support her in the ceaseless round of duty,
        inspire her in the service of many peoples.
        Give her wise and selfless ministers,
        bless her in home and family
        and grant that, through her, the Commonwealth
        may be knit together in one great brotherhood,
        a strength and joy to all its members
        and an instrument of peace in our troubled world,
        through Jesus Christ, our Lord.

George Appleton

593   King of kings and Lord of lords,
            Remember all rulers
        Whom you have appointed to bear rule
            on the earth.
        And among the first, be mindful of
            our gracious Queen,
        And prosper her in all things;
        And put into her heart good designs
            for your church,
        And for all the people committed
            to her charge.
        Grant her profound and undisturbed peace
            that in the tranquillity of her reign
        we may lead a quiet and peaceful life,
            in all godliness and honesty.

Lancelot Andrewes

594   God save the Queen, all who are dear to her and all who
advise her.
        Cleanse our national life, and raise up leaders for our land
who shall be beyond pettiness and self-seeking, and who shall

make our Commonwealth the instrument of your will among
the nations; through Jesus Christ our Lord.

Leslie D. Weatherhead

For Those in Politics

595   Sovereign Lord of men and nations, we pray for rulers and
statesmen who are called to leadership among their fellow
countrymen; give them vision to see far into the issues of
their time, courage to uphold what they believe to be right, and
integrity in their words and motives; and may their service to
their people promote the welfare and peace of mankind; through
Jesus Christ our Lord.

Basil Naylor

596   Grant, O God, and continue to give us a succession of legislators
and rulers who have been taught the wisdom of the kingdom
of Christ. Endow all members of Parliament with a right
understanding, a pure purpose, and sound speech; enable
them to rise above all self-seeking and party zeal into the
larger sentiments of public good and human brotherhood.
Purge our political life of every evil; subdue in the nation all
unhallowed thirst for conquest or vainglory. Inspire us with
calmness and self-restraint and the endeavour to get your will
done everywhere upon the earth.

John Hunter

597   O righteous Lord, may your Holy Spirit be with our rulers,
with our sovereign and all in authority under her, that they may
govern in your faith and fear, striving to put down all that is evil
and to encourage all that is good. Give your spirit of wisdom to
those who make our laws, grant that they may understand how
great a work you have given them to do; that they may not do it
lightly, but gravely and soberly, to the putting away of all wrong
and oppression and to the advancement of the true welfare of
your people.

Thomas Arnold

598   Almighty God, by whom alone kings reign and princes decree
justice, and from whom alone cometh all counsel, wisdom, and
understanding:

We, Thine unworthy servants, here gathered together in
Thy name, do most humbly beseech Thee to send down the
heavenly wisdom from above, to direct and guide us in all our
consultations:

And grant that, we having Thy fear always before our eyes,
and laying aside all private interests, prejudices, and partial
affections, the result of all our counsels may be the glory of
Thy blessed name, the maintenance of true religion and justice,
and the safety, honour and happiness of the Queen, the public
welfare, peace, and tranquillity of the realm, and the uniting
and knitting together of the hearts of all persons and estates
within the same in true Christian love and charity one towards
another, through Jesus Christ our Lord and Saviour. Amen.

House of Commons Prayer

599   O God, almighty Father, King of kings and Lord of lords, grant
that the hearts and minds of all who go out as leaders before
us, the statesmen, the judges, the men of learning and the men
of wealth, may be so filled with the love of your laws, and of
that which is righteous and life-giving, that they may be worthy
stewards of your good and perfect gifts; through Jesus Christ
our Lord.

Knights of the Garter Prayer

600   Lord, guide and direct those women who have been called
to public office: our women Members of Parliament, council
members, magistrates and school governors. Grant them
wisdom to discern between right and wrong, justice and
injustice, progress and retreat. Grant them courage to stand
alone when necessary. May they never become so involved in
service to the community that they have no time to consider
the problems and concerns of the individual. Help them to listen
patiently as well as to speak forcefully, and keep them fit and
sound in body, mind and spirit.

We ask this in your Name, Amen.

Beryl Bye

For Society

601 O God, grant us a vision of our city, fair as she might be;
a city of justice, where none shall prey on others; a city
of plenty, where vice and poverty shall cease to fester;
a city of brotherhood, where all success shall be founded
on service, and honour shall be given to nobleness alone;
a city of peace, where order shall not rest on force, but
on the love of all for the city, the great mother of the
common life and weal. Hear thou, O Lord, the silent prayer
of all our hearts as we each pledge our time and strength
and thought to speed the day of her coming beauty and
righteousness. Amen.

Walter Rauschenbusch

602 Christ, look upon us in this city,
And keep our sympathy and pity
Fresh, and our faces heavenward;
Lest we grow hard.

Thomas Ashe

603 We who stand in the world offer ourselves and our society
for your blessed healing.
We confess we have failed to love as you did.
We have been socially unjust, and our society is imperfect,
fragmented, and sometimes sick to death.
Teach us your ways in the world and in this life which we
share together.
Don't let us restrict you to a narrow ghetto labelled
'religion', but lead us to worship you in the fullness of life
as the lord of politics, economics and the arts.
Give us light to seek true morality, not in narrow legalisms
but in sacrifice and open responsibility. Show us how to
express our love for you in very specific, human service to
other men.
Lord, change our hearts from hearts of stone to hearts of

flesh, and let us give thanks to you for all of life.

Malcolm Boyd

604   Lord, the wounds of the world
           are too deep for us to heal.
           We have to bring men and women to you
           and ask you to look after them –
           the sick in body and mind,
           the withered in spirit,
           the victims of greed and injustice,
           the prisoners of grief.
           And yet, our Father,
           do not let our prayers excuse us
           from paying the price of compassion.
           Make us generous with the resources
           you have entrusted to us.
           Let your work of rescue be done
           in us and through us all.

Caryl Micklem

For Those in the Media

605   Lord God, you have placed in human hands
           great power for good or evil through television.
               We pray for those whose faces and voices are thus
               known in millions of homes;
           for those who decide policies and plan schedules;
           and those who direct and produce programmes.
               We pray that their skills and gifts
           may be devoted to what is true and good,
           so that those who watch and listen
           may be informed and entertained without being
               debased or corrupted;
           through Jesus Christ our Lord.

Christopher Idle

606 Father, we thank you that you have spoken to us
  through the words of scripture,
and chiefly through him who is the living word of God.
  We pray for all who,
by what they say and write,
influence the lives of others;
for those whose daily task is in the use of words.
  We ask for them reverence for the truth,
sensitiveness to human need,
and a true concern for the welfare of the community;
through Jesus Christ our Lord.

Basil Naylor

607 O God, who chose the written word to speak an eternal gospel
to every age, give to those who handle words as writers,
speakers, journalists and broadcasters a constant loyalty to
truth and a heart concerned with wisdom.

  May they raise, and not lower, our moral standards, and
increase, not diminish, the true welfare of mankind; for the
sake of Jesus Christ our Lord.

Timothy Dudley-Smith

For Scientific Research

608 O God, whose wisdom has set within our hearts
the quest for knowledge and dominion in the natural world,
teach us to use all science, invention and technology
  not to hurt but to heal,
  not to destroy but to build,
  not to divide but to unite your human family in
    prosperity and dignity together.
And let not our knowledge outstrip our wisdom;
through Jesus Christ our Lord.

Timothy Dudley-Smith

609 God, you know all the wonders of this age
and the skills in our human minds and hands;
you have cared for us through all of history;

therefore I pray:
     help us to use technology for the good of people,
     to heal those who have come close to despair,
     to ease the life of those in pain,
     to build good homes for those who live in shacks,
     to bring fertility to the deserts
     and good crops to our farms,
     to let the blind see again.
So may our technical marvels be your hand at work in our
world. Forgive all those who use the power of modern communicatio
to spread a false picture of the world, and forgive us all that
we have lacked discrimination to select what is good and reject
what betrays you, through Jesus Christ. Amen.
Bernard Thorogood

610 Lord God, you have revealed to this generation wonders and
     mysteries of your universe hitherto unknown.
          Forgive us because we have often turned our larger knowl-
     edge to foolish and cruel uses, and filled the world with terror
     and anguish.
          Increase in all of us the power to dwell in peace together,
     and to settle our disputes without resort to violence, that
     we may be able to put away the instruments of war, and
     use your gifts to save life, not to destroy it; through Jesus
     Christ our Lord.
Episcopal Church, USA

611 O Holy Wisdom of our God,
     enlighten all men of science
     who search out
     the secrets of your creation,
     that their humility before nature
     may be matched by reverence towards you.
     Save us from misusing their labours,
     that the forces they set free
     may enrich the life of man
     and that your name may be hallowed
     both in the search for truth

and in the use of power;
through Jesus Christ our Lord.

New Every Morning

For Social Justice

612 Help us, O God, to understand what your will is in the confusion
and unrest of our times.

Give us insight to distinguish between the signs of your Spirit
demanding change and renewal, and the signs of human greed
and lust for power; that we may be your fellow workers in
creating an order of society which acknowledges your sovereign
power and might; through Jesus Christ our Lord.

Basil Naylor

613 Lord, you have called your Church to shine as light
    in the midst of a dark and needy world:
bless and strengthen it in its testimony in every land
    for justice, truth, and freedom.
May it bring help and hope to the poor and the powerless,
    to the outcast and the oppressed;
may it maintain a bold and fearless witness
    in face of tyranny and wrong;
and may it never be ashamed of the gospel of Christ,
    but point to him as the liberator of mankind,
    the source of life and giver of peace.
We ask this in his name.

Frank Colquhoun

614 Lord, we pray for the young people whose sense of injustice
can often be roused more easily than our own. Foster their
love for their fellow-men. Clarify their thinking and use their
enthusiasm and energy aright.

Forgive us when we have failed to give them a right lead,
and grant that where we have lost opportunities they may
find them.

Help them to a right understanding of the world's needs and
protect them from corruption.
All this we ask in Jesus' Name. Amen.

Beryl Bye

615   Jesus, Son of God, friend of all social classes, grant that the rich
may so evaluate their wealth that they may generously follow
the simplicity of your dedicated life, and so help the poor to
lead a life worthy of their human dignity. Grant that all may see
themselves as your brothers and sisters, who became poor for
our sake.

Michael Buckley

For Peace

616   O God of peace, who has taught us that in returning and in rest
we shall be saved, and in quietness and in confidence shall be
our strength: by the might of your spirit lift us, we pray you,
to your presence, where we may be still and know that you are
God; through Jesus Christ our Lord.

John W. Suter

617   To be there before you, Lord, that's all.
To shut the eyes of my body,
To shut the eyes of my soul,
And to be still and silent,
To expose myself to you who are there, exposed to me.
To be there before you, the Eternal Presence.
I am willing to feel nothing, Lord,
   to see nothing
   to hear nothing.
Empty of all ideas,
   of all images,
In the darkness.
Here I am, simply,

To meet you without obstacles,
In the silence of faith,
Before you, Lord.
But Lord, I am not alone
I can no longer be alone.
I am a crowd, Lord,
For men live within me.
I have met them,
They have come in,
They have settled down,
They have worried me,
They have tormented me,
They have devoured me.
And I have allowed it, Lord, that they might be nourished and
    refreshed.
I bring them to you, too, as I come before you.
I expose them to you in exposing myself to you.
Here I am,
Here they are,
Before you, Lord.

Michel Quoist

618 O Lord, calm the waves of this heart; calm its tempest! Calm
thyself, O my soul, so that the divine can act in thee! Calm
thyself, O my soul, so that God is able to repose in thee, so
that his peace may cover thee! Yes, Father in heaven, often
have we found that the world cannot give us peace. O but make
us feel that thou art able to give peace; let us know the truth
of thy promise: that the whole world may not be able to take
away thy peace.

Søren Kierkegaard

619 In peace, let us beseech the Lord
for the peace that is from above
and the salvation of our souls;
for the peace of the whole world
and of the holy churches of God
and of all men.
For our homes, that they may be holy,
and for all our pastors, teachers and governors;

for our city (township, village) and country
and all who dwell therein;
for all that travel by land, by air, by water;
for the sick and all who need your pity and protection.
On all, have mercy, and preserve all, O God, by your grace:
for to you, O Lord, is due glory, honour, and worship;
world without end.

Liturgy of St John Chrysostom

620 Deep and silent and cool as a broad, still, tree-shaded river
Is the peace of thy presence, thou rest of our souls.
From the thousand problems of this our hurrying life
We turn, with silent joy, to plunge in thee,
To steep our souls in thy quiet depths
Where no clamour of earth disturbs our perfect content.
Thou art our home and refuge;
In thee we are safe and at peace:
Ever in the din and hurry of the world
We know that thou art near,
We know that close at hand – closer than our little life –
Floweth that silent river of thy presence and love.
In a moment we may be with thee and in thee,
In a moment be surrounded and soaked in thy peace:
In a moment, as this loud world clangs round us,
We may rest secure in the bliss of thine eternity.

John S. Hoyland

621 Deep peace of the Running Wave to you.
Deep peace of the Flowing Air to you.
Deep peace of the Quiet Earth to you.
Deep peace of the Shining Stars to you.
Deep peace of the Son of Peace to you.

Celtic benediction

622 O Lord, whose way is perfect: Help us, we pray, always to trust
in your goodness; that walking with you in faith, and following
you in all simplicity, we may possess quiet and contented minds,
and cast all our care on you, because you care for us; for the
sake of Jesus Christ our Lord.

Christina Rossetti

623   Hallowed be Thy name,
        not mine,
        thy kingdom come,
        not mine,
        Give us peace with Thee,
        peace with men,
        peace with ourselves,
        And free us from all fear.

Dag Hammarskjöld

624   Lord, make me an instrument of your peace;
        where there is hatred let me sow love,
        where there is injury let me sow pardon,
        where there is doubt let me sow faith,
        where there is despair let me give hope,
        where there is darkness let me give light,
        where there is sadness let me give joy.

        O divine master, grant that I may
        not try to be comforted but to comfort,
        not try to be understood but to understand,
        not try to be loved but to love.

        Because it is in giving that we receive,
        it is in forgiving that we are forgiven,
        and it is in dying that we are born to eternal life.

Unknown source
(Attributed to Francis of Assisi,
but first appeared 1913)

625   Lead me from death
        To life, from falsehood to truth.

        Lead me from despair
        To hope, from fear to trust.

        Lead me from hate
        To love, from war to peace.

        Let peace fill our heart,
        Our world, our universe.

International Prayer for Peace

626 We beseech thee to teach mankind to live together in peace; no man exploiting the weak, no man hating the strong, each race working out its own destiny, unfettered, self-respecting, fearless.

Teach us to be worthy of freedom, free from social wrong, free from individual oppression and contempt, pure of heart and hand, despising none, defrauding none, giving to all men – in all dealings of life – the honour we owe to those who are thy children, whatever their colour, their race or their caste.

John S. Hoyland

627 God, the king of righteousness, lead us, we pray, in ways of justice and peace; inspire us to break down all tyranny and oppression, to gain for every man his due reward, and from every man his due service; that each may live for all, and all may care for each, in the name of Jesus Christ our Lord.

William Temple

628 Give us courage, O Lord, to stand up and be counted,
to stand up for those who cannot stand up for themselves,
to stand up for ourselves when it is needful for us to do so.
Let us fear nothing more than we fear you.
Let us love nothing more than we love you,
for thus we shall fear nothing also.
Let us have no other God before you,
whether nation or party or state or church.
Let us seek no other peace but the peace which is yours,
and make us its instruments,
opening our eyes and our ears and our hearts,
so that we should know always what work of peace we may do
      for you.

Alan Paton

629 Gracious Father,
we pray for peace in our world;
for all national leaders
that they may have wisdom to know
      and courage to do what is right;
for all men and women

that their hearts may be turned to
yourself in the search for
righteousness and truth;
for those who are working to improve
international relationships,
that they may find the true way of
reconciliation;
for those who suffer as a result of war:
the injured and disabled,
the mentally distressed,
the homeless and hungry,
those who mourn for their dead,
and especially for those
who are without hope or friend
to sustain them in their grief.

Baptist Peace Fellowship

For the Unemployed

630 Heavenly Father, give wisdom to the leaders of our nation as
they seek to resolve the problem of unemployment and to
secure productive work for all.

Help the churches to minister to the unemployed in their
areas and to provide them with voluntary work wherever
possible; and enable each of us to be sensitive to their needs,
and to be ready when necessary to make sacrifices for the sake
of others, as servants of Jesus Christ our Lord.

Michael Botting

631 Heavenly Father, who wills that every individual should belong
to the human community, look with compassion on those who
suffer distress through lack of work; take from them the feeling
of rejection. Grant that they be free from want and insecurity
and may they soon find employment, as those in the Gospel
story who were called at the eleventh hour to labour in the
vineyard, through Jesus Christ, our Lord. Amen.

Michael Buckley

632   God our Father,
through and by the work of our hands
your mighty work of creation continues.
Hear the prayers of your people
and give all who seek employment
the opportunity to enhance their human dignity
and draw closer to one another
in mutual interdependence.

Anthony Castle

633   Dear God, when you created the world you made man
in your likeness – you made him a creator too –
always wanting to make things, to work, to build,
to do something worth doing.
So we pray for those who cannot work,
who are unemployed and have no work,
who have too much time and too little to do in it.
Help them to make good use of time
until they can find work to do and joy in doing it.

Rowland Purton

For the Handicapped

634   O loving Father, we pray for all who are handicapped in the race of life; the blind, the defective and the delicate, and all who are permanently injured. We pray for those worn out with sickness and those who are wasted with misery, for the dying and all unhappy children. May they learn the mystery of the road of suffering which Christ has trodden and the saints have followed, and bring thee this gift that angels cannot bring, a heart that trusts thee even in the dark; and this we ask in the name of him who himself took our infirmities upon him, even the same Jesus Christ, our Saviour.

A. S. T. Fisher

635   O Lord Jesus Christ, bound to the pillar and nailed to the cross, we pray for those who have lost their physical freedom and can no longer walk with other men and share their work and joy.

We pray for those who lie in iron lungs, and all held captive by crippling diseases, all injured in accidents or maimed by war. We remember the young, and we remember too those who have spent many years in pain and weariness. Grant, O Lord, that we who have our freedom may never forget them but may have them always in our hearts and prayers. Knowing ourselves incapable of their courage and cheerfulness, we ask with humility and reverence that the bestowals of your grace may come to them with increasing blessing. Lord, illumine their fortitude and patience with your own, uphold them in your love and possess them with your peace.

Elizabeth Goudge

636 Lord Jesus, when you were on earth, they brought the sick to you and you healed them all. Today we ask you to bless all those in sickness, in weakness and in pain:

those who are blind and who cannot see the light of the sun, the beauty of the world, or the faces of their friends;

those who are deaf and cannot hear the voices which speak to them;

those who are helpless and who must lie in bed while others go out and in:

Bless all such.

Those who must face life under some handicap;

those whose weakness means that they must always be careful;

those who are lame and maimed and cannot enter into any of the strenuous activities or pleasures of life;

those who have been crippled by accident, or by illness, or who were born with a weakness of body or mind;

Bless all such.

Grant that we, in our health and our strength, may never find those who are weak and handicapped a nuisance, but grant that we may always do and give all that we can to help them and to make life easier for them.

William Barclay

For the Sick

637   Father, your Son accepted our sufferings
to teach us the virtue of patience in human illness.
Hear the prayers we offer for our sick brothers and sisters.
May all who suffer pain, illness or disease
realise that they are chosen to be saints,
and know that they are joined in Christ
in his sufferings for the salvation of the world.

Lord, teach me the art of patience while I am well, and
give me the use of it when I am sick. In that day either
lighten my burden or strengthen my back. Make me,
who so often in my health have discovered my
weakness, to be strong in my sickness when I solely rely on
your assistance.

Thomas Fuller

638   Father, lover of life, we pray for those suffering from disease for
which, at present, there is no known cure; give them confidence
in your love and never-failing support and a stronger faith in the
resurrection. Grant wisdom and perseverance to all working to
discover the causes of the disease, so that they see in their
labours the ministry of your Son, who himself showed forth his
divine power by healing those who came to him.

George Appleton

639   Lord, the one that I love is sick and in great pain; out of your
compassion heal him and take away his pain. It breaks my heart
to see him suffer; may I not share his pain if it is not your will that
he be healed? Lord, let him know that you are with him; support
and help him that he may come to know you more deeply as
a result of his suffering. Lord, be our strength and support in
this time of darkness and give us that deep peace which comes
from trusting you.

Etta Gullick

640 Lord, we pray
    for all who are weighed down with the
    mystery of suffering. Reveal yourself
    to them as the God of love, who
    yourself bear all our suffering.

George Appleton

641 Lord of great compassion, we pray you for those who are
    nervously ill, and too weak and anxious to lift themselves above
    the fear and sadness that threaten to overwhelm them. Do you
    yourself, O Lord, lift them up and deliver them, as you delivered
    your disciples in the storm at sea, strengthening their faith and
    banishing their fear. Turning to you, O Lord, may they find you,
    and finding you may they find also all you have laid up for them
    within the fortress of your love.

Elizabeth Goudge

642 Father, we pray for the mentally ill, for all who are of a disturbed
    and troubled mind. Be to them light in their darkness, their
    refuge and strength in time of fear. Give special skills and tender
    hearts to all who care for them, and show them how best to
    assist in your work of healing; through Jesus Christ our Lord.

Timothy Dudley-Smith

643 O God the Creator and Father of all men,
    We praise you that your will is life
        and health and strength.
    Help all who are ill or in pain
        to place themselves in your hands
            in loving trust,
    so that your healing life may flow into them
        to make them well and strong,
        able and ready to do your holy will;
    through him who has made known to us
        both your love and your will,
    even Jesus Christ our Lord.

George Appleton

644 Dearest Lord, may I see you today and every day in the person
    of your sick, and, whilst nursing them, minister unto you.
        Though you hide yourself behind the unattractive disguise

of the irritable, the exacting, the unreasonable, may I still recognise you, and say: 'Jesus, my patient, how sweet it is to serve you.'

Lord, give me this seeing faith, then my work will never be monotonous. I will ever find joy in humouring the fancies and gratifying the wishes of all poor sufferers.

O beloved sick, how doubly dear you are to me, when you personify Christ; and what a privilege is mine to be allowed to tend you.

Sweetest Lord, make me appreciative of the dignity of my high vocation, and its many responsibilities. Never permit me to disgrace it by giving way to coldness, unkindness, or impatience.

And O God, while you are Jesus my patient, deign also to be to me a patient Jesus, bearing with my faults, looking only to my intention, which is to love and serve you in the person of each one of your sick.

Lord, increase my faith, bless my efforts and work, now and for evermore. Amen.

Mother Teresa of Calcutta

645 Lord, comfort the sick, the hungry, the lonely and those who are hurt and shut in on themselves, by your presence in their hearts; use us to help them in a practical way. Show us how to set about this and give us strength, tact and compassion. Teach us how to be alongside them, and how to share in their distress in the depth of our being and in our prayer. Make us open to them and give us courage to suffer with them, and that in so doing we share with you in the suffering of the world for we are your body on earth and you work through us.

Etta Gullick

646 O God of love and power, we come to you for those who are ill in body or mind, and for those who are cast down and sad.

Tell them in the midst of all their pain and anxiety that your name is Love; and since you have ordained that your own will needs our co-operation, use these our prayers.

Turn our caring into their courage, our solicitude into their succour, our faith into their will to get well; through Jesus Christ our Lord.

Leslie D. Weatherhead

647 O God our Father, who are the source of all life and health, all
strength and peace: Teach us to know you truly; take from us
all that hinders the work of your healing power, all our sins, all
our anxieties and fears, all resentment and hardness of heart;
and help us to learn to enter into stillness and peace with you,
and to know that you are our healer and redeemer; through
Jesus Christ our Lord.

Guild of Health

648 Dear Father God,
  We pray for those who suffer – especially any who are
  personally known to us.
  For those whose bodies are diseased, broken, or worn out.
  For those who have been born with a particular disability
    which they have had to learn to live with for the whole of
    their lives.
  For those who suffer mental illness, which makes them
    confused, unstable, violent, frightened or childlike in their
    behaviour.
  For those who bring sickness upon themselves through
    their own weakness, and yet find it impossible to change
    their lifestyle.
  We confess that we do not wholly understand the reason
    for much of the world's suffering, but we do believe that
    you care, and our prayers do not go unheard, because
    we pray them in the name of your Son, Jesus Christ, our
    Lord. Amen.

Beryl Bye

For the Dying

649 We pray, gracious Father, for those whose earthly life is
drawing to its close, that you will grant to them the comfort
of your presence.
  Relieve all distress, remove every fear, and give peace now
and at the last, through Jesus Christ our Lord.

Frank Colquhoun

650   O Saviour of the world, lifted up on the cross that all men might be drawn to your love, dying for the salvation of us all, we implore you to make that love and that salvation a growing reality of glory to those who face their death. Grant to them, O Lord, your gift of a perfect repentance, and then may the heaven of your forgiveness banish all fears from them forever.

Elizabeth Goudge

651   Father,
you made us in your image
and your Son accepted death for our salvation.
Help those who are now, at this moment,
at the point of leaving this life.
May they be free of pain and distress
and may their parting be in dignity
accompanied by a knowledge of your love
and the love of their families.

Anthony Castle

652   God of power and mercy,
you have made death itself
the gateway to eternal life.
Look with love on our dying sister (brother),
and make her (him) one with your Son in his
    suffering and death,
that, sealed with the blood of Christ,
she (he) may come before you free from sin.

Roman Liturgy

For Those Who Mourn

653   Grant, O Lord, to all who are bereaved, the spirit of faith and courage, that they may have the strength to meet the days to come with steadfastness and patience; not sorrowing as those without hope, but in thankful remembrance of your great goodness in past years, and in the sure expectation of a joyful reunion in the heavenly places; and this we ask in the name of Jesus Christ our Lord.

Irish Prayer Book

654 O Lord Jesus Christ, God of all consolation, whose heart was moved to tears at the grave of Lazarus; look with compassion on your children in their loss. Strengthen in them the gift of faith, and give to their troubled hearts, and to the hearts of all men, the light of hope, that they may live as one day to be united again, where tears shall be wiped away, in the Kingdom of your love; for you died and were raised to life with the Father and the Holy Spirit, God, now and for ever.

David Silk

655 Father of mercies and God of all comfort, look in your tender love and pity, we beseech you, on your sorrowing servants. Be to them their refuge and strength, a very present help in trouble; make them to know the love of Christ, which passes knowledge; who by death has conquered death, and by rising again has opened the gates of everlasting life, even Jesus Christ our Lord.

Church of South India

656 O God, we pray for your comforting spirit to bide this day upon all who mourn. Some are bereaved because of the death of loved ones. Some are sorry for sins and desire to be delivered from their burden. Some are lonely and need companionship. Some feel that life has tossed them aside and that all the major blessings have been bestowed upon others. Some have been hurt by the selfishness and carelessness of their fellow men. For all of them we pray. Help them to put their trust in and to wait upon the Lord. If they are of good courage you will strengthen their hearts. We would all faint, except we believed we shall yet see the goodness of the Lord in this land of the living. Bless all who call upon you, and even those who know not upon whom to call. In Christ's name we pray.

William H. Kadel

657 We remember, Lord, the slenderness of the thread which separates life from death, and the suddenness with which it can be broken. Help us also to remember that on both sides of that division we are surrounded by your love.

Persuade our hearts that when our dear ones die neither we nor they are parted from you.

In you may we find peace, and in you be united with them
in the body of Christ, who has burst the bonds of death
and is alive for evermore, our Saviour and theirs for ever
and ever.

Dick Williams

658   Lord, my loved ones are near me.
      I know that they live in the shadow.
      My eyes can't see them because they have left for the
            moment their bodies as one leaves behind outmoded clothing.
      Their souls, deprived of their disguise, no longer
            communicate with me.

      But in you, Lord, I hear them calling me.
      I see them beckoning to me.
      I hear them giving me advice.
      For they are now more vividly present.
      Before, our bodies touched but not our souls.
      Now I meet them when I meet you.
      I receive them when I receive you.
      I love them when I love you.
      O, my loved ones, eternally alive, who live in me,
      Help me to learn thoroughly in this short life how to live
            eternally.

      Lord I love you, and I want to love you more.
      It's you who make love eternal, and I want to love eternally.

Michel Quoist

659   Lord Jesus Christ, who shares in all our sorrows as well as our
      joys, we pray today for those who mourn the loss of someone
      they love.
            Lord, You have promised that those who believe in You shall
      live again. Remind them of Your promise.
            Lord, You rose again to prove what You said was true. Help
      them to hold on to this fact.
            Lord, You are the comforter of the sad, the protector of the
      frightened, the constant companion of the lonely. Lord, make
      Your presence real to them.
            And Lord, we pray that our love may penetrate their grief

so that they may let us share it, so that, in sharing, the load
may be lightened.

This we pray in Your Name. Amen.

Beryl Bye

660 We seem to give them back to thee, O God, who gavest them
to us. Yet as thou didst not lose them in giving, so we do not
lose them by their return. Not as the world giveth, givest thou,
O lover of souls. What thou givest, thou takest not away, for
what is thine is ours also if we are thine. And life is eternal and
love is immortal, and death is only an horizon, and an horizon is
nothing save the limit of our sight. Lift us up, strong Son of God,
that we may see further; cleanse our eyes that we may see more
clearly: draw us closer to thyself that we may know ourselves to
be nearer to our loved ones who are with thee. And while thou
dost prepare a place for us, prepare us also for that happy place,
that where thou art we may be also for evermore. Amen.

Bede Jarrett

661 Lord, as the numbness passes the pain gets sharper. I expect
to hear a familiar voice. I walk into a room, see an empty chair
and can hardly hold back the tears. I turn to share something,
an item of news, an anxiety, something I saw when I was out,
and there is no one to share it with. I don't want to be eaten
up with self-pity but, Lord, I need your pity. I'm not asking
to be brave, just to survive this awful emptiness – this grief.
They tell me that one day the pain will get easier, one day I
will finally be able to let go. That day hasn't come yet, Lord.
Until then, let me know that you are near me.

Michael Walker

662 O God, our Father, we know that you are afflicted in all our
afflictions; and in our sorrow we come to you today that you
may give us the comfort which you alone can give.

Make us to be sure that in perfect wisdom, perfect love, and
perfect power you are working ever for the best.

Make us sure that a Father's hand will never cause His child a
needless tear.

Make us so sure of your love that we will be able to accept
even that which we cannot understand.

Help us today to be thinking not of the darkness of death, but of

the splendour of the life everlasting, for ever in your presence
and for ever with you.

Help us still to face life with grace and gallantry; and help us
to find courage to go on in the memory that the best tribute
we can pay to our loved one is not the tribute of tears, but
the constant memory that another has been added to the
unseen cloud of witnesses who compass us about.

Comfort and uphold us, strengthen and support us, until we also
come to the green pastures which are beside the still waters,
and until we meet again those whom we have loved and lost
awhile: through Jesus Christ our Lord. Amen.

William Barclay

For the Mentally Ill

663   O God of light and peace, give light and peace to them that
are of a troubled mind; Grant them courage and patience, that
they may seek for the causes of their ills; and give wisdom to
those who help them to do so. And, for those whose sufferings
continue, we pray that they may be cared for in love, and that
none may add to their griefs. We ask this in the name of him
who helped the distressed, your Son, Jesus Christ our Lord.

Unknown source

664   Lord Jesus Christ, who for love of our souls entered the deep
darkness of the cross: we pray that your love may surround all
who are in the darkness of great mental distress and who find
it difficult to pray for themselves.

May they know that darkness and light are both alike
to you and that you have promised never to fail them or
forsake them.

We ask it for your name's sake.

Llewellyn Cumings

665   Heavenly Father, we remember to our comfort that you have in
your special care all broken, outworn, and imperfect minds.

Give to those who live with them the understanding and
loving Spirit of Christ;
    enlighten those who are tempted to laugh at such illness or
regard it with shame;
    and to all who are separated in this life by barriers of mind,
grant the peace and consolation of your Holy Spirit; through
Jesus Christ our Lord.

Guild of St Raphael

666   Father, we pray for the mentally ill,
    for all who are of a disturbed and troubled mind.
Be to them light in their darkness,
    their refuge and strength in time of fear.
Give special skills and tender hearts
    to all who care for them,
and show them how best to assist your work of healing;
    through Jesus Christ our Lord.

Timothy Dudley-Smith

For Enemies

667   You alone, Lord, are mighty;
    you alone are merciful;
whatever you make me desire for my enemies,
give it to them and give the same back to me,
    and if what I ask for them at any time
    is outside the rule of charity,
whether through weakness, ignorance, or malice,
    good Lord, do not give it to them
    and do not give it back to me.
You who are the true light, lighten their darkness;
you who are the whole truth, correct their errors;
you who are the true life, give life to their souls.
For you have said to your beloved disciple
    that he who loves not remains dead.
So I pray, Lord, that you will give them love for you

and love for their neighbour,
as far as you ordain that they should have it,
lest they should sin before you against their brother.
Anselm of Canterbury

668 O Lord, remember not only the men and women of good will,
    but also those of ill will.
But, do not remember all of the suffering they have
    inflicted upon us:
Instead remember the fruits we have borne because
    of this suffering –
our fellowship, our loyalty to one another, our humility,
    our courage, our generosity,
the greatness of heart that has grown from this trouble.

When our persecutors come to be judged by you,
    let all of these fruits that we have borne
    be their forgiveness.
Anonymous – found in the clothing of a dead child
at Ravensbruck concentration camp

669 *A Father's Prayer upon the Murder of his Son*

O God
We remember not only our son but also his murderers;
Not because they killed him in the prime of his youth and
    made our hearts bleed and our tears flow,
Not because with this savage act they have brought further
    disgrace on the name of our country among the civilised
    nations of the world;
But because through their crime we now follow thy footsteps
    more closely in the way of sacrifice.
The terrible fire of this calamity burns up all selfishness
    and possessiveness in us;
Its flame reveals the depth of depravity and meanness and
    suspicion, the dimension of hatred and the measure of
    sinfulness in human nature;
It makes obvious as never before our need to trust in God's
    love as shown in the cross of Jesus and his resurrection;
Love which makes us free from hate towards our persecutors;
Love which brings patience, forbearance, courage, loyalty,

humility, generosity, greatness of heart;
Love which more than ever deepens our trust in God's
final victory and his eternal designs for the Church and for
the world;
Love which teaches us how to prepare ourselves to face our
own day of death.

O God
Our son's blood has multiplied the fruit of the Spirit in
the soil of our souls;
So when his murderers stand before thee on the day of
judgement
Remember the fruit of the Spirit by which they have enriched
our lives.
And forgive.

Hassan Dehqani-Tafti of Iran

670 O God, the Father of all, whose Son commanded us to love
our enemies: lead them and us from prejudice to truth; deliver
them and us from hatred, cruelty, and revenge; and in your
good time enable us all to stand reconciled before you; through
Jesus Christ our Lord.

Episcopal Church, USA

671 Father,
according to your law of love
we wish to love sincerely all who oppress us.
Help us to follow the commandments of your new
covenant,
that by returning good for the evil done to us,
we may learn to bear the ill-will of others out of love
for you.

Michael Buckley

For Racial Harmony

672 Grant us, O Lord, to see in the immigrants who come to our
country, our neighbours to love as ourselves, equally with us

the brothers and sisters for whom Christ was born. Give us grace to welcome them into our national life, to help them to find a satisfactory place in it, and to receive from them gifts which we may have lost. Save us from racial pride, colour prejudice, personal indifference, and desire for apartness. And grant that we may all become a new race in Christ Jesus, the Lord and Saviour of all, born as a stranger far from home.

George Appleton

673 God, the Father of mankind, who in your great love made all the peoples of the world to be one family; help those of different races and religions to love, understand and accept one another. Take away all hatred, jealousy and prejudice so that all may work together for the coming of your king-dom of righteousness and peace; through Jesus Christ our Lord.

Evelyn Underhill

674 I see white and black, Lord
I see white teeth in a black face,
I see black eyes in a white face.
Help me to see persons, Jesus, not a black person,
or a white person, a red person or a yellow person,
but human persons.

Malcolm Boyd

675 Lord,
strengthen the hands of those who work
to draw together
people of different races.
May the children who play together
remain friendly
as they grow older.
May students enter deeply
into each other's worlds.
May those who live as neighbours
or work together
strive to create
truly human bonds.

Caryl Micklem

676 Heavenly Father, who made us in your image and redeemed us through Jesus your Son: look with compassion on the whole human family.

Take from us the arrogance and hatred which infect our hearts; break down the walls that separate us; and unite us in bonds of trust and understanding, that we may work together to accomplish your purposes on earth, for the glory of your name; through Jesus Christ our Lord.

Episcopal Church, USA

For the Hungry

677 Bless, O God, all who dedicate their powers today to the making of peace in the world;

Bless all who give their training and experience to feed and clothe and house the destitute;

Bless all who lend their energies and skills to teach impoverished people to till their land, to water it, and harvest it.

And give us all a lively concern for the underprivileged, and show us practical ways of helping. For Christ's sake. Amen.

Rita Snowden

678 O God our Father, in the name of him who gave bread to the hungry we remember all who, through our human ignorance, folly, selfishness and sin, are condemned to live in want; and we pray that all endeavours for the overcoming of world poverty and hunger may be so prospered that there may be found food sufficient for all. We ask this through Jesus Christ our Lord.

Christian Aid

679 Make us worthy, Lord, to serve our fellow men throughout the world who live and die in poverty and hunger. Give

them through our hands this day their daily bread, and by
our understanding love, give peace and joy.

Mother Teresa of Calcutta

680   O merciful and loving Father, look in your mercy, we pray, on
the many millions who are hungry in the world of today and
are at the mercy of disease. Grant that we who have lived so
comfortably and gently all our lives may have true sympathy
with them and do all in our power, as individuals and as a nation,
to help them to that abundant life which is your will for them;
through Jesus Christ our Lord.

George Appleton

681   Father, we deplore that in so rich a world we tolerate poverty
so harsh that men and women are embittered by it, and children
die or survive, deprived in body, mind and spirit. Forgive our
ignorance, our indifference, and our unwillingness to give the
right priority to this responsibility. As we have the knowledge
by which we can produce more than we need, stir up the
compassion of us all by all means possible, and give us the
will and the wisdom, that through political decisions, trade
agreements, and personal service, we may find the way to
share the wealth of the world, for the sake of him who was
prepared to become poor that we might be rich, Jesus Christ
our Lord.

CAFOD

For the Homeless

682   O God, who does not will that any should live without comfort
and hope, have compassion on the multitudes in our day who
have no homes, or who are overcrowded in wretched dwellings.
Bless and inspire those who are labouring for their good. Stir
the conscience of the whole nation, O Lord, and both break the
bonds of covetousness and make plain the way of deliverance
for the sake of Jesus Christ, our Saviour.

Frank Colquhoun

683   O God, the Father of our Lord Jesus Christ, who in perfect love
      for man chose to live as one who had nowhere to lay his head;
      we pray for all who are homeless, all refugees, all who must
      live in exile or in a strange land; grant them human friendship in
      their need and loneliness, the chance of a new beginning, and
      the courage to take it, and, above all, an abiding faith in your
      sure love and care; through Jesus Christ our Lord.

Christian Aid

684   Have mercy, O Lord our God, on those whom war or oppres-
      sion or famine have robbed of homes and friends, and aid all
      those who try to help them. We commend also into thy care
      those whose homes are broken by conflict and lack of love; grant
      that where the love of man has failed, the divine compassion may
      heal; through Jesus Christ our Lord.

New Every Morning

685   Lord of the stable and of the hillsides,
      we thank You for the homes that You have given us,
          For a door to shut against the night,
          For a roof and walls to keep out the cold and rain,
          For a fire at which we can warm ourselves,
          For a table at which we can gather to eat and talk.
      We pray for those who have no homes and who must live
          without privacy and security.
      We pray for those whose only home is a crowded tenement
          room or a rough shelter of planks or corrugated iron.
      Lord, in our comfort, remind us of the uncomfortable, in our
          plenty, give us concern for all those in need.

Beryl Bye

For Refugees

686   Lord,
      no one is a stranger to you
      and no one is ever far from your loving care.
      In your kindness watch over refugees and exiles,
      those separated from their loved ones,

young people who are lost,
and those who have left or run away from home.
Bring them back safely to the place where they belong
and help us always to show your kindness
to strangers and those in need.

Roman Liturgy

687 Lord Jesus Christ, you know what it was like to go as a refugee
to Egypt and later to have nowhere to lay your head, to endure
hunger in the desert and thirst upon the cross, to be badly let
down by others and suffer cruelly at the hands of men. Hear
our prayer for those who suffer these things today. Give hope
and comfort to the refugee and the homeless; have pity upon
all who are hungry or suffer pain; encourage those who feel let
down or deserted. And, as you gave your life for others, may
we spend our lives in helping others and serving God, so that
your kingdom of love on earth may reach to all mankind.

Rowland Purton

688 We pray, Lord,
for all those who have been forced to
    leave home and country.
We pray that as many as possible
    may find a new home,
    work that satisfies them
    and a country they can love.
And for those who remain in refugee camps,
    we pray that there may yet be hope
    of a new and worthwhile life.

Caryl Micklem

For Conservation

689 We thank you, Lord of all creation, for the wonder of the world
in which we live, for the earth and all that springs from it, and
for the mystery of life and growth. We pray that our gratitude
may be shown by our care to conserve the powers of the soil,
by our readiness to learn from scientific research, and by our
concern for a fair distribution of the earth's resources. We ask
these things in the name of Christ our Lord.

Basil Naylor

690 Look at your beautiful Earth, Lord;
look at what we are doing to it.
An Earth that you created especially for your children,
a paradise for our time on Earth,
and yet we neglect and destroy it.
Lord, help us to be thankful for what you have given us,
to respect our surroundings
and to do our utmost to preserve it.
For in guarding what you give us, Lord,
we are praising you for it. Amen.

Anthony Castle

691 Almighty God, in giving us dominion over all things on earth,
you made us fellow-workers in your creation.

Give us wisdom and reverence so to use the resources of
nature, that no one may suffer from our abuse of them, and
that generations yet to come may continue to praise you for
your bounty; through Jesus Christ our Lord.

Episcopal Church, USA

692 Heavenly Father, Maker of the world in which we live, give
us a love of the countryside, its lanes and fields, its woods and
streams, and open spaces; and let us keep it clean from litter
and unspoilt for those who shall come after us, through Jesus
Christ our Lord.

H. W. Dobson

General Intercessions

693 Almighty God, you have taught us to make prayers and
intercessions for all men:
We pray for the clergy, and for all who guide the thoughts of
the people; for artists, authors, musicians, and journalists;
that our common life may be crowned with truth and beauty;
For all who heal the body, guard the health of the nation, and

tend the sick; that they may follow the footsteps of Christ,
the great physician;
For all on whose labour we depend for the necessities of life;
for all who carry on the commerce of the world, that they
may seek no private gain which would hinder the good of all;
For parents and children; that purity, love, and honour may
dwell in our homes, and duty and affection may be the bond
of our family life;
For all who draw near to death, that they may know your
presence with them through the valley of the shadow and
may wake to the vision of your glory; through Jesus Christ
our Lord.

John Hunter

694 Be mindful, O Lord, of your people present here before you, and
of those who are absent through age, sickness or infirmity. Care
for the infants, guide the young, support the aged, encourage
the faint-hearted, collect the scattered, and bring the wandering
to your fold. Travel with the voyagers, defend the widows,
shield the orphans, deliver the captives, heal the sick. Help all
who are in tribulation, necessity, or distress. Remember for
good all those that love us, and those that hate us; and those
that have desired us, unworthy as we are, to pray for them.
And those whom we have forgotten, do, you, Lord, remember.
For you are the Helper of the helpless, the Saviour of the lost,
the Refuge of the wanderer, the Healer of the sick. You, who
know each person's need, and have heard their prayer, grant
to each according to your merciful loving-kindness and your
eternal love; through Jesus Christ our Lord.

Orthodox prayer

695 God the Father, and the eternal High Priest Jesus Christ, build
us up in faith and love, and grant us part among the saints with
all those who believe in our Lord Jesus Christ. We pray for all
Christian people, for rulers and leaders, for the enemies of
the cross of Christ; and for ourselves we pray that our fruit
may be abundant, and that we may be made perfect in Christ
our Lord.

Polycarp of Smyrna

696 O, you who are love, and see all the suffering, injustice, and
misery which reign in this world. Have pity, we implore you,
on the work of your hands. Look mercifully on the poor, the
oppressed, and all who are heavy laden with error, labour
and sorrow. Fill our hearts with deep compassion for those
who suffer, and hasten the coming of your kingdom of justice
and truth.

Eugène Bersier

697 O God of infinite mercy, who have compassion on all men, hear
the prayers of your servants, who are unworthy to ask any
petition for themselves, yet are in duty bound to pray for
others.

Let your mercy descend upon your Church; preserve her in
peace and truth, in unity and service; that her sacrifice of prayer
and thanksgiving may ever ascend to your throne.

In mercy remember the Queen; keep her perpetually in your
fear and favour; and grant that all who bear office under her may
serve with a single eye to your glory.

Remember our friends, all that have done us good; return all
their kindness double to them. Forgive our enemies; and help
us to forgive, as we hope to be forgiven.

Comfort the afflicted; speak peace to troubled consciences;
strengthen the weak; confirm the strong; instruct the ignorant;
deliver the oppressed; relieve the needy; and bring us all by
the waters of comfort and in the ways of righteousness to your
eternal kingdom; through Jesus Christ our Lord.

After Jeremy Taylor

698 Our heavenly Father, we commend to your mercy those for
whom life does not spell freedom: prisoners of conscience,
the homeless and the handicapped, the sick in body and mind,
the elderly who are confined to their homes, those who are
enslaved by their passions, and those who are addicted to drugs.
Grant that, whatever their outward circumstances, they may
find inward freedom, through him who proclaimed release to
captives, Jesus Christ our Saviour.

John R. W. Stott

OCCASIONAL PRAYERS

At the New Year

699 O Lord Christ, who are both Alpha and Omega, the beginning
and the end, and whose years shall not fail: Grant us so to
pass through the coming year with faithful hearts, that in all
things we may please you and glorify your name; who lives
and reigns with the Father and the Holy Ghost, ever one God,
world without end.

Mozarabic Sacramentary

700 O Lord God of time and eternity, who makes us creatures of
time that, when time is over, we may attain your blessed eternity: With time, your gift, give us also wisdom to redeem the
time, lest our day of grace be lost; for our Lord Jesus' sake.

Christina Rossetti

701 O God, whose patient ways with us and whose unfailing love for
us, surprise and humble us, go with us along the unknown paths
of this New Year. Forgive the sins of the year that has gone;
keeping near to you may we do better; live more worthily and
serve more faithfully, so that our lives may show forth a new
beauty and a deeper harmony and your holy name be glorified.
Through Jesus Christ our Lord. Amen.

Leslie D. Weatherhead

702   Grant, O Lord, that as the years change, we may find rest in your eternal changelessness. May we meet this new year bravely, sure in the faith that, while men come and go, and life changes around us, you are always the same, guiding us with your wisdom, and protecting us with your love; through our Saviour Jesus Christ.

William Temple

703   Eternal God, who makes all things new, and abides for ever the same: grant us to begin this year in your faith, and to continue it in your favour; that, being guided in all our doings, and guarded all our days, we may spend our lives in your service, and finally, by your grace, attain the glory of everlasting life; through Jesus Christ our Lord.

William E. Orchard

704   Father,
We pray for the vision which sees beyond the things of time
    and sense.
Beyond the vain attractions of this world, where we abide for
    but a few days,
To the eternal realities –
To the deathless truth and beauty of love
For whose sake you have given us being.

John S. Hoyland

Before Worship

705   Almighty God, the fountain of all wisdom, who knows our necessities before we ask, and our ignorance in asking: we beseech you to have compassion upon our infirmities; and those things, which for our unworthiness we dare not, and for our blindness we cannot ask, vouchsafe to give us, for the worthiness of your Son, Jesus Christ our Lord.

Book of Common Prayer, 1549

706 O Lord, our God, great, eternal, wonderful in glory, who
keepest thy promise for those that love thee with their whole
heart, the life of all who love thee, the help of those that flee
unto thee, the hope of those who cry unto thee: cleanse from
sin, and from every thought displeasing to thee, our souls and
bodies, our hearts and consciences, that with a pure heart and
a clear mind, with perfect love and calm hope, we may venture
confidently and fearlessly to pray unto thee.

Fourth-century prayer

707 Almighty God, the Father of our Lord Jesus Christ, and our
Father: help us as we seek through our prayers to draw near
unto thee; to bow our wills to thine, and to yield our spirits to
the influence of thy Holy Spirit. Help us as we would worship
thine eternal goodness; meditate on the unwearied mercy of
which we are constant partakers; confess our shortcomings
and sins, and give ourselves up to be led by thee in the ways
of purity and peace.

John Hunter

708 Eternal God, we come, we come again,
seeking, hoping, wanting to hear your word.

We come because, despite our best efforts,
we have failed to live by bread alone.

We come impelled by a desire too deep for words,
with longings that are too infinite to express.

We come yearning for meaning in our existence
and purpose for our life.

We come acknowledging our need for each other's
affirmation and encouragement, understanding and love.

We come confessing our dependence on you.
Lord, embrace us with your forgiveness, and claim us
by the mystery and depths of your love. Amen.

Terry Falla

709   Holy Spirit, you make alive;
bless also this our gathering,
the speaker and the hearer;
fresh from the heart it shall come,
by your aid,
let it also go to the heart.

Søren Kierkegaard

710   We thank you, our Father, for the life and knowledge which you
have made known to us through Jesus your Servant. To you be
glory for ever. As this broken bread, once scattered upon the
mountains, has been gathered together and been made one, so
may your Church be gathered together from the ends of the
earth into your Kingdom; for yours is the glory and the power
through Jesus Christ for ever.

Didache

711   Lord Jesus Christ,
I approach your banquet table
in fear and trembling,
for I am a sinner,
and dare not rely on my own worth,
but only on your goodness and mercy.
I am defiled by many sins in body and soul,
and by my unguarded thoughts and words.
Gracious God of majesty and awe,
I seek your protection,
I look for your healing.
Poor troubled sinner that I am,
I appeal to you, the fountain of all mercy.
I cannot bear your judgement,
but I trust in your salvation.
Lord, I show my wounds to you
and uncover my shame before you.
I know my sins are many and great,
and they fill me with fear,
but I hope in your mercies,
for they cannot be numbered.

Merciful Lord, take away all my offences and sins;
purify me in body and soul,

and make me worthy to taste the holy of holies.
May your body and blood,
which I intend to receive, although I am unworthy,
be for me the remission of my sins.

Ambrose of Milan

712   O God, who makes us glad with the weekly remembrance of
the glorious resurrection of your Son our Lord, vouchsafe us
this day such a blessing through your worship, that the days
which follow it may be spent in your favour; through the same
Jesus Christ our Lord. Amen.

William Bright

713   O God, the world is so much with me, late and soon. Every
day brings its tasks, its trials, its temptations. I may sometimes
resent the rush and clamour of everyday life; but if the world
was suddenly to be stilled, to an unbroken and deathly silence,
I should be distressed far more.
     I am glad, though, for the stillness of Sunday morning; for
the anticipation of the day's work and worship; for the chance
it will give of rich enjoyment, true recreation, of body, mind
and spirit; for the so welcome change from the everyday run
of things.

Leonard Barnett

Before Reading the Bible

714   O Gracious God and most merciful Father, who hast vouchsafed
us the rich and precious jewel of thy holy Word: Assist us with
thy Spirit that it may be written in our hearts to our everlasting
comfort, to reform us, to renew us according to thine own
image, to build us up into the perfect building of thy Christ, and
to increase us in all heavenly virtues. Grant this, O heavenly
Father, for the same Jesus Christ's sake.

Geneva Bible, 1560

715 O Lord, you have given us your word for a light to shine upon
our path; grant us so to meditate on that word, and to follow its
teaching, that we may find in it the light that shines more and
more until the perfect day; through Jesus Christ our Lord.

Jerome

716 Let us keep the Scriptures in mind and meditate upon them day
and night, persevering in prayer, always on the watch. Let us
beg the Lord to give us real knowledge of what we read and
to show us not only how to understand it but how to put it
into practice, so that we may deserve to obtain spiritual grace,
enlightened by the law of the Holy Spirit, through Jesus Christ
our Lord, whose power and glory will endure throughout the
ages. Amen.

Origen

717 All-seeing Father of Christ, hear these prayers. Let your
servant hear the wonderful song of Scripture. Guide my feet
along God's path; and may the royal Christ, who wards off ills
from mortal man, lead me to the Father's will.

Gregory of Nazianzus

718 Lord, who can grasp all the wealth of just one of your words?
What we understand in the Bible is much less than what we
leave behind, like thirsty people who drink from a fountain.
For your word has many shades of meaning, just as those
who study it have many different points of view. You have
coloured your words with many hues so that each person who
studies it can see in it what he loves. You have hidden many
treasures in your word so that each of us is enriched as we
meditate on it.

Ephrem Syrus

719 Let not your Word, O Lord, become a judgement upon us, that
we hear it and do it not, that we know it and love it not, that
we believe it and obey it not. Amen.

Thomas à Kempis

720 Almighty, everlasting God, Lord, heavenly Father, whose

Word is a lamp to our feet and a light on your way: Open and enlighten my mind that I may understand your Word purely, clearly, and devoutly, and then, having understood it aright, fashion my life in accord with it, in order that I may never displease your majesty; through Jesus Christ, your Son, our dear Lord, who lives and reigns with you and the Holy Ghost, ever one God, world without end. Amen.

Johannes Bugenhagen

721 Almighty and most merciful God, who has given the Bible to be the revelation of your great love to man, and of your power and will to save him; grant that our study of it may not be made vain by the callousness or the carelessness of our hearts, but that by it we may be confirmed in penitence, lifted to hope, made strong for service, and, above all, filled with true knowledge of you and of your Son Jesus Christ.

George Adam Smith

722 O Almighty God, we pray, sow the seed of your Word in our hearts, and send down upon us your heavenly grace; that we may bring forth the fruits of the Spirit, and at the great day of harvest may be gathered by your holy angels into your harvest; through Jesus Christ our Lord.

Canterbury Convocation, 1862

723 Blessed Lord, by whose providence all holy scriptures were written and preserved for our instruction, give us grace to study them this and every day with patience and love. Strengthen our souls with the fullness of their divine teaching. Keep from us all pride and irreverence. Guide us in the deep things of your heavenly wisdom, and of your great mercy lead us by your Word to everlasting life; through Jesus Christ our Lord and Saviour.

Brooke Foss Westcott

724 Eternal Light, shine into our hearts;
Eternal Goodness, deliver us from evil;
Eternal Power, be our support;
Eternal Wisdom, scatter the darkness of our ignorance;

Eternal Pity, have mercy upon us;
that with all our heart and mind and soul and strength we may
    seek your face and be brought by your infinite mercy to your
    holy presence; through Jesus Christ our Lord.

Alcuin

725   O God, we thank you for the sacred scriptures; for the comfort
the Bible has brought to the sorrowful, for guidance offered to
the bewildered, for its gracious promises to the uncertain, for its
strength given to the weak, and for its progressive revelation of
yourself.

We thank you for the men of God who speak to us still from
its pages, and for the men of God whose learning has made
those pages live.

We thank you most of all that it reveals to us your Son, the
Word made flesh.

Help us to ponder this record of your ways with men, that
your Word may be indeed a lamp to our feet and a light to our
path; through Jesus Christ our Lord.

Leslie D. Weatherhead

Before Study

726   God of Truth, who has guided men in knowledge throughout
the ages, and from whom every good thought comes, help us
in our study to use your gifts of wisdom and knowledge. Let us
read good books carefully, and listen to all wise teaching humbly
that we may be led into all truth, and strengthened in all the
goodness of life, to the praise of your holy name. Amen

Rowland Williams

727   Lord,
Grant us the knowledge that we need
To solve the questions of the mind;
Light our candles while we read,
To keep our hearts from going blind;

Enlarge our vision to behold
The wonders you have worked of old;
Reveal yourself in every law,
And gild the towers of truth with holy awe.

Henry van Dyke

728 Almighty God, the giver of wisdom, without whose help resolutions are vain, without whose blessing study is ineffectual;
enable me, if it be your will, to attain such knowledge as may
qualify me to direct the doubtful, and instruct the ignorant; to
prevent wrongs and terminate contentions; and grant that I may
use that knowledge which I shall attain, to your glory and my
own salvation, for Jesus Christ's sake.

Dr Samuel Johnson

729 Grant, Lord, to all students, to love that which is worth loving,
to know that which is worth knowing, to praise that which
pleases you most, to esteem that which is most precious to
you, and to dislike that which is evil in your eyes. Grant that
with true judgment they may distinguish between things that
differ, and above all, may search out and do what is well-pleasing
to you; through Jesus Christ our Lord.

Thomas à Kempis

730 Hear our prayers, Lord Jesus, the everlasting Wisdom of God
the Father. You give us, in our youth, aptness to learn. Add, we
pray, the furtherance of your grace, so to learn knowledge and
the liberal sciences that, by their help, we may attain to a fuller
knowledge of you, whom to know is the height of blessedness;
and by the example of your boyhood, may duly increase in age,
wisdom and favour with God and man.

Erasmus

Minister's Prayers

731 The chief service I owe you in my life, as I well know, O God,
all-powerful Father, is that every word and thought of mine

should speak of you. The power of speech that you have
bestowed on me can give me no greater pleasure than to
serve you by preaching and to show an ignorant world what
you are: the Father, the Father whose only Son is God.

But in saying this, I am merely saying what I want to do. If I
am actually to do it, I must ask you for your help and mercy, ask
you to fill with wind the sails I have hoisted for you and to carry
me forward on my course – to breathe, that is, your Spirit into
my faith and my confession of it, and to enable me to continue
the preaching I have begun.

Hilary of Poitiers

732   O Lord, I humbly beseech and implore you, grant me always the
humble knowledge that edifies. Give me that gentle and wise
eloquence which is innocent of all arrogance and exaltation of
my own gifts in the community. Put into my mouth, I pray,
the word of consolation and edification and exhortation through
your Holy Spirit, that I may exhort those that are good to be
better and, by word and example, recall those who are going
contrary to the straight path. May the words which you grant
to your servant be as sharp javelins and burning arrows which
will pierce the hearts of the hearers and kindle them to fear and
love of you. Amen.

Ambrose of Milan

733   O God our Father, let us find grace in your sight so as to have
grace to serve you acceptably with reverence and godly fear;
and further grace not to receive your grace in vain, nor to
neglect it and fall from it, but to stir it up and grow in it, and
to persevere in it to the end of our lives; through Jesus Christ
our Lord.

Lancelot Andrewes

734   Help me to spread your fragrance everywhere I go – let me
preach you without preaching, not by words but by my example
– by the catching force, the sympathetic influence of what I do,
the evident fullness of the love my heart bears to you.

John Henry Newman

735   Lead me by your Spirit. Help me; be my strength. Renew and

quicken me. Give me the Bread of Life. Gather my thought,
O Lord, and keep me from wandering and weariness. Preserve
me from the curse of much speaking, from the death of vain
busyness. Let all that I do and say be done in spirit and in
truth. Keep my love ready and willing to serve you among
men. In the midst of all our work you are a refuge of peace.
Praise, honour, and glory be to you, the Father, and the Son,
and the Holy Spirit. By your mercy, accept my ministry to the
praise of your glory. Amen.

Karl B. Ritter

736 Trouble me with the smallness of my work.
Trouble me with the greatness of your command.
Trouble me with my unholiness and my slowness to obey.
Trouble me with time running out and every lost hour.
Trouble me with my sins and the sins of all men.
Trouble me with the troubles of your church which are the work
  of men.
Trouble me, and make me to watch continually for your
  judgement.
Let me go forth desiring the coming of your glory.
Let me go forward; for your glory shall be revealed.
I thank you that my work ends and your work begins.
Lord, I believe, help my unbelief.

Karl B. Ritter

737 O God, the fountain of all wisdom, in a deep sense of my
own ignorance, and of that great charge which lies upon me,
I am constrained to come often before you, from whom I have
learned whatever I know, to ask that help without which I shall
disquiet myself in vain; most humbly beseeching you to guide
me with your eye; to enlighten my mind, that I may see myself,
and teach others the wonders of your law; that I may learn from
you what I ought to think and speak concerning you. Direct and
bless all the efforts of my mind, give me a discerning spirit, a
sound judgement, and an honest and religious heart.

Grant that, in all my studies, my first aim may be to set forth
your glory, and to set forward the salvation of mankind; that I
may give a worthy account of my time at the great day, when
all our labours shall be tried.

And if you are pleased that by my ministry sinners shall be converted, and your kingdom enlarged, give me the grace of humility, that I may never ascribe the success to myself, but to your Holy Spirit, which enables me to will and to do according to your good pleasure. Grant this, O Father of all light and truth, for the sake of Jesus Christ. Amen.

Thomas Wilson

738 Lord, make us bold to run the way of your commandments and help us to stand still before your presence, that, leading lives of quiet confidence, we may bear witness to your grace and carry your power into the world. Let your light shine through us, that men may see good works in us and give glory to the Father in heaven. So direct our lives, that in the end none to whom we have failed to show mercy and love may accuse us, and we may be received into the eternal habitations; through Jesus Christ, our Lord. Amen.

Hermann Bezzel

739 Holiness of life we crave after. Grant that our speech, our thoughts, our actions, may all be holiness, and 'holiness unto the Lord'. We know that there be some that seek after moral virtue apart from God; let us not be of their kind, but may our desire be that everything may be done as unto the Lord, for you have said, 'Walk before me and be perfect.' Help us to do so; to have no master but our God; no law but his will; no delight but himself. O, take these hearts, most glorious Lord, and keep them, for 'out of them are the issues of life', and let us be the instruments in your hand, by daily vigilance, of keeping our hearts, lest in heart we go astray from the Lord our God. Until life's latest hour may we keep the sacred pledges of our early youth.

Charles H. Spurgeon

740 Lord Jesus, merciful and patient, grant us grace, ever to teach in a teachable spirit; learning along with those we teach, and learning from them whenever you so please; that we and they may all be taught of God.

Christina Rossetti

741   Lord Jesus, teach me, that I may teach them; sanctify and enable all my powers, that in their full strength I may deliver your message reverently, readily, faithfully, and fruitfully. Make your word a swift word, passing from the ear to the heart, from the heart to life and conversation; that as the rain returns not empty, so neither may your word, but accomplish that for which it is given. O Lord, hear; O Lord, forgive; O Lord, listen; and do so for your Son's sake.

George Herbert

PRAYERS FOR THE SCHOOL ASSEMBLY

Through the Day

742 O God, help me to be cheerful all through today,
Whatever I have to do, help me to do it with a smile.
O God, help me to be diligent all through today,
Whatever I have to do, help me to do my best.
O God, help me to be kind all through today,
Whatever I have to do, help me not to be too busy to help
someone else.
O God, help me to be brave all through today,
Whatever I have to do, help me to face it and not to
dodge it.
O God, help me to be reverent all through today,
Whatever I have to do, help me to remember that you see
me, and help me to make every word fit for you to hear,
and every bit of work fit to offer to you.

This I ask for your love's sake. Amen.

William Barclay
Prayers for Young People

743 God, help us to go about life eagerly today –
Save us from grudges,
Save us from being grumpy,
Save us from thinking only of our own things.
What we have to do, let us do it with our whole hearts –

Our jobs about the house;
Our lessons at school;
Our games with others.

Rita Snowden

For our School Community

744 We pray
For prefects and monitors
    and all to whom new authority and leadership is
      now to be entrusted,
    that they may act with courage, wisdom and fairness.

For new pupils, that they may give of their best in
    spirit, mind and body,
and feel really welcome in this community.

For children who find the work difficult,
    that they may be helped to find new ways of
      developing their personalities
    and enriching their capacity for the service of others.

For games' teams, that they may play with
    enthusiasm, loyalty and unselfishness,
and with a due sense of proportion.

For school societies, that they may flourish and
    prosper, to the good of all their members.

For the teaching staff, that their work may be
    carried out conscientiously
and with the benefit of their pupils always in mind.

For the ancillary staff, that they may have strength
    and cheerfulness for their duties
and that no carelessness or ill manners on the part
    of others may make their lot difficult.

Unknown source

745 Father, we hold before you now in prayer our life together in
this school.

Help us to give to it of our best, and to receive in turn the best it has to give.

Teach us to know the joys of discovery, the warmth of friendship, the satisfaction of attempting and achieving, and the demands of truth.

Open for us week by week new windows on our world; increase our understanding of ourselves and others.

May teachers and taught alike seek first your Kingdom, to the good of this school and the glory of your Name.

Timothy Dudley-Smith

Helping Others

746 O Lord, you have given us so much; life, in a world where many are never really well; food, in a world where many are hungry; education, in a world where many never have a chance; security, in a world where many are afraid.

We cannot pay you back, but show us what we can do for others; help us to remember children and young people in other lands, especially those who are hungry and diseased, those who are homeless and afraid, those who are unwanted and suffering. Their words may be different from ours, but their hearts and minds are the same. May we offer them the hand of brotherhood and love.

Anthony Castle

747 Lord, I want to help the poor and those who are suffering, in the kind of way that you did, and not in the condescending way do-gooders are condemned for. Give me the ability to see you in the lowly of this world and to love them as you do without thinking of the cost to myself. Let me learn from them in a humble way, and then surely I won't be condemned as a do-gooder?

Michael Hollings and Etta Gullick

For our World

748   Give us, O God, the vision which can see your love in the
world, in spite of human failure. Give us the faith, the trust,
the goodness in spite of our ignorance and weakness. Give us
the knowledge that we may continue to pray with understanding
hearts, and show us what each one of us can do to set forth the
coming of the day of universal peace.

Frank Borman, from Apollo 8, 1968

749   Lord Jesus, we are constantly shown on TV, in the newspapers,
and in the cinema the horrors of the world, the evil and
perverted behaviour of mankind so that we come close to
despair. You, Lord, in your life knew failure, saw men betray
and torture each other. You knew hell on earth as we do, but
you did not despair for you loved men and trusted your father.
Keep alight in our hearts the flame of hope, make us to see the
beautiful and good things in the world, not just the drab, the
squalid and sordid. Help us to see the goodness of men, and by
our love increase this and make it grow and spread amongst the
people, for we are your instruments in the world. Make your
hope and love shine through us so that the hells of others may
be lightened and they may glimpse something of your glory.

Michael Hollings and Etta Gullick

750   Lord,
we pray for this modern world
in which faith comes hard,
where people find it difficult
to raise their eyes
above the material things
which are so necessary to life.

*We pray for those
who find it hard to believe
because they have too many things,
and for those who find it hard*

because they haven't enough.

We pray for those
who have more to eat than they need,
and those who are dying from lack of food.

*We pray for parents
who, because of their poverty,
and a lack of concern on the part of others,
must watch their children die.*

We pray for those
who suffer from disease, from confusion
and guilt, from depression and fear.

*We pray for those
who face each day with dread,
because their lives are so dominated
by the power of others.*

We pray for those
who are so lonely that life is robbed
of all loveliness and hope.

*Lord, we pray because our love for you
is a love for One whose compassion
embraces all human suffering.*

We pray because you are in our midst,
and have made people in their need
present to us, and us aware of them.

*We pray because you call us as
your disciples to reach out from ourselves
to all our fellow human beings.*
Amen.

Terry Falla

751   Lord, in the Acts, the Apostles say 'We cannot but speak of
what we have heard and seen.' I speak to you about what I
have seen and heard, Lord.
    – I see the terror of repression and war on TV.
    – I see the suffering of the poor and the oppressed.
    – I see the plight of refugees.

- I see the indignity of life for the homeless.
- I see the way in which we are destroying this beautiful
  earth.

I feel the sufferings of your people deep in my heart, Lord.
And as a black person I feel the suffering of my black
people in Britain and in Europe. I have a vision of a 'new
world', a new order. Lord, send your Holy Spirit to change
the hearts and minds of your people. Kindle in them truth,
justice, love and kindness. As for me, Lord, help me to see,
judge, act. Amen.

Gumley House School pupil

Appreciation of our World

752 Eternal Father, Creator of every planet and star,
of the wind and the seas and the rain,
give us today, we pray, the mind and heart
to rejoice in your creation.

*Forbid that we should walk through your beautiful
world with unseeing eyes.*

Forbid that the lure and comforts of technology
should ever entirely steal our hearts away from
the love of open acres and the green trees.

*Forbid that under the low roof of house or workshop,
office or study, we should ever forget
your great overarching sky.*

Forbid that when all your creatures are greeting
the morning with songs and shouts of joy,
we alone should wear a dull and sullen face.

*Let the energy and vigour which you have infused
into every living thing stir within our being.
May your life and joy pulse through us.*

And, above all, give us grace to use these beauties
of earth without us, and this eager stirring of

life within us, as a means by which we respond
to you, our Creator and our God.

John Baillie

Thanksgiving

753 Thank you, loving and caring Father, for everything that makes
us happy. Thank you for music, song and laughter. Thank
you for the good times with our friends, for the jokes and
fun together. May we never laugh at people but only with
them. Fill each day, we pray, with the joy of knowing you,
and knowing the love of our family and friends. Amen.

Anthony Castle

754 Thank you Lord! Father, most prayers are wanting prayers,
granting prayers and getting prayers. But most people when
they've received what they have, they never remember to say
thank you. Well, this prayer is for that reason. Thank you, Lord,
for my parents, friends and family. But mostly, thanks for loving
me! Thank you Father!

Gumley House School pupil

Standing up for the Good

755 Father God, help us to stand on our own feet, and think things
out for ourselves. Give us the strength we need to say 'No'
when we ought to say 'No'; even if we are the only ones to do so.

Give special help, we pray, to children who sometimes are told
to do things they know are bad, by their parents or other people;
children forced to steal things from shops, or tell lies for older
people, and who are unhappy about it. Father God, show them
what they can do, please. Perhaps they can share their worry
with somebody else older and wiser who can advise them. Give
them the courage to think things out for themselves.

Father, help us also to see the difference between being firm, standing up for what we know is right and good, and just being obstinate and stubborn for some selfish reason. It's hard for us, sometimes, to sort these things out. But please help us. Amen

Leonard Barnett

Anxiety and Peace

756 Lord, perhaps above all things today we need the gift of peace. We are anxious about so many things. We worry about our standard of living, about what people think of us, whether we can keep up the pace of life, whether we have an identity. Anxiety drives so many people out of their minds. Save us from anxiety; show us how to accept that your love for us is real and that nothing can separate us from it; give us that interior peace which is untouched by the outer storms of life. When we get excited, worried, anxious, say to us calmly, quietly as you did to the waves and winds which disturbed your disciples' little boat – 'Peace, be still'. Amen.

Michael Hollings

757 Help me, O God, to put away the fears of childhood;
    Fear of being alone, and of the dark;
    Fear of doing distasteful things, and hurting myself;
    Fear of strangers, going to fresh places, meeting people;
       doing unfamiliar things;
    Fear of failure.

Teach me rather, O God, to fear
    Compromising with the truth by silence or speech;
    Losing what good name I have;
    Bringing hurt or shame upon my family and friends;
    Breaking my word;
    Betraying Christ.

Leonard Barnett

758 Lord, we need your help.
We need a calm mind; grant us your peace.
We need a clear head; grant us your wisdom.
We need to be careful; grant us your patience.
We need to be inspired; grant us your enthusiasm.
Keep us from all panic as we put our trust in your power to
keep us this day.

K.A. Clegg

Friendship

759 Help me, O God, to be a good and a true friend:
to be always loyal, and never to let my friends down:
Never to talk about them behind their backs in a way which I
would not do before their faces;
never to betray a confidence or talk about the things about
which I ought to be silent;
always to be ready to share everything I have;
to be as true to my friends as I would wish them to be to me.

This I ask for the sake of him who is the greatest and the truest
of all friends, for Jesus' sake. Amen.

William Barclay

760 Lord Jesus, you had friends and felt lonely and abandoned when
at the end of your life, they left you to suffer alone. Help us to be
good friends, loyal and reliable, ready to help whenever we can.
While we have special friends, please help us to be friendly with
everyone, remembering that you asked us to love one another
as you have loved us. Amen.

Anthony Castle

761 Let us pray for our friends,
that they may lead happy and useful lives;
Let us pray for any friends
with whom we have quarrelled,
that we may have the chance to be reconciled;
Let us pray for those who are living in new surroundings

and lack friends.
Let us pray for those who have lost their friends
by the way they live;
Let us pray for those who befriend the friendless.
God our Father,
make us true and loyal friends.
Grant that all our friends.
may lead us nearer you.

Caryl Micklem

Making Mistakes

762 Dear Father, help us
to make mistakes courageously
this week.

*We know we cannot possibly hit
the mark in everything we try,
so let us try and keep trying.*

Let us not weep when we fail
to fulfil our hopes and intentions,
but help us to keep striving.

*May we be understanding
with the mistakes of others.*

Help us to be a community marked by
caring and comforting,
healing and sustaining,
enabling and reconciling,
so that together
we may demonstrate our love
for you, for each other,
and for all people.

*Thank you, Father, for the ability
to learn from mistakes, and to hone
our minds, skills, and spirits
so that the supreme goal,*

even Christ, may be closer
through the efforts,
the mistakes, and the successes,
of this week. Amen.

Terry Falla

763 Heavenly Father, things do not always go well. We fail at home,
with our friends and here at school. No one can be a success all
the time. Your Son, Jesus, knew what failure could be, yet he
did not give up. Help us, too, to have faith, and trust in you and
believe that good can come from apparent failure. Please use
our failure to help us to learn more about ourselves and lead
us to real personal growth. We ask this through Jesus Christ
your Son. Amen.

Anthony Castle

For Greater Maturity

764 O God, help me to have in my life the virtues which all people
value and admire.

Give me wisdom always to know
  What I ought to do;
  What I ought to say;
  Where I ought to go.

Give me courage,
  To do the right thing when it is difficult;
  If need be, to be laughed at for my faith;
  Never to be ashamed to show my loyalty to you.

Give me justice,
  Always to be fair in thought and word and action;
  Always to think of the rights of others as much as of
    my own;
  Never to be content when anyone is being unjustly treated.

Give me self-control,
  Always to have my impulses, passions and emotions under
    perfect control;

Never to be swept into doing things for which I would
be sorry;
Never to do anything which would hurt others, grieve those
who love me, or bring shame to myself.

Hear this my prayer for your love's sake. Amen.

William Barclay

765 Almighty Father, help us to come to a true maturity in our lives.
Help us to learn love and respect for others; a respect which will
spring from the ability to see things not only from our own point
of view, but that of our parents, teachers, friends and especially
those people we find difficult to like. We ask this through Christ
your Son who died for us all. Amen.

Anthony Castle

766 Help me, Lord God, not to take the easy way out and repeat
what I so often hear other people say, 'It's not my fault.' May I
have enough maturity to accept responsibility for all my actions,
bad as well as good. Amen.

Anthony Castle

The Real 'Me'

767 Lord, I don't know what I am really like. I put on a different
face and outlook with each person I am with. I am the good
son, obedient and biddable when I am with my mother, agreeing
with her opinions. I am bright and rebellious with my friends at
school; boastful and showing off when I'm with girls. When I
am alone with no one about I don't know which me is the real
one and it is frightening, so I turn on the radio and identify with
the mood of the singers. Is there a me or just a collection of
disguises and masks with emptiness behind? Help, Lord! Give
me a glimpse of what you would like me to be and strength to
become it; if I put on the appearance other people expect of
me, surely I can take on the reality you want me to have? Give
me the courage to follow your Son and become like him, for I
think this is the only way I will find myself.

Michael Hollings

768 O God, you can see my inmost thoughts and know me better than I know myself. You understand the impulses I feel, the ambitions I have, the silent loneliness I experience. Forgive me my sins against truth – the untruth within me, the half-truths, the evasions, the exaggerations, the trying silences that deceive, the masks I wear before the world. Help me to see myself as I really am, fill me with the courage I shall need if I am to seek the truth and live in truth.

Anthony Castle

769 O God, I know quite well that I bring most of my troubles on myself.

I leave things until the last minute, and then I have to do them in far too big a hurry to do them properly, and so I often come to school with lessons half-learned and work half-done.

I don't spend all the time I ought to spend in work and in study, although I always mean to.

I get angry and impatient far too easily, and the result is that I upset myself and everyone else.

I do things without thinking first, and then I am sorry I did them.

I hurt the people I love most of all, and then – too late – I am sorry for what I said or did.

It is not that I don't know what is right. I do know – but the trouble is that I mean to do it and then don't do it.

I need your help to strengthen me and to change me.

Please help me to do what I cannot do and to be what I cannot be by myself.

This I ask for your love's sake. Amen.

William Barclay

Against Prejudice

770 Father God, some of us know what it is to be afraid to talk to people of a different religion.

We are afraid because of what our parents will say or do to us.

We are afraid because of what our neighbours will say or
    do to us.
Give us courage.
    Teach children and grown-ups in this and every land to show
love to people no matter what colour they are or by what name
they are called.

Prayer of a child in
Northern Ireland

771   Almighty God, help us not to judge others by appearances. Help
      us, Lord, to understand that no matter what race or colour we
      are, or what age, we are all equally your sons and daughters.
      May we never intentionally and deliberately give hurt or offence
      to anyone. Help us to realise that if we are all your sons and
      daughters, that makes us brothers and sisters in your family.
      We need your help to understand this and live it out in our
      lives. Amen.

Anthony Castle

772   Our Father, God,
      as you confront us with your Word
      and meet us in the world,
      may we discover
      and keep rediscovering:

      That '*true peace*
      is not merely the absence of tension,
      but the presence of justice and brotherhood',

      That '*the ultimate tragedy*
      is not the brutality of the bad people,
      but the silence of the good people',

      That '*with your help and the world's,*
      we can speak, share, and show forth
      a substitute for selfishness and silence',

      That, as your people, we are
      an open letter about Jesus Christ:

      '*A letter written not with ink*
      but with the Spirit of the living God,

Written not on stone tablets
but on the pages of the human heart'.

> Terry Falla
> The first three quotations are
> from Martin Luther King,
> and the fourth from
> The Apostle Paul (2 Corinthians 3:3)

Enjoying Sport

773 Our Father, we thank you for giving us
and all your creatures a love of play.

Thank you for the pleasures
of eye and limb and mind
working in harmony, and for the
healthy environment we enjoy.

Help us to learn
from submitting to rules,
from belonging to a team,
and from accepting an umpire's verdict,
that self-discipline is worthwhile.

May the experience
of learning the skills of our sport,
of engaging in fair competition,
and of working to keep fit,
teach us the value of developing
all your gifts.

Help us to enjoy our victories
without losing respect for our opponents;
when we lose, make us generous toward them
and keen to improve ourselves.

Help us, with honest effort,
to fulfil our potential,
and to encourage our opponents
to do the same.

Keep us fair in judgement,
clean in play,
disciplined in mind and body,
as befits followers
of the Lord Jesus Christ.

Amen.

David Griffiths

For Animals

774 Great Father in heaven, thank you for making animals to be our friends. Give us pity for all sick animals, for hunted and caged animals, for animals that are ill-treated and teased, and for any that are lost and frightened. Make us brave to defend any animal when we see it being cruelly treated. May we be the friends of all dumb creatures and save us from causing them any suffering through our own thoughtlessness.

Brenda Holloway

775 Heavenly Father, the Bible tells us that you are the creator of the world; that you made all the animals and brought them to the man, Adam, to name them. You intended us to be in partnership with the animals, to watch over and care for them.

Stop, then, Almighty God, and help us to stop, all the cruelty that we hear animals suffer. There is no need for them to be hunted and trapped for their fur; no need for them to be experimented on for safer cosmetics; other ways can be found to make products safe.

We pray for our pets, may we respect and care for them.

We pray for guide dogs, guard dogs and other animals that work for human beings, may they be well loved and treated.

We pray for farm animals and poultry in factory farms, may they receive all they need for a happy life.

We pray for the wild animals of the countryside, may they suffer no cruelty from human beings.

We pray for all the animals caged in our zoos and parks, may their keepers provide them with enough space and

care to ensure for them a dignified existence.
Father Creator, we pray for all animals, domestic and wild, that share our world, may none ever be abused or treated with cruelty, for we believe that you love all of your creation. Amen.

Anthony Castle

INDEX OF SUBJECTS

Love 203
Love for God 278–304
Love for Others 305–322

Married people, for 207–210
Maturity 764–766
Media, for those in the 605–607
Mentally ill, for the 663–666
Minister's prayers 731–741
Missionaries 578
Mistakes, making 762, 763
Morning prayers 1–38
Mothering Sunday 101–103
Mothers 101–103
Mourn, for those who 653–662

Nation, for the 588–591
Nature 333
New Christians, for 580–585
New Year, at the 699–704

Offering the day 10
Old Age 219, 220, 319
Opportunities, using 2
Ox, prayer of the 259

Parents 182, 189, 196
Passion of Christ 121
Patience 321, 391–399
Peace, for 616–629, 756–758
Pentecost 147–167
Persecutors, for 668–669
Perseverance 391–399
Politics, for those in 595–600
Poverty 681
Praise 229–242
Prejudice 672, 770
Psalm 130 (adapted) 364

Queen, for the 592–594

Racial harmony, for 672–676
Real 'me' 767–769
Reconciliation 365–369

INDEX OF SOURCES

BIOGRAPHICAL NOTES

Alcuin (c.732–804)
Of noble Anglo-Saxon family, he became headmaster of the renowned York Cathedral School. Meeting the Emperor Charlemagne in 781, he was persuaded to be his educational counsellor. He is famous for revising the liturgy of the Frankish church.

Alford, Henry (1810–1871)
Dean of Canterbury, writer and the editor of the Greek Testament.

King Alfred (849–901)
Enlightened Saxon king of Wessex who saved England from conquest by the Danes and promoted Christianity and a great revival of learning.

Ambrose of Milan, St (339–397)
While still governor of the province of Milan, Ambrose was chosen by popular acclaim as its new bishop. He is thought to have been the first to introduce the singing of hymns into Christian worship. Beyond his hymn writing and scriptural studies he is famous for converting the great Augustine of Hippo.

Anatolius
Fifth-century Christian writer.

Andrewes, Lancelot (1555–1626)
Theologian and court preacher who energetically defended and advanced Anglican doctrines.

Anselm, St (1033–1109)
Archbishop of Canterbury, monk and philosopher, founder of Scholasticism.

Appleton, George (b.1902)
Writer, formerly Archbishop of Perth, Australia and Archbishop of Jerusalem, now retired.

Arndt, Johann (1555–1621)
Pastor and Lutheran theologian, author of mystical writings.

Arnold, Thomas, Dr (1795–1842)
Educator, influential Headmaster of Rugby Public School

Ashe, Thomas (1836–1889)
English poet and man of letters.

Augustine of Hippo, St (354–430)
Converted late in life, Augustine brought the education and cultural values of his time to his appointment as Bishop of Hippo. Philosopher, theologian and defender of orthodoxy against various heresies. His literary activity was the most copious of all Roman antiquity.

Baillie, John (1886–1960)
Sometime Professor of Divinity at the University of Edinburgh and Principal of New College; author of *A Diary of Private Prayer*.

Baldwin of Canterbury (d. 1190)
Archbishop of Canterbury. Scripture scholar and writer. Helped to lead a crusade to the Holy Land where he died.

Barclay, William (1907–1978)
New Testament scholar, prolific writer of over 60 books and spiritual mentor to millions.

Barnett, Leonard (b.1919)
Methodist minister, religious writer, journalist and playwright.

Barth, Karl (1886–1968)
Influential theologian who initiated a radical change in Protestant thought.

Basil the Great, St (329–379)
One of the great Fathers of the early church, Basil defended the orthodox faith against Arianism. He became bishop and wrote many works on monasticism, theology and canon law.

Beethoven, Ludwig van (1770–1827)
One of the greatest composers in the history of Western music.

Benson, Edward White (1829–1896)
Educator and Archbishop of Canterbury, responsible for liturgical reform in the Anglican church.

Bersier, Eugène (1831–1889)
Writer and minister of a congregation of the Free Reformed Church in Paris; Eugène worked for Church unity and wrote on Church history and liturgy.

Birtwhistle, Allen
Methodist minister, at one time in pastoral charge of Wesley's Chapel, London.

Bisseker, Harry (1878–1965)
Anglican priest, theologian, writer and Scripture scholar; headmaster of Leys School, Cambridge, for fifteen years.

Blake, William (1757–1827)
Poet, painter, engraver and visionary creator of an emotionally direct method of thought and artistic expression.

Bloom, Anthony (b.1914)
Former doctor of medicine and soldier, now the Russian Orthodox Metropolitan Archbishop for Western Europe.

Boehme, Jacob (1575–1624)
Shoemaker of Silesia who imparted his mystical experiences through writings, most of which were published posthumously.

Bonaventure, St (1217–1274)
Theologian, Minister General of the Franciscan Order and Cardinal.

Bonhoeffer, Dietrich (1906–1945)
Protestant theologian who supported ecumenism but died for his opposition to the Nazis.

Book of Common Prayer, 1928
Liturgical book of the churches of the Anglican Communion. First authorised in 1549, radically revised in 1552, minor revisions being made in 1559, 1604 and 1662. A proposed revision of 1928 was rejected by Parliament; however this revision was accepted and used by the Protestant Episcopal Church of the USA.

Borman, Frank (b.1928)
Astronaut who, with Lovell and Anders, made the first manned flight around the moon, December 1968.

Botting, Michael (b.1925)
Rector of Aldford with Bruera, Chester; writer and joint Director of Training for the Diocese of Chester, honorary canon of Ripon Cathedral.

Boyd Carpenter, W. (1841–1918)
Bishop of Ripon, Royal chaplain, prolific writer and notable preacher.

Boyd, Malcolm
Episcopalian priest well known for his book of 1965 *Are You Running With Me, Jesus?*

Bradwardine, Thomas (1290–1349)
Chaplain to King Edward III, theologian and mathematician, called 'the profound doctor'; elected Archbishop of Canterbury, but died before being enthroned.

Bright, William (1824–1901)
Theologian, scholar and writer; Canon of Christ Church, Oxford.

Brooks, Phillips (1835–1893)
Bishop of Massachusetts who won an international reputation for his sermons; composer of 'O Little Town of Bethlehem'.

Browning, Elizabeth Barrett (1806–1861)
English poet whose reputation rests chiefly upon her love poems.

Buckley, Monsignor Michael (b.1924)
Catholic theologian, writer, liturgist and former director of Woodhall Pastoral Centre; well-known for his peace work in Northern Ireland.

Bugenhagen, Johannes (1485–1558)
A priest colleague of Martin Luther who organised the Lutheran Church in northern Germany.

Bunsen, Christian K. J. (1791–1860)
Liberal Prussian diplomat, scholar and theologian.

Burke, Carl (b.1917)
A Baptist minister and one-time chaplain to Eire County Gaol NY; author of the best-selling *God Is For Real, Man* and subsequent books.

Bye, Beryl
Wife and mother who has become an established writer of prayers and children's books.

Caedmon (flourished 657–680)
The Venerable Bede tells how Caedmon, an illiterate herdsman, had a dream in which he was told to sing of 'the beginning of things'. By virtue of his hymn of creation, Caedmon has the distinction of being the first Old English Christian poet.

Calvin, John (1509–1564)
Theologian, ecclesiastical statesman and one of the most important figures of the Protestant Reformation.

Camara, Helder (b.1909)
Archbishop of Olinda and Recife in Brazil, champion of the poor and human rights.

Canisius, Peter (1521–1597)
Jesuit scholar who has been called 'the second Apostle of Germany'.

Canton, William (1845–1926)
English poet.

Carmichael, Amy (1868–1951)
Missionary in South India who founded the Dohnavur Fellowship.

Carpenter, Mary (1807–1887)
English philanthropist, social reformer and founder of free schools for poor children.

Castle, Anthony (b. 1938)
Head of Religious Studies in an Essex high school; writer, compiler and editor of numerous books in the field of pastoral care and spirituality.

Cennick, John (1718–1755)
An evangelist and writer who worked with the Wesleys in the West Country of England and in Ireland; later joined the Moravian Church.

Chamberlain, Elsie (Rev.)
Minister and broadcaster, producer in 1950s of BBC feature 'Lift up your hearts'.

Channing, William (1780–1842)
American Congregationalist, later Unitarian, minister, author and moralist, known as the 'apostle of Unitarianism'.

Chapman, George (1550–1634)
Poet and dramatist, translator of the classics.

Chapman, Rex (b. 1938)
Writer and prayer-book compiler; former school chaplain, now canon of Aberdeen cathedral, currently the bishop's adviser for Education.

Clement of Rome (dates uncertain)
One of the earliest successors of Peter in the see of Rome. The letter he wrote to the Christian community at Corinth, about the year 96, contains the oldest Christian prayer known outside scripture.

Colquhoun, Frank (b. 1909)
Anglican Canon Emeritus of Norwich Cathedral and former editor of *The Churchman*, well known for his books of prayers.

Columba of Iona, St (521–597)
With twelve disciples, the Abbot Columba erected a church and monastery on the island of Iona. This was their springboard for the conversion of Scotland to Christianity. He and his associates spread the gospel in Britain more than any other contemporary group. Many poems and some hymns are ascribed to Columba.

Coptic Liturgy of St Basil/Coptic Liturgy of St Cyril
The ancient church of Egypt, later known as 'Coptic', has a simpler liturgy
than other Eastern churches. It goes back to the traditions of early Egyptian
Christianity and comes in several forms – the most used is that of Basil, the
least used is under the name of Cyril.

Cosin, John (1594–1672)
Bishop of Durham, a liturgist whose scholarly promotion of traditional worship
and doctrine established him as one of the fathers of Anglo-Catholicism.

Couturier, Paul (1881–1953)
French priest and worker for Christian Unity, one of the founders of the
annual Week of Prayer for Christian Unity.

Cowper, William (1731–1800)
English poet, one of the most widely read of his time. His popularity sprang
from the simple directness of his work.

Cranmer, Thomas (1489–1556)
Archbishop of Canterbury in the reign of Henry VIII who compiled the Book
of Common Prayer, and died for his beliefs under Mary Tudor.

Cumings, Llewellyn (b.1929)
Writer and contributor to compilations of prayers; rector of Denver in the
Diocese of Ely, England.

Cyprian of Carthage (d. 258)
He led the church of Carthage as bishop during the Decian persecution. He
wrote to fulfil his pastoral leadership with particular charity and concern for
those who fell away from the church.

Dearmer, Percy (1867–1936)
Theologian, prolific writer, sought-after lecturer and finally Canon of
Westminster Abbey.

de Foucauld, Charles-Eugène (1858–1916)
French soldier and explorer who after conversion became a Trappist monk
then later a hermit, first in Palestine, then in Algeria, where he worked among
the Tuareg tribesmen and was murdered.

de Gasztold, Carmen Bernos
Teacher, who wrote the celebrated *Prayers From the Ark*, during the German
occupation of France. After a breakdown she was taken in by the nuns of the
Abbaye at Limon-par-Igny, where she still lives.

Dehqani-Tafti, Hassan
Exiled bishop of the Episcopal Church in Iran; before being driven from
Iran by the Islamic revolution his son, Bahram, was murdered on 6th
May 1980.

de la Colombière, Claude (1641–1682)
French Jesuit, court preacher to Mary, James II of England's queen; spiritual director of Margaret Mary Alacoque. Falsely accused of complicity in the Titus Oates plot.

Didache (or *The Teaching of the Apostles*)
The oldest surviving Christian church order, probably written in Egypt or Syria in the second century. Its sixteen chapters were quoted in the fourth century by Eusebius in his *Church History*.

Donne, John (1572–1631)
Famous preacher at St Paul's, London, where he was Dean, a leading poet of the seventeenth century.

Dostoevsky, Fyodor (1821–1881)
Russian novelist whose penetration into the recesses of the human heart has had a profound influence on the twentieth-century novel.

Dudley-Smith, Timothy (b. 1926)
Former Suffragan Bishop of Thetford, and President of the Evangelical Alliance (1987–1991), writer of popular religious books and modern hymns.

Duncan, Mary L. (1814–1840)
Hymnwriter.

Edmund of Abingdon, St (1175–1240)
Distinguished scholar and outspoken Archbishop of Canterbury. His virtue and literary works strongly influenced the English church.

Eliot, T. S. (1888–1965)
Poet, playwright and critic, a leader of the modernist movement in poetry, literary doyen of his age.

Ephrem Syrus (306–373)
(Also known as Ephraem of Edessa or Ephrem the Syrian). Born at Nisibis (in modern Turkey), he moved to Edessa (Syria) and founded 'the Persian school', for Christians of Persian origin. He taught there until his death. A contemplative soul, Ephrem's prolific theological and poetic writings earned him the title of 'lyre of the Holy Spirit'.

Erasmus, Desiderius (1466–1536)
The greatest patristic and classical scholar of the Northern Humanist Renaissance.

Evely, Louis (b. 1910)
Belgian Catholic spiritual writer.

Falla, Terry
Australian Baptist Minister; married with a family. Author and compiler of collections of prayers, presently working as a University chaplain.

Fénelon, François (1651–1715)
Archbishop, mystical theologian and man of letters whose liberal views exerted a lasting influence on French culture.

Francis of Assisi, St (1181/82–1226)
Founder of the Franciscan orders of men and women, leader of the religious movements of the early thirteenth-century reform of the church.

Francis of Sales (1567–1622)
Roman Catholic bishop of Geneva who was active in the struggle against Calvinism; founder of the order of Visitation Sisters. Honoured by the title of Saint by the Roman Catholic Church.

Fuller, Thomas (1608–1661)
Scholar, preacher and one of the most witty and prolific authors of the seventeenth century.

Furlong, Monica (b. 1930)
Convert to Christianity, former journalist, now an established novelist, poet and spiritual writer.

George, Rosa
Former lecturer in Spirituality at St Stephen's, Oxford; co-writer, with Michael Hollings, of several compilations of prayers.

Gibran, Kahlil (1883–1931)
Philosophical essayist, novelist, mystic, poet and artist originally of the Maronite Christian community of Lebanon, but settled in the USA.

Goudge, Elizabeth (1900–1984)
Writer of novels, children's stories, and plays, as well as religious biographies and anthologies.

Gray, A. Herbert (1868–1956)
Writer and Presbyterian minister on staff of the Student Christian Movement and involved in pastoral work in several London churches.

Greet, Dr Kenneth (b.1918)
Theologian, secretary general of the Methodist Conference and writer on religious and social questions.

Gregory of Nazianzus, St (d.390)
Ordained priest by his father, the Bishop of Nazianzus, he later resigned a bishopric because he could not face the practical daily problems. A sensitive and prolific writer, with Basil and Gregory of Nyssa, he brought Arianism to an end.

Grou, John Nicholas (1731–1803)
Preacher and spiritual director. At the time of the French Revolution, John, a Jesuit, fled to England.

Guardini, Romano (1885–1968)
Italian-born German Roman Catholic theologian and writer.

Gullick, Etta
Former Anglican lecturer in Spirituality at St Stephen's, Oxford; compiler, with Michael Hollings, of a number of popular collections of prayers.

Hammarskjöld, Dag (1905–1961)
Economist, statesman and second Secretary General of the United Nations; his leadership enhanced the prestige and effectiveness of the UN.

Harries, Richard (b.1936)
Bishop of Oxford, former Dean of King's College, London; lecturer, broadcaster and writer, particularly on prayer and spirituality.

Harvey, F. W. (b.1912)
Playwright and script-writer.

Heber, Reginald (1783–1826)
Hymnwriter and poet; widely travelled Bishop of Calcutta.

King Henry VI (1421–1471)
King of England and a pious and studious recluse whose incapacity for government was the chief cause of the Wars of the Roses.

King Henry VIII (1491–1547)
King of England who early in his reign published his famous book on the Sacraments in reply to Luther and received from the Pope the title 'Defender of the Faith'. Yet his drive for an heir brought about a great ecclesiastical revolution and by 1534 he had become head of the church in England, severing all connections with the papacy.

Herbert, George (1593–1633)
Devotional poet of the metaphysical school of John Donne, ended his days as a saintly country parson.

Hickes, George (1642–1715)
Bishop, author of *Hickes' Devotions* published in 1700.

Hilary of Poitiers, St (315–367)
Converted to Christianity through studying Holy Scripture; although married, the people of Poitiers chose him as their bishop. Profound thinker and brilliant theologian, Hilary's greatest treatise was *On the Trinity* from which his prayers spring.

Hippolytus of Rome (d.235)
A bishop and vigorous opponent of heresy. He opposed church authority but after his condemnation to hard labour in mines, he was reconciled to the church and died a martyr.

Hollings, Michael (b.1921)
English Roman Catholic parish priest, author and compiler of a number of books of prayers.

Hopkins, Gerard Manley (1844–1889)
Jesuit priest and one of the most individual of Victorian poets; his poetry combined perception, force of intellect and religious feelings.

Horneck, Anthony
Chaplain to King Charles II and author of *The Crucified Jesus*.

Houselander, Caryll (1901–1954)
English writer and poet, worked with child victims of World War II.

How, W. Walsham (1823–1897)
Bishop of Wakefield, remembered for his books of sermons and prayers.

Hoyland, John S. (1887–1957)
Writer and lecturer at Woodbrooke College, Birmingham; decorated for public service in India.

Hunt, Leigh (1784–1859)
Essayist, critic, journalist, poet and editor of influential journals.

Hunter, John (1849–1917)
Congregational minister, speaker, hymnwriter and compiler of *Devotional Services*.

Idle, Christopher (b. 1938)
Anglican Rector of the parish of Limehouse, London, part-time journalist and hymnwriter.

Ignatius, of Loyola, St (1491–1556)
Founder of the Society of Jesus (Jesuits) and one of the most influential figures in the Catholic Reformation of the sixteenth century.

James, Walter (1828–1910)
Writer, rector of Fleet, Hampshire, England; later canon of Lincoln Cathedral.

Jarrett, Bede (1881–1934)
Dominican priest, historian, scholar, lecturer; at the time of his death was the prior of Blackfriars, Oxford.

Jenks, Benjamin (1647–1724)
Nonconformist clergyman, speaker and writer.

Jerome, St (347–420)
One of the most learned of the Fathers of the church, Jerome became a hermit for a short period, before becoming a priest and founding a

monastery at Bethlehem. A prolific writer, he is best remembered for his Latin translation of the Bible which profoundly influenced the early Middle Ages.

John XXIII, Pope (1881–1963)
Angelo Roncalli, one of the most popular popes of all time, inaugurated a new era for the Roman Catholic Church by convoking the Second Vatican Council.

John Chrysostom, St (347–407)
A renowned preacher (hence the name Chrysostom – 'golden-mouthed'), John was appointed Archbishop of Constantinople. His reforming zeal offended the rich and powerful. He was deposed and banished. Recognised as a biblical interpreter and Father of the church.

John Paul II, Pope (b. 1920)
Karol Wojtyla, the first Polish pope, elected on 16th October 1978. In his own right a poet, dramatist, philosopher and theologian.

Johnson, Samuel (Dr) (1709–1784)
Poet, essayist, critic, journalist, Doctor Johnson is regarded as one of the outstanding figures of English eighteenth-century life.

Johnson, Samuel (Rev.) (1696–1772)
Nonconformist clergyman, speaker and writer; author of the influential *Father, in Thy Presence Kneeling*.

Julian of Norwich (1342-died after 1416)
Celebrated mystic and recluse whose *Revelations of Divine Love* is considered one of the most remarkable documents of medieval religious experience.

Kadel, William H.
Presbyterian pastor, first president of Florida Presbyterian College, later president of Pittsburgh Theological Seminary.

Keble, John (1792–1866)
Anglican priest, theologian and poet who originated and helped lead the Oxford Movement.

Kempis, Thomas à (1379–1471)
Reputed author of *The Imitation of Christ*, written between 1390 and 1440. He was a representative of the '*devotio moderna*'.

Ken, Thomas (1637–1711)
Anglican bishop, hymnwriter, royal chaplain to King Charles II. Deprived of his see in 1691 for opposing William of Orange.

Kierkegaard, Søren (1813–1855)
Religious philosopher and critic of Rationalism, regarded as the founder of Existentialist philosophy.

Kingsley, Charles (1819–1875)
Anglican clergyman, teacher and writer whose novels influenced social developments in Victorian Britain.

Langton, Stephen (1150–1228)
English cardinal whose appointment as Archbishop of Canterbury precipitated King John's quarrel with the pope.

Larsson, Flora
Married to a Swedish Salvation Army officer, Flora is British, and as a Salvationist has worked in many countries round the world.

Laud, William (1573–1645)
Archbishop of Canterbury, religious adviser to King Charles I, his policies towards religious dissidents contributed to the outbreak of the English Civil War.

Law William (1686–1761)
Author of influential works on Christian ethics and mysticism

Lawrence, Sir Henry Montgomery (1806–1857)
English general and political administrator; lived all his life in India where he was involved in the Sikh wars and mortally wounded at the siege of Lucknow.

Lewis, C. S. (1898–1963)
Scholar, novelist and author of many books on Christian apologetics, also famous for his classic stories for children.

Luther, Martin (1483–1546)
Biblical scholar, Augustinian monk, linguist and a prolific writer, who posted his 95 theses and precipitated the Protestant Reformation.

Macdonald, George (1824–1905)
Congregational minister, freelance preacher, novelist, poet and writer of Christian allegories, best remembered for his children's stories.

Macnutt, Frederick B. (1873–1949)
Canon of Canterbury Cathedral and chaplain to King George V (1931).

Markham, Edwin (1852–1940)
Lecturer and poet, best known for his social protest poems.

Marmion, Columba (1858–1923)
Irish Benedictine Abbot of Maredsous Abbey, Belgium, eloquent preacher with a special ministry to fellow priests.

Marshall, Peter (1902–1949)
Writer, preacher and chaplain to US Congress.

Martineau, James (1805–1900)
Unitarian theologian and philosopher whose writings emphasised the primacy of the individual conscience.

Matheson, George (1842–1906)
Blind clergyman, lecturer and prolific writer.

Mechthild of Magdeburg (1210–1297)
Also known as Mechtilde of Helfta. A medieval mystic whose writings are ardent and romantic, the principal collection being *The Flowing Light of the Godhead*.

Merton, Thomas (1915–1968)
US journalist who joined the Cistercian Order (Trappist monk) and became a celebrated counsellor and spiritual writer.

Meyer, F. B. (b.1927)
Lecturer in theology; American writer on history and religious subjects.

Michalon, Père
French priest dedicated to the furtherance of Christian Unity, co-worker with Paul Couturier.

Micklem, Caryl
United Reformed Church minister and spiritual writer.

Milner-White, Eric (1884–1963)
Dean of York; lecturer in history and spiritual writer.

Moody, Dwight L. (1837–1899)
Prominent American evangelist who set the pattern for later evangelism in large cities.

More, Thomas (1477–1535)
Eminent scholar, humanist and statesman, chancellor of England, who died for refusing to accept Henry VIII's Act of Succession. Honoured with the title of Saint by the Roman Catholic Church.

Naylor, Basil (b.1911)
Canon Charles B. Naylor, Anglican chancellor and canon of Liverpool Cathedral.

Newman, John Henry (1801–1890)
Eminent churchman and man of letters, led the Oxford Movement in the Church of England, later became a cardinal of the Roman Catholic Church.

Nicholas of Flue (1417–1487)
Married man and father of ten children who at fifty became a hermit and a spiritual counsellor.

Niebuhr, Reinhold (1892–1971)
One of most important American theologians of the twentieth century, who had extensive influence on political thought.

Nimitz, Chester W. (1885–1966)
After the Pearl Harbor attack, Admiral Nimitz was appointed Commander-in-Chief of the US Pacific Fleet: the Japanese capitulation was signed aboard his flagship, the *USS Missouri*.

Nouwen, Henri (b. 1932)
Roman Catholic theologian, lecturer and writer in Pastoral Theology, now a Trappist monk of the Abbey of Genesee, New York.

Oldham, John H. (1653–1683)
Poet and educator, pioneer of the imitation of classical satire in English.

Olier, Jean-Jacques (1608–1657)
Founder of the Sulpicians, a group of secular priests dedicated to training candidates for the Roman Catholic priesthood.

Oosterhuis, Huub (b. 1933)
Ordained a Jesuit priest, his pastoral work has revolved around the student community of Amsterdam, where he participated in the renewal of the Dutch Liturgy.

Orchard, William E. (1877–1955)
A Presbyterian minister, preacher and lecturer who strove for better ecumenical relations between the churches; became a Roman Catholic priest.

Origen (185–254)
Brilliant head of the Alexandrian school, and prolific writer who is acknowledged as the greatest theologian the Greek church has produced. His father died a martyr and he himself died as a result of the torture endured during the Decian persecution.

Osgood, Samuel (1808–1885)
American portrait painter, painted famous figures like Edgar Allan Poe.

Oxenden, Ashton (1808–1892)
Anglican Bishop of Montreal, Canada, prolific writer of short popular religious works.

Oxenham, John (1852–1941)
Pseudonym of William Dunkerley, businessman turned novelist and poet, co-edited *The Idler* with Jerome K. Jerome.

Parker, Matthew (1504–1575)
Scholar, Archbishop of Canterbury and moderate reformer under Queen Elizabeth I.

Parker, Theodore (1810–1860)
American Unitarian theologian, pastor and social reformer active in the anti-slavery movement.

Pascal, Blaise (1623–1662)
Mathematician, physicist, religious philosopher and writer; he defended Jansenism and is famous for his *Pensées*.

Paton, Alan (1903–1990)
One of South Africa's foremost writers who through circumstances became a reluctant but eminent politician.

Patrick, St (385–461)
Missionary-bishop credited with bringing Christianity to Ireland and probably in part responsible for the Christianisation of the Picts and Anglo-Saxons.

Polycarp of Smyrna (70–156)
Bishop of Smyrna and disciple of the Apostle John, who was burnt to death at the age of 86. His martyrdom is reliably described in a letter to the Christians at Philomelium. In his final prayer he remembers his priestly functions.

Prewer, Bruce (b. 1931)
Minister of the Uniting Church in Australia at Pilgrim Church, central Adelaide. Bruce, married with a family, has a special interest in social justice issues.

Pseudo-Athanasius
St Athanasius (c. 295-c. 373) was a staunch opponent of Arianism; some ancient writings, in his style and ascribed to him, are not from his pen. For want of a better title these are attributed to 'Pseudo-Athanasius'.

Purton, Rowland
Teacher and author of many popular anthologies and compilations for use at the school assembly.

Pusey, Edward Bouverie (1800–1882)
Anglican theologian, scholar and a leader of the Oxford Movement, helped found the first Anglican sisterhood.

Quoist, Michel (b. 1921)
Sociologist and Roman Catholic parish priest, his popular book *Prayers of Life*, published in 1963, was responsible for a new realism in prayer.

Rabbula of Edessa (d. 436)
Bishop of Edessa, Rabbula was a great opponent of Nestorianism. He is said to be the author of a Syriac translation of the New Testament.

Rahner, Hugo
Brother of Karl Rahner, and like him a Jesuit scholar and priest.

Rahner, Karl (1904–1984)
Renowned German Roman Catholic theologian, lecturer and writer.

Rauschenbusch, Walter (1861–1918)
Baptist clergyman and theology professor who led the Social Gospel movement in the United States.

Richard of Chichester, St (1198–1253)
Bishop of Chichester and friend of St Edmund of Canterbury. His great love and concern for the poor won him the title of the 'model diocesan bishop'.

Ridley, Nicholas (1503–1555)
Protestant reformer and Bishop of London, considered one of the finest academics of the English Reformation; died for his beliefs under Queen Mary Tudor.

Ritter, Karl Bernhard (1890–1976)
German Reform minister, theologian and compiler of collections of prayers.

Rossetti, Christina (1830–1894)
Youngest member of an illustrious family, Christina was a devout Anglican who wrote sacred poetry of a high standard.

Saward, Michael
Vicar of Ealing and Prebendary of St Paul's Cathedral; writer and broadcaster.

Serapion of Thmuis (d. after 339)
At the end of the last century an important collection of prayers was found on Mount Athos. These bear the name of Serapion, Abbot of the monastery of Thmuis, Egypt, from the year 339.

Severus of Thrace (d. 304)
A priest of Heradea in Thrace (Greece). He was martyred in c. 304.

Shaw, Gilbert
Writer of spiritual books, *The Face of Love* and others.

Silk, David (b. 1936)
Archdeacon of Leicester, pastoral minister and liturgist.

Simeon, the New Theologian (949–1022)
After many years as the superior of a monastery, Simeon was deposed for rigorism. Recalled after a year's exile he preferred to found a small monastery near Constantinople where he wrote many short treatises. His title was for his particular interpretation of mysticism.

Smith, Delia
Popular writer, broadcaster and TV presenter of culinary programmes; also an established writer on prayer and spirituality.

Smith, Sir George Adam (1856–1942)
Scottish Free Church preacher and Semitic scholar who helped make higher criticism of the Old Testament acceptable.

Snowden, Rita
Prolific writer of inspirational books; deaconess and first elected woman Vice-President of the Methodist Church, New Zealand.

Spencer, George (1799–1864)
Youngest son of 2nd Earl Spencer, ordained to Anglican ministry, later became a Roman Catholic; better known as Father Ignatius Spencer, he was the companion of the famous Passionist preacher, Dominic Barberi and great, great uncle of Diana, Princess of Wales.

Spurgeon, Charles Haddon (1834–1892)
Gifted and popular Baptist minister and preacher who weekly drew thousands to the Metropolitan Tabernacle, London; his collected sermons fill 50 volumes.

Stevenson, Robert Louis (1850–1894)
Poet, literary critic, author of travel books, but best remembered for his romantic adventure stories.

Stitch, Wilhelmina
Writer of popular religious verse in the 1930s.

Stobart, Hugh (1883–1952)
A lieutenant-colonel who was awarded a DSO in the First World War; later a businessman involved in food production companies.

Stott, John R. W. (b. 1921)
Scholar, theologian, writer, honorary chaplain to Queen Elizabeth II and rector emeritus of All Souls church, Langham Place, London.

Tagore, Rabindranath (1861–1941)
Indian poet and philosopher who received the Nobel prize for Literature in 1913.

Tallis, Thomas (1510–1585)
Considered the most important English composer of sacred music before William Byrd.

Tauler, Johann (1300–1361)
Dominican preacher who, with Meister Eckhart and Heinrich Suso, was one of the chief Rhineland mystics.

Taylor, Jeremy (1613–1667)
Theologian and writer who held the post of chaplain to Archbishop Laud and later King Charles I. After the Restoration he was appointed Bishop of Down and Connor.

Teilhard de Chardin, Pierre (1881–1955)
Jesuit priest, philosopher and palaeontologist, famous for his theory that man is presently evolving to a final spiritual unity.

Temple, William (1881–1944)
Archbishop of Canterbury, leader in the ecumenical movement and in educational and labour reforms.

Teresa of Calcutta, Mother (b. 1910)
Founder of the Order of the Missionaries of Charity dedicated to serving the poor and abandoned, particularly in India. Awarded the Nobel Peace Prize in 1979.

Thorogood, Bernard
United Reform Church minister and General Secretary of that Church.

Traherne, Thomas (1637–1674)
Writer and last of the mystical poets of the Anglican clergy with a temperament inclined to the Celtic mysticism.

Underhill, Evelyn (1875–1941)
Mystical writer and sought-after religious counsellor who helped establish mystical theology as a respectable discipline.

van Dyke, Henry (1852–1933)
Presbyterian minister, poet, short-story writer and essayist who was popular in the early twentieth century.

van Zeller, Hubert (1905–1983)
Benedictine priest, writer and retreat-giver.

Vanier, Jean (b.1928)
Son of a former Governor General of Canada, philosophy lecturer, now member of a French lay institute; famous for the foundation of L'Arche, an association of small groups that care for the handicapped.

Vaughan, Charles J. (1816–1897)
Writer, preacher and Dean of Llandaff, often simply known as 'Dean Vaughan'.

Vives, Johannes Ludovicus (1492–1540)
Spanish scholar at the English court, humanist and student of Erasmus.

Walker, Michael
Baptist minister, lecturer in Christian Doctrine at the South Wales Baptist College.

Wallace, Jamie (b.1929)
Baptist minister and honorary pastor of Earls Barton Baptist Church, Northamptonshire.

Warren, Alan (b.1932)
Anglican canon and Provost of Leicester.

Weatherhead, Leslie D. (1893–1976)
Theologian, eminent preacher and pastor at City Temple, London; President of Methodist Conference 1955–1956; prolific writer of a wide range of Christian books.

Wesley, John (1703–1791)
Anglican clergyman, energetic preacher and evangelist, who, with his brother Charles, founded the Methodist movement.

Westcott, Brooke Foss (1825–1901)
Regius Professor of Divinity at Cambridge from 1870; later Bishop of Durham.

Williams, Dick (b.1931)
Writer and compiler of collections of prayers; Rector of Croft with Southworth in the Diocese of Liverpool. Diocesan newspaper editor.

Williams, Rowland (1818–1870)
Anglican divine, preacher and lecturer.

Williams, Susan (b.1932)
Teacher, photographer and poet, married to Dick Williams; they have three children.

Wilson, Thomas (1663–1755)
Bishop of Sodor and Man; published first book in Manx, helped translate the New Testament into Manx.

Winstone, Harold (b.1917)
Theologian and eminent Roman Catholic liturgist, now retired; founder and former director of St Thomas More Centre for Pastoral Liturgy, London.

Woolman, John (1720–1772)
American Quaker leader and preacher who worked for the abolition of slavery.

Wordsworth, Christopher (1807–1885)
High Church Anglican, headmaster of Harrow School, later Bishop of Lincoln; best remembered for his hymns.

Xavier, Francis (1506–1552)
Greatest Roman Catholic missionary of modern times; as a Jesuit he brought Christianity to India, the Malay Archipelago and Japan. Honoured as a saint by the Roman Catholic Church.